THEORIES AND PRACTICES OF LIBRARY MANAGEMENT

By

Rakeshkumar Shantilal Prajapati

B.Lib., M.Lib.

Librarian

Swami Vivekanand Sarvoday Bank Education College

Mehsana (Gujarat)

(India)

DISCOVERY PUBLISHING HOUSE PVT. LTD.

NEW DELHI-110 002

Published by:

Tilak Wasan

DISCOVERY PUBLISHING HOUSE PVT. LTD.

4383/4B, Ansari Road, Darya Ganj

New Delhi-110 002 (India)

Phone : +91-11-23279245, 43596064-65

Fax : +91-11-23253475

E-mail : discoverypublishinghouse@gmail.com
sales@discoverypublishinggroup.com
parul.wasan@gmail.com

web : www.discoverypublishinggroup.com

***First Edition:* 2013**

ISBN: 978-93-5056-382-3

Theories and Practices of Library Management

Printed at:

Dynamic Printers

Delhi

Contents

Preface

Library Management is not a new concept. Library management is a sub-discipline of institutional management that focuses on specific issues faced by libraries. Library management encompasses normal management tasks as well as intellectual freedom, anti-censorship, and fundraising tasks. Issues faced in library management frequently overlap those faced in management of non-profit organizations. Developed with the inception of libraries, its original concept, that lacked systematic procedures and scientific application, has undergone a remarkable change to cope up with the present era of advanced information technology which demands of efficient system and speedy service. Telecommunication and computers have given a new face to libraries and its services.

In the present book, *Theories and Practices of Library Management,* attempts have been to include all the latest informations related to library systems, procedures, automation and several activities of the libraries which have an effect on the readers' service.

—Author

1

Accountability in Library Management

INTRODUCTION

If libraries were to be judged on their own merit, in isolation from their parent organisations, the majority in the ASEAN countries can be said to be excellent, even in comparison with libraries in more developed countries. However it is only when libraries are judged in the context of their parent organisations that their contribution is seen to be more peripheral rather than integral.

For example, most university libraries are not fully integrated into the teaching-learning process which forms the core business of universities. This is partly due to pedagogical constraints, in that teaching-learning strategies at the university do not encourage resource-based learning, causing libraries to be side-lined.

It may also be due to the fact that librarians are not regarded as "academic" by the academia, "inferior" in status and ability. These are realities that exist at universities and in different other ways at other types of library environments. At the national level, it is librarians who have always assumed that libraries are critical to national development while not many outside the library community acknowledge the importance of the library's role.

There are sufficient indicators that reflect this lack of recognition:

* Changes in nomenclature from 'librarians' to 'information professionals/specialists,' 'librarianship' to 'information science' propagated by librarians themselves, beginning in the 1970's. It is as if prior to the 1970s, libraries had not been involved with information provision and dissemination.
* Librarians not awarded the same recognition as other professions and this is reflected in schemes of service and salary scales despite the fact that librarians have academic and professional qualifications at entry point.
* The proliferation of members of other professions taking the lead role in information provision and dissemination.

The issue therefore is, against this background, are librarians in the position to cope with the demands and challenges of the 21st century?

ARE LIBRARIES READY FOR THE 21ST CENTURY?

To fight, one has to recognise the enemy – so it is with libraries. Unless libraries understand what is demanded of them by the 21st Century, it would be difficult for them to face the onslaught of the changes that the century will bring. To prepare themselves for the onslaught, they would need to not only assess their current "strengths" and "weaknesses" but to also recognise the "opportunities" or "threats" presented by the 21st century.

A SWOT analysis of libraries is important because it provides libraries with a more 'clinical' approach to library development, minimising trial and error in the process.

The SWOT analysis is not based on research data but based on the perception and certain assumptions on the part of the authors, resulting from their reading of the relevant information literature as well as their experiences as Chief Librarians. The SWOT analysis is used merely to illustrate the need for librarians to be introspective and understand their capabilities as well as to be aware of developments taking place in their surrounding environment.

Internal Environment:

* *Strength*:
  - Collection
  - Reputation
  - User Education
* *Weakneses*:
  - Collection
  - Staff
  - Funds
  - Usage
  - Peripheral role
  - Non-integrated Strategic Plan

External Environment:

* Opportunity:
  - Lifelong education
  - Innovative technology
  - Knowledge management
  - Globalisation
  - National policies and Objectives
* *Threat*:
  - Proliferation of information providers
  - Globalisation

DEFINING THE LIBRARY'S ENVIRONMENT

INTERNAL ENVIRONMENT

Any assessment of the library's strengths and weaknesses must be based on user feedback in the form of complaints or user studies or benchmarking. In the absence of such feedback however and purely for the purpose of this chapter, the authors have drawn on their own experiences as Chief Librarian and Consultant Librarian to identify the strengths and weaknesses of the library.

Strengths

Three areas can be identified as the library's strength, notably:

* Collections
* Reputation
* User Education

Collections

Collections are the library's greatest strength because without collections, there can be no library. The strength of the collections however depends on its size and uniqueness. In the 1950s and 1960s, the size of the collection is the measure of the library's worth. As such weeding exercises were seldom undertaken for fear that large libraries will lose their competitive edge. Today, the issue of size is not the main criteria to assess the library's stature because with the advent of digital libraries, the world's collections are easily accessible. The uniqueness of collections however has became a more important criteria for assessing the library's strength because of their heritage value and their potential as a national asset.

In the case of Malaysia, the various Malaysiana collections at the National Library of Malaysia, at the 17 public university libraries, at government research agencies in the form of research collections, at the State Public Libraries in the form of the state collections, are examples of unique collections that are found in the country.

Collectively, the collections found in all types of libraries in any country can be deemed to be the country's national asset. The fact that they are professionally organised for easy retrieval makes library collections indispensable for national development. However, while the monetary value of these collections may be easy to quantify by totalling the annual budgets of each library, their academic and cultural value are priceless. But the main issue in question is: Are the collections used? However priceless the collections, their value will come to naught unless used.

Reputation

Libraries exist today because people believe in the traditional concept of the libraries as being at the heart of learning. Since the education system provides the nation's manpower and serves as the catalyst for national development and advancement, libraries are accorded the same value. They believe that a literate population is the country's foremost asset and critical for national advancement. This belief has prevailed till today but it is a perception that has not been substantiated by library usage. It is obvious that while libraries are still regarded as an important tool for education and a mechanism for development of manpower for the country, reputation alone is not sufficient. The perception that libraries are important must be replaced by a more realistic view of the library's worth.

User Education

Teaching users how to retrieve materials via the library systems, whether manual or electronic, has long been undertaken by libraries. However, user education programmes have become more urgent in recent years when library systems became ICT-based. The underlying premise of all user education programmes is that however excellent the library's collections and systems are, if not used they serve no purpose.

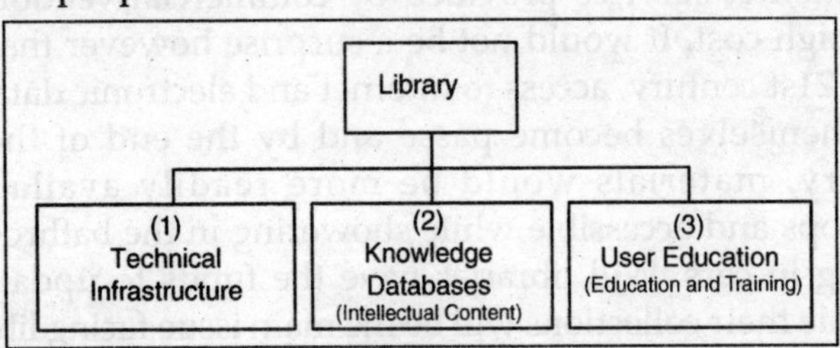

Fig. 1.1

User education programmes are now offered by most libraries, both formally or informally. It is the best way to promote libraries and library use because not only do these programmes enable librarians to come into direct contact with the clients, demonstrate to the clients the proficiency of librarians in both the academic aspect of library work as well as the technical aspect, it also provides libraries with the opportunity to.

* Be integrated into the teaching and learning process in the case of university libraries or
* Develop literacy skills among members of society in the case of public libraries.

Weaknesses

Unfortunately, there are more weaknesses than strengths in our analysis of the internal environment:

Collections

Generally, notwithstanding the size of their collections, libraries have in their collections, materials that contain data more archival than current. They are excellent for scholars and researchers from the academia but users of the 21st century are weaned on ICT and expect information at a press of the button.

Library collections are mainly passive collections, sitting on library shelves for years, unused. Consisting mainly of printed secondary and tertiary sources, they stand the risk of being replaced by e-books, e-journals and internet. It has become very common for libraries to have e-books, e-journals and internet services provided by commercial vendors at a very high cost. It would not be a surprise however that later in the 21st century, access to Internet and electronic databases will themselves become passé and by the end of the 21st century, materials would be more readily available in palmtops and accessible while showering in the bathroom or driving in cars. Will libraries have the funds to update and upgrade their collections will be the main issue facing libraries in the 21st century.

Unless libraries have collections that are relevant and can meet the demands of the 21st century, library collections comprising of secondary and tertiary data, will be rendered obsolete. The main weakness of library collections however lies in the fact that they are not used to the optimum, giving rise to management debates on whether or not it is cost-beneficial to maintain libraries when alternatives are available on-line.

Staff

In order for libraries to be dynamic, library staff must have the right qualifications and competencies for the job in hand, as well as the right attitude towards service. In the current situation, the majority of library staff can be said to be generally passive and not proactive. This is where library education plays a part. Librarians of the 21st century must be multi-skilled, have sound subject knowledge and good leadership. Library schools would have to be more responsive to these needs and take into account that librarians of the future will not be sitting at a desk in a library but will work in a virtual environment with PC(s) as colleagues. Multi-skilled, she will need to communicate well, preferably in several languages, be knowledgeable in specialised subject areas, innovative in the use of ICT, personable and independent.

Funds

Lack of funds is a perennial problem faced by all libraries. Notwithstanding the fact there are libraries that are well-endowed funds are never adequate to fulfill all objectives. This has resulted in libraries undertaking resource-sharing of collections and services to reduce expenditure and optimise usage. In some countries, libraries have embraced the concept of 'corporatisation' through which libraries have imposed membership fees and service charges. Other libraries depend on sponsors and donors for funds. The issue is: will libraries in the 21st century have to be self-funding?

Usage

The most important issue in library usage is the need to provide evidence of usage. Much of the professional literature has alluded to the fact that despite their importance, libraries are not used to the optimum. Also, with the establishment of digital libraries, which makes remote access easy, library visits will soon be more for pleasure than for information gathering. In a recent survey of undergraduates at the University of Malaya Library only a small percentage visit the library every day (17.2%), with the majority (54%) visiting a few times a week. The survey also shows that the majority of students do not use the electronic databases preferring the printed books instead. There is a need to market library services to increase usage, whether on-site or remote.

At the OUM Library, statistics obtained from log-ins of e-books and e-journals show that:

* Remote access is greater than on-site access and
* Usage of e-books higher than e-journals.

Peripheral Role of Libraries

Is the role of library passive or proactive? There is no real evidence to show that libraries are integrated into the core business of their institutions, especially academic libraries and special libraries. In the case of University libraries, while there is no evidence of a correlation between usage of library resources and academic achievement evidence of Faculty-library integration can be discerned by asking the following questions:.

* *Teaching*: Is there resourcebased teaching? Are library resources integrated into teaching activities?
* *Learning*: Is there resource based learning? Are library resources integrated into learning activities?
* *Research*: Is there evidence that the more specialised the research, the less need there is for library resources?

With regard to the library's role in learning, in a survey undertaken at the University of Malaya, to determine whether the user education programme is useful for their learning, the majority of students surveyed replied in the affirmative.

EXTERNAL ENVIRONMENT

To be prepared for the 21st century, libraries would have to be aware not only of developments taking place in the world outside library walls but to interpret these developments into "opportunities" or "threats" for libraries. Those that can be considered as "opportunities" must be taken advantage of while taking steps to be prepared for those that are considered as "threats". These "opportunities" and "threats" found beyond library walls must however be seen in the right perspective, against the background of the library's capabilities or its "strengths" and "weaknesses".

Weaknesses

What can be interpreted as 'opportunities' can be subjective, depending on how the librarians perceive them to be.

For the purpose of this chapter, the authors have identified five areas:

* Innovative Technology.
* Globalisation.
* Life-long Learning.
* Knowledge Management.
* National Policies and Objectives.

Innovative Technology

The phrase "innovative technology" is deliberately used here to denote the innovative aspects of technology because not since the wheel has there been a development so global that it has not touched every aspect of life and every level of society, *e.g.* e-learning, e-government, e-business. From the Parliament to shopping, technology has become part of life. Reaching the moon, artificial intelligence, cloning of genes have become mundane news – innovative technology has made them possible.

The advantages provided by innovative technology can be summarised as:

* More efficient work processes, with less mistakes and greater output
* Provides global access to information
* Encourages independent learning

But the issue that confronts libraries in the 21st century is: To what level should librarians be trained in technology?

In the case of libraries, innovative technology has been identified to facilitate:

* Day-to-day tasks such as acquisitions, cataloguing, loans etc.

* Interaction with users via the use of portals. The development of information gateways or portals has made it possible for library and information professionals to upgrade their services. Information portal can offer users one stop work stations where they can search across a multitude of resources and retrieve electronic and book resources in one station. Information portals can provide integration of sources for searching and for location and delivery of materials – in whatever format they exist. Portal brings the opportunity to develop elibrary services – to meet the growing expectations of the student population.
* Enables user education programmes to be conducted in large groups with hands-on sessions. Undertaking user education programmes provides libraries with the opportunity to optimise usage because users are taught lifelong learning skills such as information–retrieval skill and ICT skills. Implementing a portal can change the environment in which users discover information and get better access to the wealth of contents.

Globalisation

The term "globalisation" is associated mainly with business – giving rise to concepts such as 'global economy', 'global markets', 'global competition' or hyper competition', etc. A global economy is one in which goods, services, people, skills and ideas move freely across geographic borders.

Relatively unfettered by artificial constraints, such as tariffs, the global economy significantly expands and complicates a firm's competitive environment". Is globalisation relevant for libraries?

The authors are of the opinion that since 'information delivery' is a business and globalisation is basically a business concept than globalisation will have an impact on libraries. Innovative technology has made it possible for business to be conducted in a global environment but how does globalisation affect librarians?

Self-Efficiency vs. Outsourcing

Concept of self-sufficiency has given way to global outsourcing by cutting out the role of the middle man, including the librarian. This has implications for the library in matters relating to human resource and organisation structure.

Examples:

* *Acquisitions*: Librarians do not need to go though local agents. There are many more companies on Internet who can acquire anything for libraries, ranging from equipment to books.
* *Cataloguing*: OCLC is a case in point although it does not contain records for non-English items.
* *Information Services*: It is a matter of time before information services are conducted on a global basis replacing libraries and librarians except for the provision of local information which however may be taken over by local companies with enough entrepreneurial acumen to take over the information market.

Demand for Wide-ranging Information

Imagine providing information services for the whole world, when most libraries cannot even satisfy the information needs of their own clientele. Theoretically, however, this is what globalisation could generate. Do librarians have the potential for it?

In reality, no. Working on the premise that no one person can provide all information on everything, it will be a massive task but if libraries do not do it other more enterprising professionals would. It is worth a thought. For example, libraries in Malaysia need not confine themselves to providing information merely about Malaysia but through databases subscribed and information networks established via the universities and ministries, librarians can play a role. This will have implications for the library in terms of collections, human resource and job expertise and skills. The question that begs to be asked at this juncture is: Do we still need libraries and librarians in the face of globalisation?

Life-long Learning

The move towards a more democratic form of education in the 1960s and 1970s resulted in a shift in the concept of education from one that was authoritarian and elitist to one that advocated 'equal opportunity in education'. 'Equal opportunity in education' was seen as the democratic right of all individuals-irrespective of race, status, age or ability but at the same time 'equal opportunity' does not mean the same treatment for everyone.

For equal opportunity to be meaningful, however, education must be extended on a continuous lifelong basis with opportunities for success provided at every stage of the continuum.

Any attempt at early elimination would render the democratisation process ineffective and make a mockery of the principle of 'equal opportunity' Conceptualising education as a lifelong process was an effort at translating democratic principles into educational practice. Democratising education on the principles of equal opportunity meant a re-appraisal of traditional aims and methods.

Unlike the traditional concept, the modern concept of education believes that education should produce a learning society, not a learning minority. In simple language, higher education should be catering to the masses. The change in emphasis in educational aims and objectives has made it necessary for teaching and learning methods to be reviewed, giving rise to a productive learning environment with the focus on learning and the learner rather than teaching and the teachers, in greater emphasis given to differentiation in needs, abilities and personalities in the development of independent and active learning the democratisation of higher education has given the concept 'equal opportunity' a new meaning, encompassing a wider scope of educational aims and objectives. It has given modern education certain characteristics.

Greater and More Flexible Access to Higher Education

Greater access does not mean mainly increasing the number of people enrolled in mainstream university programmes but also to provide opportunities for those previously "excluded" for various reasons. Propagating lifelong education would ensure that any one who wishes to acquire qualifications at any stage of his life would be able to do so because there are alternative means by which the opportunity is provided

Learner-centred Approach to Learning

The importance given to the learner in the modern approach to education ensures that learner needs are given priority. In lifelong learning, the focus is on teaching the learner how to learn, not what to learn. In modern terms, it would mean "empowering" the learner such that he can be independent and resourceful throughout his lifetime of learning experiences. This also means that the learner is given the opportunity to learn at his own pace and according to his own style.

He can undertake his learning anywhere, anytime, anyhow. Learning therefore becomes flexible, at a pace dictated by the learner and in accordance with negotiated objectives.

Variety of Teaching Strategies

With the learner's interest at the heart of the teaching-learning process, the method and strategy of instruction need to adapt. Instruction has now to be skills-based, not subject-based, consistent with the need to prepare learners for lifelong learning, so as to teach them how to learn rather than what to learn. Instruction is individualised to cater to individual differences of the learners making it necessary for small-group teaching rather than the whole-class approach which assumes that learners learn at the same pace. A greater variety of teaching strategies have been devised in recent years to cope with the learner-centric pedagogy such as interdisciplinary team-teaching, project work, problem-based teaching and with greater ICT capability, web-based teaching, e-teaching, etc. What implications does lifelong learning have for libraries?. Bearing in mind that lifelong 'students' are now not confined to the 5-14 age cohort but more likely 5-65 years age cohort as the learning population moves from primary schools to universities, libraries will have to reassess its collections, services and delivery systems to accommodate this learning continuum.

There will be traditional as well as non-traditional universities. In the case of the non-traditional universities offering open and distance learning programmes, libraries will need to focus more on digital collections, services to be more flexible providing for remote access and delivery systems need to be efficient. The issue is: When libraries move from providing library-centred to usercentred services, the library can no longer be a building but a system.

Knowledge Management

The concept of Knowledge Management (KM) is basically one that advocates sharing of knowledge within a company or agency such that with the sharing of knowledge it will help the company or agency to combat competition and provide it with the competitive edge.

It is a process that involves:

* *Knowledge creation*: Recording information from top management downwards and vice versa. It includes documenting unwritten knowledge or in other words, documenting experiences of people relevant to the company operations. This is not an easy task because the information may not be current and people are not forthcoming, preferring to be secretive.
* *Knowledge organisation*: Documenting and using retrieval systems to store and make accessible the necessary information. What to document, how detailed and for whom are issues related to KM. In certain agencies, there will be a committee or jury of specialists to decide which information to document and store.
* *Knowledge dissemination/sharing*: KM was introduced to reduce barriers in information/knowledge sharing

in companies to facilitate decision-making and prevent unnecessary duplication of effort. Knowing what others are doing in other department will help departmental heads to make more informed decisions. Knowledge sharing is more effective if it involves all levels of staff – from top management downwards and vice versa. The logic of sharing strategic and operational knowledge is to make processes more efficient and intradepartmental communication more effective. As for its role in ensuring the company's monetary gains it has been reported in the professional literature to be 'successful'. KM has also been described as "organisational learning" because in sharing the information or knowledge the whole organisation goes through a learning process. The success of KM is difficult to quantify because it is difficult to measure the success of knowledge-sharing or to ascertain to what extent organisational learning takes place.

But what does KM mean to libraries?

* The library can become the Centre for Knowledge Management in the institution by being involved in documenting, organising and disseminating the information or knowledge gathered from within the organisation This is particularly viable for all libraries, e.g. in the case of university libraries information about teaching, learning and research activities can not only be documented via published reports but also by interviewing the VC, Deputy VC's, Deans, lecturers, students, Ministry of Education officials, etc. In special libraries at government agencies or private companies, there may be problems with access to confidential information like pricing of commodities, marketing policies, marketing research results, etc. In Malaysia, these are a few successful agencies undertaking KM. From their experience, it can be said that the success of KM depends on the support of the management

of the organization while the main problem is that colleagues are not cooperative and not forthcoming with information, especially tacit information.

* The library can create primary "live" information, instead of dealing with "passive information" which is often secondhand, outdated, irrelevant and insignificant.
* Staff must be trained or retrained in certain areas in order to function effectively. The ability to interview effectively, the ability to relate to people without either intimidating them or being intimidated by them, knowledgeable in relevant subject areas, proficient at handling ICT information delivery systems, etc.
* Allows library to be creative because there is neither universal approach to KM, nor one or best way of implementing it.
* Recognition that information is an important commodity but like any other product needs good marketing strategies. If the library wants to function as an information centre it has to convince its own market and society at large of the importance of its role as information provider.

National Policies and Objectives

All countries have long-term strategic plans. In Malaysia, it is a 25-year plan which forms the basis for national development till 2020. Briefly, the V2020s aim is to make Malaysia an industrialised nation by the year 2020. In order to achieve this aim, nine thrust areas were identified to drive the V2020. One of the thrust areas is to make the Malaysian society a knowledge-based society. In this case of Malaysia, not only is the public sector committed to achieving the strategic objectives of V2020 but the private sector as well. Knowing where the nation is heading towards and the role played by each sector of society is important to the library and although the role of libraries is more indirect than direct, libraries do have in their custody the nation's intellectual wealth which should be optimized in the development of the knowledge society.

Considering the wealth of information resources located at libraries throughout Malaysia, if they had been read and used, Malaysia does not need to wait till the year 2020 to have an information-rich society.

Threats

Proliferation of Information Providers

A potential threat is the proliferation of non-library information providing companies and agencies that provide information via Internet. They may impose charges for the information but the information is usually current. How can libraries compete when the collections available at libraries are mainly secondary information found in print and electronic media?

There are three areas that the new breed of information providers has found foothold:

* Delivery systems
* Content development
* Content management

At the International Conferences of Asian Digital Libraries, held in Kuala Lumpur in December 2003, it was remarkable to listen to ICT specialists who have devised systems for information delivery. The focus was systems rather than content but it gave a good indication of what is imminent in the near future. Much as librarians were awed by the current developments, it also gave the impression that unless libraries take on a more pro-active approach, libraries will be by-passed as information centres. So the issue is: Can libraries compete?

Globalisation

There are two aspects in globalisation – the positive and the negative, depending on how one views it.

There are two potentials:

* Ability to outsource certain aspects of library functions such as acquisitions, cataloguing and information sources.

* Provide information services beyond home shores. It will be a daunting task as there will be a need to upgrade staff expertise but notwithstanding this, we need to explore the possibility.

From the negative point of view, it will spell the end of library services as we know it now, specifically with regard to information delivery. The library will remain the centre for loans and reference, using print and electronic resources. These materials can be accessed on-site or from the home or office. But the critical issue is currency and variety of information that cannot be supplied by libraries. Globalisation will then take away from the library its information delivery function because in speed and variety libraries will not be able to compete with information centres worldwide despite the cost.

ACCOUNTABILITY IN LIBRARY MANAGEMENT

Having defined the environment it is obvious that while in the internal environment there are more weaknesses than strengths, in the external environment there are more opportunities than threats. How then can libraries take advantage of the opportunities that the 21st century has to offer when library resources are inadequate and their role more peripheral than integral?

The answer is to strategise – through well-designed strategic plans, efficient organisation, capable leadership and effective control measures. It is only when these management tools and strategies are in place can libraries ensure the achievement of their goals and objectives. The onus therefore lies with the libraries to maximise their opportunities and be accountable for the success of their performance. Seen in this light, accountability therefore is the key factor to whether or not they can meet the demands and challenges of the 21st century

STRATEGIC PLAN

A well-designed plan would provide direction, minimise uncertainty and impact of changes, reduce waste and establish standards for goal achievements.

The planning process incorporates the following steps:

* Setting of goals and objectives
* Formulating strategies
* Developing action plans
* Coordinating activities
* Monitoring accomplishment of goals
* Review/ revise plan

For the libraries, it is crucial that they understand what their core business is, which is SERVICES. Their core business must be integrated into the core business of their organisations

In designing the strategies, the library has to first determine a strategic focus which will be incorporated in its:

* Vision,
* Mission and
* Objectives statements.

Where does the issue of accountability arise in the formulation of the strategic plan? It is in the quantitative methods used to measure the accomplishment of goals and objectives, in the time frames given to accomplish each activity and in the quality measures used in the performance such as monitoring, setting standards (ISO) and benchmarking. But however brilliant the plan, unless implemented, it is useless.

ORGANISING

The organisation structure should facilitate the achievement of goals so it is important that the organisation structure is designed to facilitate work flow (whether via function, specialisation or process), define the chain of command (whether hierarchical, flat, etc.), define the span of control (the wider the less effective) and clarify issue such as centralisation vs. decentralisation.

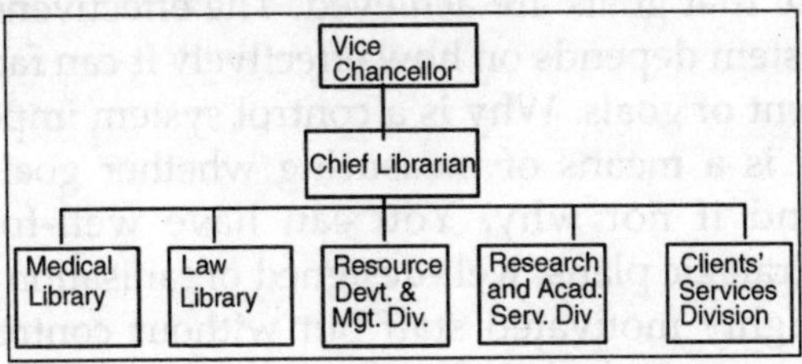

Fig 1.2. Example of a Simple One-site Organisation Structure

The library management would have to structure the organization in such a way as to ensure that the organisation structure facilitates rather than hinder the achievement of goals. The library management is therefore accountable in this aspect.

LEADING

Leading is influencing others to carry out tasks towards the achievements of goals. There are different types of leaderships but there are certain traits or characteristics that reflect good leadership:

* Develop corp of excellent staff
  - Staff development plan
  - Motivation
  - Competency training
  - Leadership training
  - Performance measurement
* Monitor activities
* Monitor achievement of goals
* Flexible and adaptable leadership
* Establish value culture – leadership by example

Leadership is not confined to being the Chief Librarian or the Library Director but leadership is found at all levels. Leaders may be managers but not all managers are leaders. The quality of human resource in any organisation depends on the quality of leadership. In this way, the library manager should be held accountable if staff cannot perform and goals cannot be achieved.

CONTROL

Control measures must be in place to monitor activities and ensure that goals are achieved. The effectiveness of any control system depends on how effectively it can facilitate the achievement of goals. Why is a control system important?

* It is a means of measuring whether goals are met and if not why. You can have well-formulated strategic plans, well-designed organisation structure, highly motivated staff but without control there is no measure of goals achievement.

* It is a management tool that can be used to monitor and measure activities with greater objectivity.

There are basically three types of control measures that libraries can use:

* Monitoring
* ISO
* Benchmarking

CONCLUSION

The demands and challenges of the 21st century should serve as a catalyst for reviewing the library's relevance to its organisation but unless it is held accountable for its performance *vis-à-vis* the organisation, it will remain ineffective and peripheral.

2

Becoming a Library Manager

Chances are that at some point-while in library school, while working as a paraprofessional, while working as a front-line librarian, or even while utilizing your favourite library-you had visions of how you could arrange things better if you "ran the zoo". Chances are that at some point after becoming a library manager, you realised that now that you *do* run the zoo-or at least the monkey house-it can be harder than you envisioned to implement those changes you have always wanted to make.

Merely sitting in the zookeeper's seat, further, may transform both your perspective and your priorities. Many of us are accidental managers; that is a given. What is not a given is the way you approach and grow into your management position. Parenting expert Dr. Spock once reassured parents everywhere with the classic line: "Trust yourself, you know more than you think you do."

The same can be said for most accidental library managers. Everything you have learned-as a library worker, from previous supervisors, on the job, from mentors, from volunteer work, from committee involvement, in nonlibrary managerial positions, from classes, from workshops, from the professional literature, as a parent, or from coworkers-will be useful as you settle in. Start from the assumption that you know more than you think you do and that you can trust in your own common sense.

You know how to treat people the way you would yourself like to be treated. You know how you would like the library, or your own small part of it, to work. You know how you respond to stress, to challenges, and to other people. Now, move forward from here. Library management comprises more than just making the changes you have always wanted. You must make those changes in the optimal fashion for your institution, in the context of its larger goals, other departments' activities, and your patrons' needs. You must learn to prioritize your own and your staff's tasks and goals, and to carry out these tasks in a logical order that allows each of your moves to build on your previous actions.

Your interactions with and management of the various members of your staff always need to work towards allowing the institution to carry out its mission and to serve its customers. Management as a whole involves achieving institutional goals through the people and resources available to you. Adult Services, Mount Prospect Public Library, Illinois, explains: "My biggest challenge was learning what it means to be a manager. It's not just writing reports and keeping an eye on the budget, but it's also a lot of interaction with others".

LIBRARY SKILLS AND MANAGERIAL CHALLENGES

Our skills and background as librarians can both help and hinder our managerial exfforts. If we think consciously about these linkages, we can learn to become more effective in any managerial position.

Positive connections include:

* *The ability to collect and analyse information:* Throughout your managerial career, you will need to utilize these skills in activities ranging from creating a budget, to strategic planning, to writing a marketing plan.
* *The urge to share information:* Any organization benefits from the free flow of information; close-mouthed managers foster inefficiency, rumors, and resentment.

* *The ability to organize knowledge:* Again, this will be useful in activities as large as strategic planning and as seemingly small as keeping updated and organized personnel files.
* *The tendency to build networks:* No manager can "go it alone," and librarians' propensity to share information, stories, experiences, and acquired knowledge with one another will stand you in good stead here.
* *The belief in the principle of equity of access and treatment:* As useful when it comes to staff as when dealing with library customers.

On the other hand, tendencies you need to be careful of as a library manager include:

* *The notion that "the patron is always right:"* When you extend your wish to make life comfortable for your patrons to bending over backward to make life easy for your staff, you run the risk of not pushing your people to their fullest.
* *The wish to avoid conflict:* Studies and personality tests consistently show that librarians tend to tip the introverted and conflict-avoiding side of the scale. This is a generalisation, but watch for these tendencies in yourself and be willing and able to step in to manage conflicts among your employees and with your patrons.
* *Emphasis of the philosophical over the practical:* Library school tends to foster a black-and-white worldview of philosophical idealism; managers eventually need to learn to compromise.

Additional linkages will be emphasized in the appropriate chapters, but always be open to understanding the ways in which your background as a librarian affects your work as a manager. Make a conscious effort to manage as a librarian. Overall, remember that you are a *library* manager, and that the ways in which you manage your people and institution need to be true to the principles and practices of librarianship. Ultimately, working effectively as a library manager demands developing a new way of thinking and behaving, while remembering your roots as a librarian or building a background in librarianship.

MAKING THAT TRANSITION

As you adjust to your management role, the first transition from managed to manager can be the hardest. As a nonmanagement employee, you may have been provided with an orientation, directions, and fairly explicit instructions on your day-to-day duties when settling into a new position. As a manager, you may be thrown into a new job with little direction or instruction on how to proceed; management positions are often largely what you make of them. Although you will have a broad outline of your administrator's, board's, or institution's expectations, part of your job will actually be to define your own specific responsibilities and role within your department, library, or section.

Even after the first transition or two gives you an idea of what to expect, the transition into any managerial position can be tricky throughout your career. Transitional periods are inevitably stressful for both you and your new staff, as everyone involved is dealing with a fairly major change and needs to renegotiate relationships and work patterns. But while your staff members' daily work will most likely remain relatively constant, providing them with an underlying stability to draw upon while weathering the changes your arrival brings, you will face the additional task of redefining yourself as a supervisor, a department head, or an administrator. The first few months in a managerial position can be critical in establishing your credibility, settling comfortably into your new role, and setting out your management style and strategies.

This transitional period, while difficult, also presents the opportunity to begin as you mean to continue, to build relationships and alliances with your staff, supervisors, and colleagues, and to lay out your vision for your department, section, or organization. It is always harder to switch gears later than to chart your course from the outset. Take time, however, to get to know your staff, their personalities, their strengths, and their weaknesses before launching into a major change initiative. In some ways it can be especially difficult to take over a position from a previous manager who seems to have run the zoo in a less than optimal manner. Library staff will have developed an understandable mistrust of those in a management role.

Much of your time at the outset may be spent undoing the damage your predecessor left behind, rather than in moving forward with your own initiatives and ideas. As one manager survey respondent notes: "Be aware that your staff may not trust you or your motives at first." This can be frustrating, so work on maintaining your own energy and enthusiasm. New library managers often come in brimming with ideas, but need to have the willingness first to learn the library's organizational culture and to lay the groundwork of trust needed for their initiatives' success. Also think about the ways in which succeeding an ineffective manager can actually work in your favour.

Any moves you make may lead to improvements—and there will be a general predisposition towards change. If you were promoted from within, having suffered with the rest, you will also have insight into what not to do when you move into a management role. Another manager survey respondent even explains her theory of management as: "Having seen library management done badly, I try to think: what would my old boss have done-and do the opposite." One staff survey respondent suggests: "Never forget what it's like to have a bad boss, and don't turn into one yourself." If you have experienced a history of incompetent or ineffective managers, though, it may take you some time to overcome your own distrust of management and realise that you are now one of "them". Librarians who are promoted into a managerial position from within will find that their former coworkers will have particular preconceptions and expectations for their behaviour as a manager, based on past conversations and behaviour as an employee. Your former colleagues may no longer be quite sure how to interact with you. Oregon State

University Librarian for Systems Applications says that: "the biggest surprise for me was that people I had worked with for more than five years viewed me as a different person simply because I had become a manager."

They would sometimes agree to concepts that I presented, even though in reality they had very different views on the issue. I found this disconcerting because I wanted and expected them to express their honest opinions. As any manager, your relationships and interactions with nonmanagerial staff members will inevitably change. Katharine Salzmann, Archivist/Curator of Manuscripts, Southern Illinois University at Carbondale, explains:

"I don't know if it was exactly a surprise, but the biggest adjustment I had to make was simply realizing that I was a 'boss.' I wasn't fully prepared for the role and how people's expectations of me would change, or how my working relationships with individuals would change."

This is not to say that you cannot have good, friendly working relationships with your staff members, but your relationships as manager and managed will tend to take on a different flavour than that of your relationships with your professional peers. You need to consider how important it is to you to be liked, as opposed to being respected as a manager. If you have tended to find most of your friends through work, you may need now to extend that circle outside your institution's walls. If, on the other hand, you come from the outside to assume a management position in a given library, your first step before defining any new goals will be to familiarize yourself with the institution's existing mission and organizational culture, as well as with the people who will be working for you. You will need to settle into your new environment and to give people a chance to settle into the inherent change your arrival brings.

You will of course have your own theories, ideas, and priorities-as well as responsibility for those imposed from above and outside. If you appear to be swooping in with a completely new agenda, however, you will undoubtedly meet with fierce resistance from existing staff. People need a compelling reason to move out of their comfortable routines, and need to feel as if they are a part of any change. Make it a point to learn from and work with your staff from the very beginning.

Realise also that the fact that your administration made the decision to hire from the outside rather than promote from within may mean that it is consciously looking for new perspectives and fresh ideas. Capitalize on this desire for change by enlisting administrative, institutional, and/or board support for your initiatives from the outset. Your goals have a greater chance of success if they receive consistent support throughout the management hierarchy of your organization. Successful management is undoubtedly more complicated than just "doing the opposite" of what your previous less-than-competent boss used to do.

A good first step, though, as you begin defining your role as a manager, is to think back to all of your experiences as someone who has been managed, inside or outside of a library environment. Identify both the role models you do, and those you do not, wish to emulate. Debbie Hackleman notes that "in some cases I learned by observing others–both what worked well and what I would choose to do differently. Observing negative examples is often quite useful." Of course, it is always easier to identify negative experiences and to dwell on what not to do. This is a useful beginning, and you should always keep your previous managers'–and your own–missteps firmly in mind. Dwelling on the negative, however, fails to provide us with a solid foundation for deciding what *to* do, for making the decisions that help propel both our careers and institutions forward, and for establishing our own management style. The next task, therefore, involves deciding where to go and how to begin. Before implementing any changes, you will need to identify the goals for your institution, section, or department, within the larger goals of the organization, larger institution, or system.

You need to provide yourself and your staff with a larger context for your work, in order to successfully define both what you do and why you do it. Lastly, realise that, in any management situation, you will also be compared to your predecessors. Whether comments tend to run along the lines of: "That's not how Ms. X used to do it," or: "We're so glad not to have to waste our time pleasing Mr. Y anymore," it will take staff some time to settle in and become accustomed to your way of managing things.

Remember, you are not the first person to ever face this transition-and, if you should ever leave your position, your staff will be equally as glad to explain to your successor just what she is doing differently. Do not get hung up on people's tendencies to bring up the past; libraries are long-lived institutions, and each library's history includes a long line of managers and management styles. Focus on carving out your own place and creating your own part of your institution's history.

WHAT A LIBRARY MANAGER DOES

The ways in which library managers spend their time of course vary among institutions and different levels of management-and in a sense, this is what this entire book is about! But there are some similarities among the roles and responsibilities of most managers. The basic job of any manager is to direct her resources and people towards accomplishing the defined goals of the institution. Higher-up managers may be responsible for defining these larger goals; section or department managers may set goals for their part of the whole in terms of the larger mission of the library; and libraries, as service institutions, need overall to define and to prioritize these goals in terms of the needs of their patrons or customers. As a library division manager at the Josephine County Library System, Oregon, explains: "Fight for the patrons, and every decision that is made should be made because it will make it easier for the patron." Any traditional managerial activity fits into this broad definition. You supervise and evaluate library staff in order to ensure that they work effectively to provide the services your patrons need and expect.

You keep the technology and facilities in your institution humming along so that customers have a comfortable, safe, and useful place to work, as well as the tools to meet their informational needs. You help create a culture of customer service, realizing that your approach and that of your employees goes a long way towards creating an atmosphere in which you can effectively serve your community. The way in which you manage people largely defines their attitudes towards their work, which in turn defines how smoothly the organization runs. You hold the authority to make decisions within your institution, and are responsible for making those decisions in the way that will best accomplish institutional goals. You are responsible for ranking the importance of various activities in terms of these goals, for prioritizing goals themselves, and for allocating resources to best accomplish library goals.

WOMEN IN MANAGEMENT

Although librarianship is still a female-dominated profession, many observers have noted that men hold a disproportionate number of administrative positions, that they tend to receive higher compensation than women in the field, and that subfields of the profession with a higher concentration of male workers tend to be higher-paid. These discrepancies are beginning to change in some subsets of the profession; female *Association of Research Libraries* (ARL) directors, for example, now make slightly more than their male counterparts, although there are fewer of them overall. This change in the salary structure of the top positions at large research institutions, however, fails to extend to other management positions and library environments. Female library managers can network with others to work to conquer these and other challenges. ALA's Library Administration and Management Association, for example, has a women administrator's discussion group.

ALA also has a *Committee on the Status of Women in Librarianship* (COSWL), which has among its goals that of helping women advance into managerial positions, and maintains a Feminist Task Force. Although still under-represented, especially in "top" jobs, relative to their presence in the profession, women make up an ever-increasing proportion of those in library management positions. This in turn results in an ever-increasing number of other female managers with whom you can network. You can also network with female managers in other professions; there are a number of organizations for professional women that will help you. Women are also more likely to face interruption of their careers for family reasons.

The lower pay in librarianship relative to that in many other professions means that female librarians may be more likely to take time for child care, elder care, and other personal responsibilities than will their more highly paid nonlibrary partners. Work to create the same flexibility and opportunity for your staff as you would appreciate from your institution. Be open to job sharing, flexible schedules, and telecommuting options, when the type of position and an individual's personality and work ethic make these ideas a reasonable possibility. A number of library responsibilities can be effectively carried out off-site, including functions such as collection development and Web design.

Libraries that fail to support flexible work options risk losing some of their best employees. Further, be supportive of pay equity efforts; do not dismiss them now that your own salary has increased with the assumption of your managerial duties. Some argue that women have a distinct managerial style, that their ways of interacting with people inevitably differ from the "male" style of management and communication. Depending on who you read, you will find arguments that female styles of management are either a better or a less effective way of managing. Remember that you will need to develop your own style—as appropriate to your organizational culture, your staff, your own personality, and your library's goals.

NON–LIBRARIANS AS LIBRARY MANAGERS

Non-MLS holders face particular challenges as library managers. Those new to the library environment may find that, although their existing managerial skills are transferable, it still takes time to understand and fit into the library world. Paraprofessional mid-level managers may encounter a prejudice for the MLS among degreed administrators and other department heads. Non-MLS library managers must develop a deep understanding of the functions of their institution, especially of the particular section or project for which they are responsible.

As one manager survey respondent stresses:

* "I think it is essential for a library manager to know the basics of the functions he or she is managing. For example, I wasn't familiar with the specific tool my cataloger used at my last job, but at least I knew cataloging, so I could help her when needed and know when she was or wasn't doing her job."

You need to understand the work your staff is doing in order to properly evaluate whether they are doing this work well and efficiently. The process of developing this insight may be as simple as taking the time to observe and ask questions, or it may take some reading or coursework, depending on your situation and background. While MLS librarians value the degree, they also generally value experience and expertise. The best way to impart that value and to elicit their respect is by example.

PARAPROFESSIONAL MANAGERS

Paraprofessional managers occupy a unique place in a library's hierarchy. Although you may fill a managerial position that appears in an equivalent level on an organization chart as your MLS peers, you may have a more difficult time promoting your ideas to those administrators that have an unconscious preference for the degree—and you may receive a lower salary. This observation is not intended to rekindle the ongoing debate over the value of the MLS, but rather to make you aware of some of the issues you might face as a paraprofessional manager in many library environments. If your organization will help cover the costs of a degree and you can see a clear career path for yourself, you can consider going back to school and earning your MLS.

The fantastic combination of a library degree and your previous library and management experience should equate to higher salaries and more options in your future, if you intend to stay in the library field. Many librarian managers got their start in paraprofessional positions and then earned the degree after working in the field for a number of years, enabling them to move up and to advance their careers in library management. In any case, realise that library school, while it may prepare people to be librarians, rarely prepares them for a career in management. Your MLS counterparts have no particular advantage *as managers*. The library skills and outlook that help create a good library manager, further, are by no means unique to degree holders.

VOLUNTEER MANAGERS

You may be entering a library management position in a small and/or remote library as a volunteer manager, on a full- or parttime basis, without specific library experience—and without compensation! Much of the information in this book will also be applicable in a volunteer situation, but you will need to adapt any advice, as appropriate, to smaller libraries and to your unique circumstances. As a volunteer manager, you also may be responsible for all library activities, from organizing a collection, to checking out materials, to managing others. Non-MLS library managers thrown into or assuming one of these library management positions should investigate Dave Sutton's *So You're Going to Run a Library: A Library Management Primer*, which is a useful guide for any manager new to libraries, especially in small institutions. If you are a volunteer manager, congratulations on feeling so strongly about the value of libraries that you are willing to donate your time and effort to keeping one going in your community or in your institution. One of your first steps should be to try to find a more experienced library manager to serve as your mentor and to help answer your inevitable questions about both librarianship and management. Again, here, a willingness to learn and to grow in your position will serve you well. Part of being a good volunteer manager may also include inspiring others to volunteer, as well as constructively directing and praising their energies.

NON–LIBRARIANS (NEW TO LIBRARIES)

If you enter library management from another profession, you may be taken aback by the amount of controversy the appointment of a nonlibrarian to a library administrative-especially a director-position in a larger institution can cause. This can be especially difficult if you begin calling yourself or are hired as a "librarian." As a non-MLS administrator, realise that you have walked into an ongoing argument about the importance of the MLS degree.

Some of the professionals who have spent the time, money, and effort to earn a master's in library and information science feel strongly about the value of the degree, pointing out that non-M.D.s who work in doctor's offices are never called doctors; public school employees without degrees and certification are not considered qualified to work as teachers. Institutions that call nondegree holders "librarians" and award them with administrative posts, in this view, merely contribute to an erosion of the value of the MLS degree.

This feeling is exacerbated by a general public perception that all library workers are "librarians" and questions such as: "You have to have a master's degree for this?!" as well as an ongoing internecine argument about the value of the degree and about the quality and rigor of some graduate programmes. Your assumption of an administrative position can stir up all of these feelings and arguments, but realizing that the tension stems from a number of factors can help you take criticism less personally and prepare yourself to field people's concerns. If there seems to be an argument or an undercurrent of feeling among staff that you are less entitled to your position due to your lack of an MLS, you may begin to feel defensive about your ability to do the job.

This is a situation in which you will do best by expressing your willingness to learn from your staff. As Mary Pergander, Head Librarian, Lake Bluff Public Library, Illinois, notes of her pre-MLS management experiences: "I did not know as much about libraries as my staff did.

I trusted them to teach me, they trusted me to lead them. It worked out fine." Although you may understand the basic similarities among the duties involved in administrative positions in different environments, only time will demonstrate your ability to serve effectively as a *library* administrator. Acknowledging the strengths and knowledge base of your employees, while also demonstrating the unique perspective and skills you bring to your position, is the best combination to begin winning over your staff.

Any good manager learns from her staff in any environment; you will need to do so more overtly, and will need to rely on your professional staff in areas where your knowledge is lacking. Make a point of learning about the issues that affect today's libraries. Keep up to date, for example, by reading Weblogs and library news sites each morning. Start with major resources such as *American Libraries* and *Library Journal*, each of which posts breaking library-related news stories online.

Then, branch out further to include a couple of resources in your library's area of specialty. Librarians value information and the informed. Your interest in issues important to the field will help you assimilate into the library culture. As one respondent to the staff survey states: "My current manager does not have an MLS, nor does he have much knowledge of libraries. While I do appreciate his dedication to his work and his willingness to take action, I wish he would take more opportunities to understand and observe our work." Also be sure to join relevant local and national associations and to network with other managers, library workers, and librarians.

MANAGING YOURSELF

Beyond this commitment to learning, there are also a number of personal qualities that will help you become a better manager—as well as those you should try to curb.

Habits and patterns to overcome include:

* Procrastination. Many libraries are able to hum along for quite a while even when some managerial tasks are put off, masking the fact that their internal

foundations are crumbling. Do not let a façade of well being allow you to put off potentially unpleasant tasks such as managing conflicts or making needed budget cuts.

* Impatience. Although in certain situations impatience can be quite useful in getting tasks done on a timely fashion, it has little value when dealing with library staff. As Amanda E. Standerfer, Library Director, Helen Matthes Library, Effingham, Illinois, suggests: "I would tell a new library manager to be patient. Not everything is going to work out in the first few months or years. I wanted to fix everything right away, and it just wasn't possible."
* Defensiveness. New managers sometimes develop an unfortunate tendency to take comments personally, or to jump to lay blame on others. While defensiveness may grow out of uneasiness in your new position, your staff will be more concerned about your behaviour than the reasons behind your actions. Accept that you will make mistakes; be willing to take blame as well as credit and to learn from your errors.
* Miscommunication. Effective communication goes beyond communicating clearly and providing staff with pertinent information, and includes watching your own behaviour and communication style. There is no room for sarcasm towards your staff, for example.

Habits to cultivate include:

* *Listening*. You need to pay attention to, and learn from, your staff, peers, customers, and administration. As Kari Baumann, Branch Manager, Centennial Park Branch Library, Greeley, Colorado, says: "I think the most important thing any new manager can do is to listen—to her staff, and to library staff that she doesn't supervise— to understand the organization as a whole."
* *Assertiveness and self-confidence*. Many new library managers have difficulty transitioning, not only into

dealing with staff as a manager rather than as a peer, but into dealing with their own bosses and colleagues in a self-confident and effective manner. Take charge from the beginning. Start out as you mean to continue. Understand the power that you have in the organization, and do not be reluctant to use it to influence people and influence change in your library. Librarians with a tendency to be less extroverted can find this more difficult, but a certain level of assertiveness is necessary in order to maintain your influence in the organization.

* *A willingness to be proactive.* Why wait for problems to pile up or for complaints to find you? Look for ways to improve library service, working conditions for staff, workflow, or funding, and then act on achieving your goals in these areas.
* *Communication.* The importance of maintaining open and frequent communication with anyone you supervise—or report to.
* *Lifelong learning.* Library manager can afford to stagnate in her position.

People skills are essential to any effective manager—especially in libraries!—and much of the discussion here and throughout the book reflects that fact. Of course people skills are also important in most subfields of librarianship, but they are especially necessary for managers in any library setting, type, or department.

CHARTING A MANAGEMENT PATH

The earlier you start consciously charting your career path as a library manager, the more successful you will be in your career as a whole. Some schools are proactively meeting the concerns of students seeking additional education in the management aspects of library science.

If you are just joining the profession and you have a clear vision of a library career path that includes management, you can investigate graduate library and information science programmes that offer a heavier emphasis on the administrative side of the field. Several schools now have joint programmes that offer a heavier exposure to the management aspects of librarianship; Kent State and UCLA, for example, each offer a joint MLIS/MBA degree programme, which can be especially useful to those whose career goals include management of a very large institution.

Mentors and Role Models

Earlier, the discussion focused on deciding whom *not* to emulate during your career as a library manager. Equally, if not more important, are the qualities of those you do choose to emulate. If you have lacked good managerial role models in your career so far, you can consider enrolling in a formal mentoring programme–either within your own institution, or one sponsored by a library-related or other organization. Alternatively, seek out more informal mentors – online, through networking at local events, through contacting people writing on issues that interest you.

Seek out expertise wherever it lies, and be willing to ask your mentors for their support and help. Realise also that it can be useful to find multiple mentors to help you with the various facets of and different decisions involved in your position. Everyone has his or her own area of expertise, and a mentor can be anyone with experience or knowledge that you lack. Author and Webmaster Priscilla Shontz advises: "Find yourself some good mentors, either at your organization or elsewhere. This is important in any position, but in a management position you can sometimes feel very alone–especially if you manage a small library where you are the only manager. It can be incredibly helpful to have friends, mentors, and colleagues to whom you can turn when you have a question or when you just need to vent! For example, if you manage a branch library, you may want to develop relationships with other branch managers, so you can ask for advice when facing a decision or problem. Library activist suggests that new managers "find a mentor to help show you the ropes in your organization and give you pointers on management skills."

A one- or two-year graduate programme, of course, can be hard pressed to fit in all the coursework needed to prepare someone to become a librarian, let alone to teach management skills as well. However, the lack of practical information presented in even the most basic library management courses was overwhelmingly cited as a problem by manager survey respondents—and, given the predicted upcoming wave of library retirements, this should be a concern for schools charged with preparing future library managers to fill these anticipated upper-level vacancies.

Many respondents to the manager survey suggested that more hands-on courses would have been useful, especially those incorporating role-playing, jobshadowing, and/or presentations and advice from actual working managers in different library settings. Others suggested internships or other real-world activities. A number of library managers do take advantage of continuing education opportunities to fill in the gaps left by their alma maters, or to build up their skills in specific areas. As a manager, you will likely need to take responsibility for your own ongoing learning and professional development. There may be no one above you that will suggest you take a class, attend a conference, or otherwise push yourself professionally, whereas as a nonmanagement librarian you may have been used to your supervisor suggesting that you engage in these activities.

Never fall into the trap of assuming that, because you have progressed to a certain point in your career, you need no further professional development. Realise also that more official professional development activities such as workshops and meetings serve as excellent networking as well as professional development opportunities, and can keep you energized and focused on your career and your profession. Cessa Vichi, a library division manager at the Josephine County Library System, says: Attending any training is always beneficial for ideas, new ways of looking at old problems, inspiration and growth as a leader.

As a leader, the responsibility for organizational/division growth falls on you. New ideas, fresh input, and different approaches are vital to learning and growing as a leader." You can locate official professional development and management training opportunities in a variety of ways, from reading your local library system's newsletter to attending ALA conferences. Also, be open to learning through your professional reading. Professional development includes all of your lifelong learning, from reading to on-the-job experience. Lifelong learning means precisely that: learning through all of your experiences, whether planned or not.

Always try to think beyond your current job, and about how you can learn, grow, and move forward in your library career. Take advantage of professional development and networking opportunities. Look at these not as an imposition on your time, but as an opportunity to reenergize, learn, and open to new possibilities. Libraries, especially today, do not remain stagnant–you need to stretch yourself to keep up! Warren Bennis and Robert Thomas note: "The ability to learn is a defining characteristic of being human; the ability to continue learning is an essential skill of leadership. When leaders lose that ability, they inevitably falter. When any of us lose that ability, we no longer grow."2 As a librarian, you possess an inherent advantage over managers in other types of organizations. A major task of any manager is to identify and assimilate the information that will help her do her job. Who better to take on that task than information professionals? The only difference here is that, instead of compiling this information on behalf of your patrons, you are doing so for yourself and as is relevant in your own context. Most managers are made, not born, and you can use your library skills to help make your own way.

3

Librarians' Skills and Qualifications

INTRODUCTION

The appearance of the internet and the WorldwideWeb, as a final stage of an evolution started many decades ago with the introduction of computers and network technologies, has created a new information and social environment, radically different from the functional environment of the traditional library. This fact has led to a considerable research and discussion concerning the form, the role, the position and the functions of the social institutions known as "libraries" within this new context.

At the same time, and as it might be expected, another discussion is under way, concerning what may be considered as the human parallel of the institution, that is the librarian or the information professional that runs the library. This discussion concerns many aspects and problems of the information professional in the new environment and especially the types, the education needed, the skills and qualifications required, the extent to which the profession should or will change etc. In an attempt to determine and understand these changes and, mainly, to analyse the data that will lead the profession to the new century, several works with various types of predictions, analyses and proposals regarding the future of the profession have been published. A brief overview of the relevant literature follows so that the findings of our research are considered in the suitable context. According to these works, thus, the modern librarian should be a professional that possesses standards and values that function effectively and smoothly in a technological environment.

He fully understands and knows sufficiently the conventional library practices. He constantly wishes to change, to develop and to learn. He adapts easily in a permanently altered environment of information, he has experience in education and possess a considerable amount of communication skills. His survival will be ensured by the fundamentals of his science and the skills and roles that emerge from them. The role of intermediate and instructor will still be essentials and librarian will focus into helping the user identify the information he needs and providing tools for evaluation and use.

Audunson believes that the modern academic courses in LIS should aim to create the "complete librarian", while Researchers points out that the education should not only focus on the technical matters of Library Science, such as the creation of a digital library, but should also be orientated towards the development of survival and affective skills. In the modern environment procedures and practices in education should convergence with those found in an actual working environment.

Librarians must emphasize in the learning environment they create themselves and not solely to technology. He also demonstrates ten tendencies of the contemporary environment of information that influence librarian's function and role such as: virtual is a place not a format, communities of interest are no longer bounded by geography and every profession's relevance is in question. According to him, one of the most important future roles is that of information councelor. Identification of the most important issues that affect – within the modern environment – the behaviour and attitudes of every librarian is also accomplished by Melchionda. Technostress and techno-phobia, lack of standardisation and quality, competition with search engines and commercial tools are few of the factors that influence the role of librarian in the modern environment.

An important issue should be the examination of the real cause of changes in the librarian's profession, regardless of time frame, and through a more realistic point-of-view. In fact, the goals of our profession are still the same and they are affected from the expectations of the market, the working environment and ethics. Specialization or hybridization should not pose a dilemma, since the profession must be considered as a whole set that is constantly changing and revised. Regarding the "hybridization" of our profession, Biddiscombe believes that the hybrid library poses the need for "hybrid" information professionals.

Although it is difficult for one person to acquire a large number of skills, he states that every modern librarian must be able to recognize informational needs, manage users and encourage people with different skills to work in the same team. Such "hybrid" teams will play an important role as far as management of future information systems is concerned. Librarians should also focus on evolving their internet skills and four basic points regarding that evolution should be mediation and assistance, teaching and training, partnerships, design and production.

Also, according to Pace every online library experience should be consisted of quality, expertise, integrity and longevity. Concerning the skills needed by a modern librarian, Fisher analyses a set of skills and points out that at the same time with the traditional roles, the librarian will create organizational information management systems, will use the techniques of Information Architect, will manage access in digital documents and will support every possible learning procedure. A profile of skills and qualification is also demonstrated by Partridge and Hallam, according to which qualifications are divided into technical and generic ones.

Ashcroft identifies six basic skill categories:

* Professional.
* Marketing and promotion.
* Evaluation.
* Communication – negotiation – collaboration.
* Censorship.
* Personal transferable skills.

In addition, Marion conducted a research on job advertisements and she concluded that a new category of "digital librarian" is not yet necessary and library is still a part of an evolving automated environment, rather than of a digital one. She also found communication skills to be the most wanted qualification. Kwasik's analysis on job ads regarding skills for serials librarians found communication skills to be the second most desired qualification. In general, she found traditional skills to be more desired than then ones originating from the digital world. The importance of ICT skills is underlined by Biddiscombe as he believes are necessary for any learning, educational or research procedure in a learning environment, but at the same time, information specialists should maintain some of their traditional skills and qualifications.

Steele and Mechthild also believe that ICT skills, along with communication and administration ones will be essential for every modern librarian. They also state that the use of many terms in order to describe the new librarian is the result of the uncertainty of what the role of a librarian should be.

Concerning the roles served by a modern librarian, Fourie's literature survey identified several roles:

* Publishing;
* Negotiating;
* Teaching;
* Advising;
* Retrieving – researching; and
* Archival management.

In addition, she suggested three more:

* Environmental scanning;

* Active identification of new niche markets; and
* Action research.

Moreover, England states that the librarian will function as researcher, organizer and publisher, member of the digital library design team, teacher and consultant, while Garrod analyses seven roles for a modern librarian, such as metadata specialist, marketing – public relations and learning facilitator. Finally, Nageswara and Babu's research reflects some of the most current trends in LIS as impressed through the roles they identify; search intermediary, facilitator, trainer – educator, web site builder – publisher, researcher, interface designer, knowledge manager, shifter of information resources.

RESEARCH

A total of 200 job advertisements were studied from UK, Canada, Australia and the USA in 2006 and 2007. The aim of the research is to have the qualifications and the skills of librarian's profession investigated, as they are impressed through the job ads. The elements of this research – substantially the qualifications and skills that the libraries ask for – were used so that a basic profile for a modern librarian would be created, which presents the skills through classes and subclasses. The job ads concern positions in various types of libraries and their departments.

Table 3.1. Skills and Qualifications Identified through Job Advertisements

Skills/qualifications	%
Degree in LIS	82
Working experience	68
Communication skills	65
Collection development – management	53
Service orientation	38
Working in a team	38
Administration – organizational skills	36
Knowledge of current developments in LIS	32
User education	30

(Contd...)

Table 3.1 Continued....	
Skills/qualification	**%**
Digital collection development – management	27
Use of software applications	27
Library automated systems	25
Creation – management of web pages	25
Personal traits	22
Knowledge of library's subject content	21
Working alone	20
Markup languages	16
Databases	13
Programming languages	12
Use of p/c	12
Sets priorities	11
Networks	11
Programme management	10
Problem solving	10
Foreign languages	10
Development of personal career	9
Attention to detail	8
Metadata	7
Serial collections management	6
Knowledge of current developments in ICT	6
Marketing	5
Critical thinking	5
Multimedia	5
Alliances – consortia	4
Administration experience	3
Digitalization	2
Typing	1

FINDINGS

The findings of this research are:

* A total of 38 skills and qualifications were identified through the job ads. Their percentage of appearance was recorded and it's the basic element for the final findings of this research.

* Degree in LIS and working experience skills were expected to be the ones with the highest percentage, and should be considered "de facto" for all librarians, without any further value into this research's findings.
* Communication skill appears in over 60 per cent of the ads and should be considered a desirable skill for every modern librarian. We can assume that this need for communication skills, no matter if the librarian works in technical or public services, comes from the rapid development of the web and the increase of possible ways and means of communication among LIS professionals and the librarian and the user.
* Development of digital collections skill appears in the 10th place. The "equivalent" originating from the traditional environment appears in twice as many advertisements. This finding is an important one regarding the need for development of a completely new set of skills that will originate from the digital world. Instead, it is concluded that the skills that the librarian has developed for decades and regard the knowledge and use of traditional library systems are still important.
* Interpersonal skills, in general, have a high percentage of appearance in the job ads.
* The need for administrative-organizational skills underlines that a modern librarian should have the ability to manage and organize weather it is about the library and its departments or research groups and projects.
* ICT skills often have a higher percentage than the "digital skills". Although ICT skills have a relatively low percentage, we can expect that this will change in the future. General use of software and the knowledge of creating and maintaining web pages are two of the most desirable skills in this category.
* Skills related with the management and use of digital

content have a small demand and that was an interesting finding. Especially when compared with the "traditional" skills we can conclude that, at the time being, professional practice dismisses the need for a new category, the "digital librarian".

* Probably the most important aspect of professional development and advancement for the modern librarian is adaptation of current skills in new practices and motivation in acquiring new skills when needed.
* The qualifications and the personal skills a librarian must possess does not change according to the developments in technology, but goes along with the change in organisational and administrative structure of information services.
* Qualifications for a modern librarian are a mix of old and new ones and that synthesis derives from the need in organising documents and information in a hybrid environment.
* Social skills are important not only for professionals working in public services, but should be considered a distinct category of skills, along with professional skills, important for every modern LIS professional.

PROFILE

There has been an analysis in two major categories: professional and general skills. As professional are comprehended the skills that are directly interwoven with the working practices, the use of professional standards and the daily activity of the librarian regarding various technical services. In this category are included the practices of traditional librarianship, new tendencies that prevail in the management of digital content, the general ICT skills and, finally, various subclasses of general administrative and educational type.

In the category of general skills in which it would, rather, be more appropriate the term social skills, are included all those abilities that the librarian develops daily through his working environment without, however, being related directly with his daily occupation with activities such as cataloguing. The belief that was expressed in various cases, often by persons that did not originate from the traditional librarianship, for the necessity of developing a new set of qualifications and skills, directly and uniquely originating from the digital world, is erroneous.

Table 3.2. Profile of skills and Qualifications

Professional skills	Generic (Social) Skills
Process: Management of conventional materials	Personal traits
Automated library systems	Individual talents
Collection development	Critical thinking
Collection management	Attention to detail
Experience in selecting, acquiring and processing conventional material	Problem solving
	Self-marketing
Serials collection management	Ethics
Process – management of digital materials	Business skills
Metadata tools	*Interpersonal skills*
Design and management of databases	Working in a team
Evaluation of internet informational materials, sources and services	Communications skills
	Ability to work alone
Collection development	Understanding user demands and informational needs
Multimedia	
Digitalization	Leadership
Electronic publishing	Service orientation
ICT skills	Participation – development of library consortia
Markup languages	*Experience*
Design, creation and maintenance of web pages	Reference experience
Technical knowledge in computers	Knowledge of library's subject content

(Contd...)

Table. 3.2 Continued...

Professionsl Skills	**Generic (Social) Skills**
Use of software applications (O/S, Office, etc.)	Ability to accept change
Distance education software	Administration experience
Programming languages	Prioritize work
Networks	Insight in transferring traditional operations in an online environment
Ability to compare software, hardware and technologies	*Lifelong learning – continuing education*
Administrative – organizational skills	Planning personal career
Library facilities management	Ability to learn constantly
Financial resources management	Knowledge of current developments in LIS
Human resources management and evaluation	Knowledge of current developments in ICT
Evaluation of library services	
Interviewing skills	
Marketing	
Projects management	
Understanding organizational structure	
Education	
LIS degree	
Participation in conferences – seminars	
Participation in library associations – organizations	
User education – online education	
Typing	
Foreign languages	

Even though the librarians are facing challenges for new and emerging skills, the most important aspect of this change is to be able to adapt the existing skills – many of which are traditional librarianship skills – and the ability to remain flexible in a working environment that is constantly changing. Thus, we can talk not only about a new set of skills and qualifications, but, rather, about the suitable mentalities that should be developed and be adapted in the working culture.

The librarians need to maintain those skills that gave them respect in the traditional environment and they should, simultaneously, continue being open in new ideas, being interested to approach user needs and develop all those new skills they need, in order to ensure access to information. And we must keep in mind that the state of the evolving librarian is not a new condition, but rather a continuation of what librarians have always done.

4

Quality Management Approaches in Libraries

INTRODUCTION

The increasing expectations of users have challenged libraries to improve their quality of services. Limited by increasingly tighter budgetary restrictions, library managers feel more pressure to fully exploit available resources. Therefore, several libraries and information services have adopted quality management practices in recent years.

Among the various initiatives implemented include:

* ISO 9000 standards,
* 5S movement, and
* benchmarking.

By adopting quality management, the library's image and service quality can be improved, and librarians can increase productivity while focusing on the customer's needs. Quality management has been extensively applied within the manufacturing industry for over a decade.

More recently, the service industry has increasingly emphasised this area. The public sector has also put forward major initiatives to improve quality. Closely examining available quality management techniques in service industries and the public sector reveals their effectiveness and positive impact on the customers. Quality management is increasingly integrated into library services, following their perceived success in manufacturing industries, with particular emphasis on improving service quality.Libraries have developed numerous programmes to fulfil user requirements. In general, libraries concentrate mainly on maintaining administrative activities, building the collection, and serving the users.

Therefore, the functions of a library can be broadly categorised as administrative management, technical services and public services. Administrative management defines the objectives of the library, allocates the resources to achieving such objectives, co-ordinates related activities, and assesses the performance of related services. Technical services largely focus on building the collection and making the collection more accessible for users.

The activities of technical services include acquisition, information organisation, and preservation. While all library activities strive to, public services serve the customers most directly. Related activities consist of circulation, reference and access service. Library services can be viewed as an open system with materials, resources and information needs of customers as input. In other words, the activities involved in providing and using library services are more interrelated than isolated.

While the library only exists for serving customers, the service delivery system should be user-oriented. Although all functions and activities focus on customers, the direct interaction between library and customers occurs in public services. That is, librarians working in circulation, reference and access service respond and translate the customer's expectations to the technical service department and administrative management.

Depending on the ability of public services to accurately interpret customer requirements, all functions of the library can be directed to satisfying the quality requirements and information needs of customers. Quality management in libraries and information services has received considerable attention, with a majority of those investigations describing quality concepts, quality management principles, related processes, and limitations. From the perspective of library services, adopting quality programmes increases the effectiveness of the library and satisfies increasingly higher customer expectations.

Most quality management- related literature is based on experience drawn from industrial organisations, particularly on the manufacturing of tangible products delivered to the end-user at a later stage.

Past years have witnessed the increasing acceptance of quality management into services-related and non-profit organisations, such as education. Despite the significant level of adaptation within service organisations and the public sector, there exists missing link between quality management principles/tools and the implementation of quality management in libraries and information services.

Johannsen foresaw the risk:

- . . . As the general principles of quality control have originally been developed in private sector and industrial environments, you may expect problems, when you wish to use those principles to manage quality of an intangible resource, information, in organizations, where structures, culture, management style, business strategies and customers are often very unlike industrial organizations.

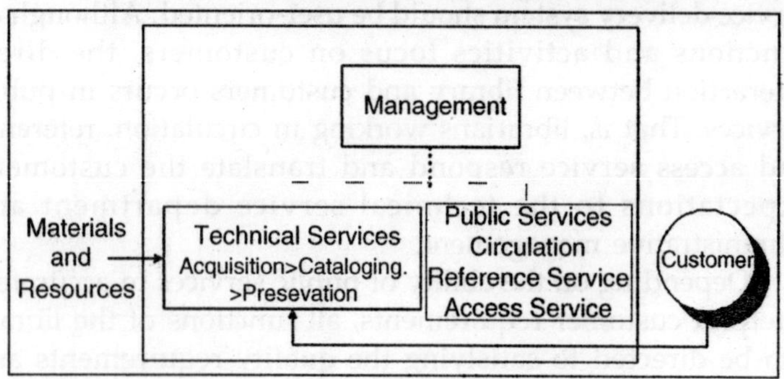

Fig 4.1. A Systemic View of Library Services.

Effectively→ implementing quality management in libraries and information services requires an understanding of the following:

* The unique characteristics of library operations
* The nature of interaction between librarians and customers
* The making of recommendations on the application of appropriate quality management concepts and techniques.

QUALITY MANAGEMENT APPROACHES

Quality management approaches can be categorised broadly into three stages according to the evolution of management control. Management can implement control before an activity commences, while the activity occurs, or after the activity has been completed. Consequently, three types of control are feedforward, concurrent and feedback. The most desirable type of management control is feedforward control that is future-directed and takes place in advance of the actual activity.

Feedforward control is advantageous because it allows management to prevent anticipated problems rather than having to cure them later and to avoid wasting resources. Concurrent control, as its name implies, takes place while an activity is in progress. When control is enacted while the activity is being performed, management can correct problems before they become too costly. The most conventional means of control relies on feedback. The feedback control takes place after the activity.

However, a disadvantage of this approach is that the damage will have already occurred by the time that the manager has the information to take corrective actions. Consequently, feedforward control is the most economic approach and can meet the requirement of customers, followed by concurrent control and feedback control, respectively. Interestingly, quality management approaches developed and applied to assess and improve product quality can be related to types of management control from the perspective of an open system.

Quality management approaches were originally developed as being product-oriented. Feedback control, an inspection-based quality control approach, was introduced to detect inferior products at the after-production stage. Realising that quality could not be improved by merely inspecting the finished product, subsequent efforts switched the emphasis of quality management from inspection to process control: from feedback control stage to concurrent control stage.

The underlying premise regarding quality in the concurrent control stage is that quality is equivalent to meeting or exceeding customer expectations. Manufacturing products that reflect the diverse needs of customers, is more of a function of good design than of good control of a process. Therefore, quality management has gradually shifted to emphasis on the design phase: from concurrent control stage to feedforward control stage.

Quality by Inspection

The inspection-based system was perhaps the first scientifically designed quality control system to evaluate quality. The system is applied to incoming raw materials and parts for use as inputs for production and/or finished products. Under this system, some quality characteristics are examined, measured and compared with required specifications to assess conformity. Therefore, the inspection-based system is a screening process that merely isolates conforming from non-conforming products without having any direct mechanism to reduce defects. Reducing the damage to final products, sampling plans were developed to control product quality. Although an effective technique, a quality control system based on sampling inspection does not directly achieve customer satisfaction and continuous improvement. Producing fewer defects through process improvement is the only means of reducing defects.

QUALITY BY PROCESS CONTROL

Defects inevitably add to the production cost and waste resources. Therefore, a business strives for zero defects. The quality management system based on sampling inspections has been replaced by the approach of continuously improving the process. This concept, as pioneered by Deming, moves from detecting defects to preventing them and continuing with process improvement to meeting and exceeding customer requirements on a continuous basis. The continuous cycle of process improvement is based on the scientific method for addressing problems, commonly referred to as the Deming cycle.

Deming's approach consists of four basic stages:

* A plan of what to do;
* Do or carry out the plan;
* Study what has done; and
* Act to prevent errors or improve the process.

The planning stage consists of studying the current situation, gathering data, and planning for improvement.

Related activities include:

* Defining the process, its inputs, outputs, customers, and suppliers;
* Understanding customer expectations;
* Identifying problems;
* Testing theories of causes; and
* Developing solutions.

In the do stage, the plan is implemented on a trial basis to evaluate a proposed solution and provide objective data. The study stage determines whether or not the trial plan is working correctly and if any further problems or opportunities are identified. In the final stage, act, the final plan is implemented and the improvements become standardised and implemented continuously. This process then returns to the plan stage for further diagnosis and improvement. The Deming Cycle can enhance communication between the staff involved and help employees to use the wheel to improve processes.

Some of the specific tools used to improve processes are control charts, process capability studies, seven tools, seven new tools, and seven creativity tools. However, the appropriate tools must be applied for the specified purpose. For example, cause-and-effect diagrams and process flow charts could be more appropriate during the planning stage of the Deming wheel, whereas control charts may be most appropriate during the stage of checking.

QUALITY BY DESIGN

The Deming approach shifted the focus of quality management a step back from inspection to process control. The approach of quality by design makes a further step back from process to design. By definition, Quality by design implies that quality must be built in early in the development and design stage. By doing so, the final product can satisfy the customers.

Two important techniques for designing quality products are:

* Quality function deployment (QFD) and
* Failure Mode and Effect Analysis (FMEA).

Quality function deployment is a structured approach that:

* Identifies and ranks the relative importance of customer requirements;
* Identifies design parameters that contribute to the customer requirements;
* Estimates the relationship between design parameters and customer requirements and among different design parameters; and
* Sets target values for the design parameters to best satisfy customer requirements.

A QFD matrix is frequently used to translate prioritised customer requirements into identifiable and measurable product specifications and engineering requirements to reduce functional variation and costs, thereby facilitating the decision-makers in making designrelated decisions. Many investigators have successfully applied QFD in product and service design. Failure Mode and Effect Analysis is a methodical approach to examine a proposed design for possible ways in which failure can occur.

FMEA consists of:

* Identifying and listing modes of failure and the subsequent faults;

* Assessing the probability of these faults;
* Assessing the probability that the faults are detected;
* Assessing the severity of the consequences of the faults;
* Calculating a measure of the risk;
* Ranking the faults on the basis of the risk;
* Attempting to resolve the high-risk problems; and
* Verifying the effectiveness of the action by using a revised measure of risk.

In addition to providing preliminary information on reliability prediction, product and process design, FMEA helps engineers identify potential problems in the product earlier, thereby avoiding costly changes or reworks at later stages. Closely scrutinising quality management reveals that many techniques are based on experience derived from manufacturing tangible products. Whether or not quality management practices can be transferred to a service industry delivering intangible services has received considerable attention.

Many investigators confer that:

* The service and manufacturing industries differ in terms of the characteristics of quality,
* Different criteria must be used for measuring these industries, and
* The focus of quality management is rather different than similar.

The final manufacturing products can be measured objectively, while the quality can be managed by output control. Meanwhile, the deliverables of services are frequently intangible, which is difficult to measure objectively. In addition to the simultaneously delivery and consumption of services, the quality certainly cannot be managed by either output control or process control. Brophy and Coulling indicated that with the broad applications in the service sector, the sector has come to the recognition that some aspects of quality management must be approached somewhat differently in the service industry.

The most distinguishing characteristic between service and manufacturing industries is that in the former, there is usually a direct interaction between the customer and the service. Libraries and information services have intensive direct interaction and also indirect contact with the customers. Because of the immediacy of the interface, libraries must develop their own framework when integrating quality management approaches into libraries.

FRAMEWORK OF QUALITY MANAGEMENT APPROACHES IN LIBRARIES

Having different characteristics, library services require special approaches of quality management that go beyond the simple adoption of manufacturing techniques for a product. Quality management related to library functions can be viewed in three phases: before service, during service, and after service. Library services ultimately focus on satisfying the information needs of customers. Before services are provided, the technical service departments should have required books and information resources collected and value-added to enhance their value to the customers.

Therefore, the customer-oriented library should regard technical services as resource development system to ensure that every customer has resources properly acquired, organised, displayed or accessed. Having direct contact with customers, the public services should be regarded as information service delivejry system and focus on providing information to customers accurately, promptly, and responsively to help customers solve problems, and build up customers' knowledge and ultimately enhance their productivity.

Administrative management should be regarded as the service support system to coordinate and allocate resources as well as provide support for technical services and public services to satisfy customers' needs, and to evaluate service performance periodically and to continuously improve service quality. Figure shows the quality management approaches and techniques associated with the stages of service delivery in libraries.

Resource Development System

Largely concerning itself with backstage activities, a resource development system is the off-line preparation for public services and has no direct contact with customers. For services in which the customer need not be present, the service transaction can be de-coupled and standardised. For example, acquisition is considered to be a customised service. Convenient access to Web-accessible public access catalogue, however, has weaned customers from present interaction with live librarians to interaction via online purchase request and, consequently, only routine order preparation and communication is required.

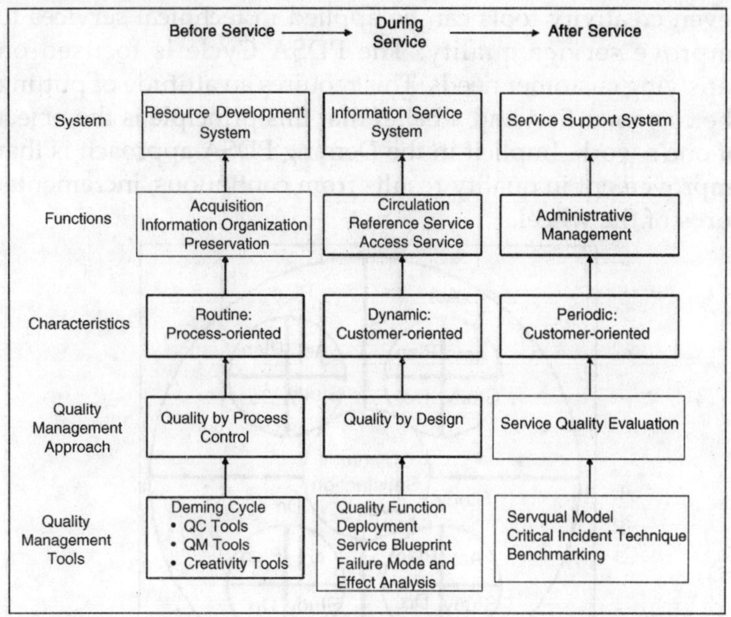

Fig 4.2. Framework of Quality Management Approaches in Libraries.

Most activities related to technical services have technical and procedural standards to follow, accounting for why each function is characterised by a high routine and process-orientation. International or domestic rules govern the cataloguing, classification, and information organisation. In addition, standardised practices also exist for acquisition and preservation, *e.g.* how order requests are to be formulated and transmitted.

In fact, many practices in technical services are standardised by actual work routines and formalised based on a detailed and systematic study during library automation. Therefore, the quality management of a resource development system should emphasise the concurrent control of process to ensure that all books and resources have been accurately collected, accessed and valueadded appropriately. Quality by process control is the best quality management strategy for a resource development system.

Deming's PDSA cycle, together with the seven quality control tools, the seven quality management tools, and the seven creativity tools can be applied in technical services to improve service quality. The PDSA Cycle is focused on satisfying customer needs. This requires an attitude of putting the customer first and a belief that this principle is the object of one's work. Implicit in the Deming PDSA approach is that improvement in quality results from continuous, incremental turns of the wheel.

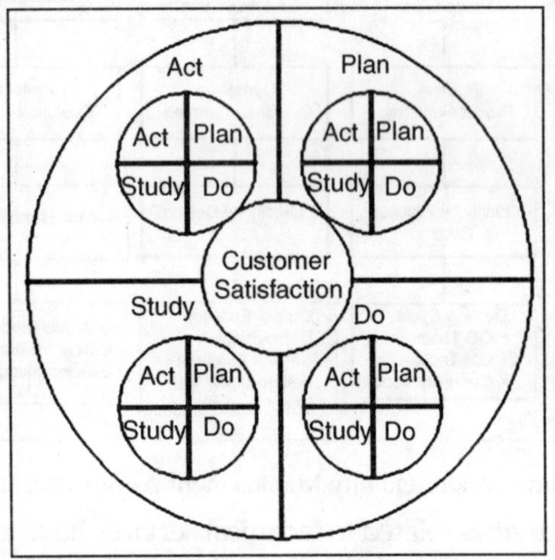

Fig 4.3. The Deming Circle

Seven simple tools — cause-and-effect diagrams, run charts, scatter diagrams, flowcharts, Pareto diagrams, histograms and control charts — have been termed the Seven Quality Control. In the early 1970s, as Total Quality Control (TQC) expanded to service and administrative areas, it became clear that the 7QC tools were not always appropriate.

So, the seven new QC tools or the seven management tools – affinity diagrams, interrelationship digraphs, tree diagrams, matrix diagrams, prioritisation matrixes, process decision programme charts, and activity network diagrams–were developed under the leadership of Nyatanni. Among these the affinity diagram is a tool for organising language data. After ideas are brainstormed and written on cards, they are grouped together with similar ideas. A header card is created which captures the meaning of each group of ideas. This is a creative, right brain, activity.

The Seven Creativity Tools are problem definition, brainstorming, brainwriting, creative brainstorming, word and picture association, advanced analogies, and the morphological chart. While the original seven QC tools are oriented towards the analysis of quantitative data, the seven management tools and seven creativity tools are designed to handle unstructured, verbal information in group-base problem-solving or decision- making processes. All these tools can be used separately or complementarily. For example, the acquisition department can use control chart to evaluate the performance of dealers, and build partnership with the best dealer.

The serial department can use the cause-and-effect diagram not only to analyse the causes of missing issues but also use relation diagrams to control the order status of critical serials to ensure the completeness and promptness of serials collection. In addition, the Pareto diagram can be used in the cataloguing department to collect the data on bibliographic verification and copy cataloguing for further analysing the feasibility of enhancing productivity and shortening the processing time.

INFORMATION SERVICE SYSTEM

The information service system is a service delivery system that has direct contact with customers. In circulation, access and reference services, the customer often serves as the co-producer and works with the librarians and the library system to produce a final product which enhances knowledge, skills, or promotes the enjoyment of leisure activities. The service encounter is always initiated by the customer. Therefore, the major function of an information service system is dynamic and customer-oriented. Because of direct interaction with public service librarians, customers require the service to be done right the first time and to be consistent every time.

Consequently, quality by design is the best quality management strategy for information service system. Quality management tools that can be applied are quality function deployment, failure mode and effect analysis, and service blueprinting which is specially designed for effectively managing the service encounter. Reference service has direct encounters with customers, and the service quality depends highly on the performance of the reference librarians and their interactions with customers. Therefore, the design of reference service can adopt the techniques of quality function deployment.

Library activists proposed a modified framework of quality function deployment for reference service. There are four phases to facilitate communicating service requirements from the customer to the activities related to quality management of reference service delivery. The first phase is to identify the customer's needs and requirements. The second phase is to define the service requirements and design the co-service system so that the right quality is built in from the very beginning of service design.

The third phase consists of process planning which is a matter of selecting the co-service process "best" producing what the customer needs. Phase four involves the planning of the quality management activities. It emphasizes translating reference processes into quality management activities in order to ensure quality both before and during the reference encounter. The first task of applying QFD to reference services is to identify customer needs, which are descriptions in the customer's own words of the benefits they want the reference services to provide. The opinions posted on the library web site or BBS, customer complaints, records of reference interviews, previous user studies, and so on, will all contribute to the list of customer needs.

In reference services, the primary customer needs might be categorised as "good employees", "right answers" and "nice environment". In order to manage the customer needs, the primary needs need to be structured into a hierarchy. For example, the primary need for "good employee" might be elaborated as "good attitude" and "good skills" in serving customers. And the "good attitude" is subdivided into "kind and polite", "does not have to wait", "assists users in looking up information" and "properly dressed".

Each customer need is, then, to be met in terms of professional terminology – that is, service requirements. For example, the words "kind and polite" express the customer's concept, but librarians need these words translated into their vocabulary in order to actually build a service delivering standards and quality management activities. In delivering reference service, "kind and polite" may be described in terms of the responsiveness, approachability, attentiveness, and courtesy. The service requirements of reference services translated from customer needs might be grouped into answer, process, and environment, using an Affinity Diagram.

For example, the quality of answer might be evaluated according to two perspectives – results and sources. And the quality of source might be evaluated according to the indicators of credibility, acceptability, accessibility and availability. After the service requirements have been identified and prioritised, the most important requirements must be linked to reference process to design the co-service system to satisfy the customer needs.

Circulation and access service is the major contact between the customer and the library, and is usually the starting point for customers to use all other library services. With information networks, most customers can remotely access the webpac or search networked databases. After identifying the availability of certain books or documents, the customer is physically present in the library to check out those books or photocopy the required documents. If the collection or documents needed by the customers are unavailable, the customers can also apply for an interlibrary loan or document delivery service. Encounters between the customer and library are integral and continuous, with each customer possibly encountering many points of services and interacting with varying service facilities and librarians.

Therefore, the circulation and access service should be designed by integrating all of the service points to provide seamless services to customers. The service blueprint is a customer-focused service process analysis tool. Figure gives an example of a typical service blueprint for access service. A service blueprint is a detailed map or a flow chart of the service process. However, creating a flow chart can only depict the workflow of internal operations from the perspective of the librarian.

Such a flow chart neither provides understanding of the interaction between the librarian and the customer; nor can it integrate these encounter points with related activities that support these encounters. Therefore, the concepts of "line of interaction" and "line of visibility" are used in a service blueprint to improve service encounters. Consequently, the service delivery process can be simultaneously viewed from the perspectives of the librarian and the customer. The line of interaction differentiates actions performed by the customer from actions performed by the librarians. Customer actions are placed above the line.

Actions performed by the librarians are located below the line. These actions are charted on the service path proceeding from left to right. Along the line of interaction, the encounter points, *i.e.* the points in the service process where the customer receives the access services, can be easily specified. The line of visibility in a service blueprint distinguishes those processes that are visible to the customer from those that are behind the scenes.

This concept facilitates the understanding of the interconnection between "below-the-line" and "above-the-line" service processes and the recognition that the latter processes where the customers' experiences directly depend on the former processes that customers do not experience.

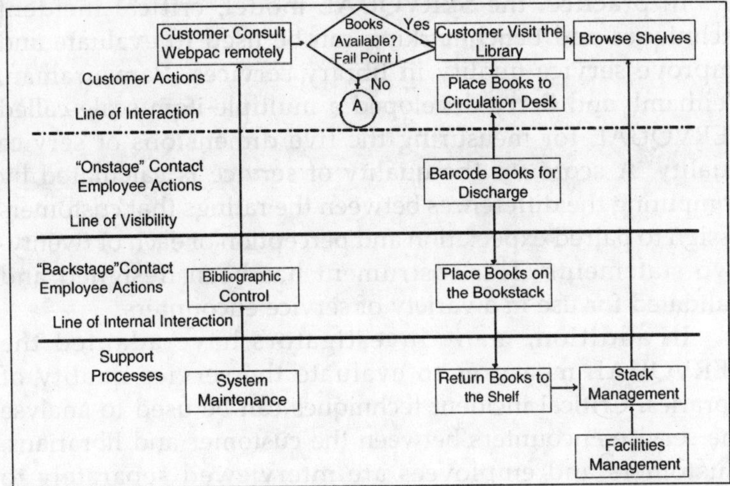

Fig 4.4. Framework of Service Blueprint - A Case of Access Service.

The blueprinting exercise also provides librarians with opportunities to identify potential fail points and, then, use the failure mode and effect analysis to design "foolproof" procedures to avoid such an occurrence, thereby ensuring the delivery of high-quality services. The purpose of failure mode and effects analysis is to identify all the ways in which a failure can occur, to estimate the effect and seriousness of the failure, and to recommend corrective design actions. An FMEA usually consists of specifying the following information for each critical component: failure mode, cause of failure, effect on the product or system within which it operates, corrective action, and comments.

SERVICE SUPPORT SYSTEM

The performance of a customer-oriented library should be evaluated on the basis of quality and quantity. Quantitative evaluation in terms of output measure is the basic element of a statistical report, which is mainly prepared for accountability not for improving service. Meanwhile, customer satisfaction significantly contributes to improving service quality. Based on the evaluation results, the service support system should allocate resources to those services that customers deem as having low satisfaction.

In practice, the SERVQUAL model, critical incident techniques and benchmarking can be used to evaluate and improve service quality in library services. Parasuraman, Zeithaml, and Berry developed a multiple-item scale called SERVQUAL for measuring the five dimensions of service quality. A score for the quality of service is calculated by computing the differences between the ratings that customers assign to paired expectation and perception of each of twenty-two statements. This instrument has been designed and validated for use in a variety of service encounters.

In addition, many investigators have adapted the SERVQUAL measures to evaluate the service quality of libraries. Critical incident techniques can be used to analyse the service encounters between the customer and librarians. Customers and employees are interviewed separately to describe their experiences of the service experience. By doing so, the cause of success or failure of the service encounter can be analysed; the critical factors of service encounters can be identified as well.

Correspondingly, staff training and development courses can be designed to enhance the capacity of librarians and library instruction. Moreover, information literacy programmes can be designed to equip the capacity of customers. For every quality dimension, some organisations have earned the reputation of being "best in class" and, thus, a benchmark for comparison. Benchmarking, however, involves more than comparing statistics. It also includes visiting the leading organisation to learn firsthand how such outstanding performance has been achieved.

CONCLUSION

Manufacturing-based models and techniques for managing quality may be unproductive unless a clear understanding of the particular nature of the service sector is used to re-focus the model and select an appropriate set or sequence of tools or techniques. This chapter presents a novel framework for incorporating quality management into library and information services. All libraries can select the appropriate techniques for their programme with the framework dimensions proposed herein. Quality management approaches and techniques can help libraries, but do not always guarantee the outcome.

Libraries wanting to continuously improve their service quality and completely satisfy customers must create a customer oriented culture in their organisation. First, a framework of total quality management must be established for the library by promoting a quality culture before applying any particular technique. The techniques must be considered as an integral part of the total quality system. Importantly, managers must identify and suggest appropriate methods by analysing issues such as organisational culture, competence, skills, missions, and accessibility of resources and information. Above all, what is required is the support and commitment of senior management to make the application of these approaches and techniques meaningful and useful.

5

Integrated Library Management System

INTRODUCTION

Until recently the place of the *Integrated Library Management System* (ILMS) within the service context of libraries has been unchallenged. ILMS represent considerable technology investment by libraries. In 2002, libraries spent more than US$530 million on library systems and related services, with vendors making 39% of their estimated overall revenue from maintenance of such systems. For libraries, the ILMS is *the* corporate system. The success of library process change and information retrieval has been built around the functionality, or otherwise, of the ILMS. These systems have provided a solid foundation for both collection management and resource discovery.

Times however are changing. The information landscape is increasingly fluid and the role of the ILMS in this context is being questioned. Information retrieval is no longer limited to library-controlled resources. Students prefer access via Google rather than the library catalogue. Libraries themselves are recognizing the transient nature of electronic content. Content supplier generated MARC records are being downloaded into library catalogues as transient, not permanent, record markers of electronic content.

This chapter will look at the pressures the changing information environment is placing on the continuing development of the ILMS as the central point of access to library mediated information resources. The focus of this research is the academic library environment. A case study of the Victoria University Library experience within the changing E-Service environment will be outlined. The findings of this study will then be set against a broader survey undertaken on the uses made of ILMS in 26 major Australian university libraries and one U.S. university library.

The hypotheses used to shape this research were:

* *Hypothesis 1 (H1)*: ILMS cannot cope with the range of E-Service requirements of libraries and their users, as they are bound to the MARC format and the bibliographic record. ILMS are being bypassed in their support of Library E-Services.
* *Hypothesis 2 (H2)*: E-Service requirements are met by a range of different systems – some proprietary, some home-grown, some even part of the ILMS. The range of systems required is causing dissatisfaction with current ILMS and introducing complexity into the management of library systems.

LITERATURE REVIEW

There can be no doubt that much of the literature in this area speculates on the future role of libraries – none of which is particularly clear. Since 1995, or what Tenopir calls the "post web world", libraries have been seen as in danger of "substitution". The web is becoming "a ubiquitous source of information" giving an "illusion of depth and comprehensiveness" that leads to a questioning of the value of libraries and their collections. This review will not speculate on these future roles, but will focus instead on the certainty of changing technology, increasingly digital information resources and societal shifts that have changed user expectations of library services.

STRATEGIC ROLE OF THE ILMS WITHIN LIBRARIES

The ILMS is "a key piece of infrastructure of the library". Its key value to libraries is its ability to offer a catalogue and to manage workflows. The ILMS is still seen as preeminent in offering "intelligent and convenient access to catalogue data *i.e.* effective access points which translate user needs with great precision and multi-layered end user interfaces which can be adjusted to different levels of user sophistication." It is also seen as the most cost effective way to handle infrastructure tasks such as "acquisitions, cataloguing and circulation".

In fact its most cost effective feature is this integration of "workflows and processes...closely tied to data flow", even if this "integration of technical services often don't get equal weight in library decision criteria". Libraries have traditionally performed a role of physical repository, housing print materials, with a catalogue that provides access to these locally held resources. The accessibility of the web has seen this shift, and catalogue records describing local print materials now sit side by side with records providing links to external web resources.

While the inclusion of these electronic sources may "enrich" library collections, they are also "inherently problematic" because they do not have the traditional standards base for inclusion that print materials do. The scope of what a library catalogue system describes has broadened in a way that is only exceeded by the expectations of its digitally-literate end users. Libraries are constrained in the amount of investment they can make on new systems. The marketplace is dominated by a restricted number of major vendors and once acquired, systems are retained for a considerable period.

"Although few would characterise their current automation system as perfect, libraries rarely leave current systems out of dissatisfaction with support or functionality. Migrations are just too costly". Library system companies "[have] pulled out all stops to retain customers and entice them to migrate to their replacement systems". These replacement systems need to offer "tools to both help manage the electronic content they purchase and create content from digital products". Whilst vendors are trying to change their systems to meet these demands there is also a questioning about whether one ILMS can offer all these functions.

Certainly add-on products are increasing in their use. As Kenney points out "integration, metasearching, open source software and the internet are all pushing the ILS in new directions". Investment in "standalone products for linking and digital management accounted for nearly 13% of the ILS market last year".

ACADEMIC LIBRARIES: A USER CONTEXT

The growth and availability of access to information via the internet and associated technology has transformed the expectations of the client population as well as their service preferences. New technologies and developments have altered the perceived link between information and libraries. For students of previous generations the library stood clearly as the first place to "begin" research and offered a number of options within its physical locations including "librarian, journal indexes or perhaps the more modern CD ROM".

These students were "educated in a world dominated by the physicality of libraries" and as a result thought of "information residing in a particular place". The coming of the "digital age" has fundamentally altered this. Research is no longer tied to a physical location. This next generation of students described variously as the "millennial generation", "digital generation", "Generation Y" "dot com generation" or "n-gen" may not be able to remember a time when their home did not contain a personal computer.

They are characterised by the use and processing of information for education and learning. Their entire education "probably involved technology". This generation is often adept at "multiprocessing", undertaking several tasks simultaneously, such as using their computer while listening to music or talking on the phone. In locating information their first instinct is the search engine rather than a library.

In 2002 the U.S. based Pew and Internet Life project published findings that indicated that 73% of the current college students participating in their sample used the internet more than the library for information searching. This same study also confirmed the preference for multitasking, describing students "browsing web pages while working on an assignment".

Related to this change in access to information and technology are the fundamental changes that have occurred in views of education and its role in society. Lifelong learning is the major educational movement discussed in relation to learners of this generation. Education as a continuing process throughout life in order to "maintain employment" coupled with the quest for "self improvement" and enhanced ability to solve multiple problems are major drivers for this. Seely Brown refers to a "new literacy" going beyond text and image and encompassing information navigation.

Tapscott expands on this idea with his "eight shifts of interactive" learning. He outlines a number of key differences between the old "broadcast learning" and the new "interactive learning". The areas of major shift include the move away from linear learning to hypermedia, the importance of discovery as opposed to instruction, an emphasis on learner-centred customisation and learning how to learn. The move to lifelong learning and the role of teacher as facilitator are also important elements of this model.

The range of services, functionality and "instant gratification" offered by sites such as Amazon and Google has much to do with the transformation of user expectations. Libraries need to incorporate the best features of commercial services into the best aspects of their own services. Pace suggests "not until consumer sites' features are folded into our traditional interfaces can libraries hope to make a library experience as engaging as an online experience".

In noting that "Amazon.com is used by many in lieu of public access catalogs", Kenney *et al* raises the idea that libraries need to adopt some of the practices of these services including "recommending like materials" or quantifying the value of information to the potential client.

VICTORIA UNIVERSITY LIBRARY : A CASE STUDY

Victoria University Library is neither large in academic library terms nor particularly well funded. It however demonstrates clearly the key characteristics of the literature *i.e.* the growth of digital information and its impact on information and staffing resources as well as the growth of systems developments to cope with these changes. Victoria University is a 'Dawkins University' created in 1990 from the amalgamations of various Technical Colleges and a College of Advanced Education. Currently it is the largest provider of educational services in the Western Region of Melbourne, with some 30,000 Technical and Further Education students and 15,000 Higher Education students.

CHANGES IN INFORMATION RESOURCES AND SERVICES

The University Library ranks 38th out of 38 Australian University Libraries in terms of serial acquisitions and 35th in terms of monograph acquisition. Its material allocation budget has remained relatively stable over the past three years at around AU$2.5 million, with its most notable expenditure characteristic being the increasing dominance of electronic information resources. This trend has been especially noticeable in the last three years, with electronic information resources moving progressively from consuming 13.73% of the serial budget to 18.6% to now being estimated at 50% of the 2003 serial budget.

At the end of 2002, the Library held 32,048 electronic serial titles "accessible via the University Network" and had "in addition 5,118 hard copy subscriptions". The expected impact of digital monographs has not really occurred. Post the Digital Copyright Amendment legislation in 2001, the use of electronic reserve has exploded, with views per quarter climbing steadily in 2003 from 25,000, to 35,125, to this current quarter being 100,727.

There is increased pressure for more online resources. In 2002 there was a 41% increase in the use of online database services. Some difficulty has been experienced in restructuring to cater for the 'virtual campus', as it is difficult to shift staff to the new job roles of web page maintenance as well as maintenance of electronic information resources and license management. New service support initiatives have also been launched to support this new environment, such as our e-mail reference service. There has also been a move towards the use of online forms by clients for interlibrary loans and making book purchase suggestions.

LIBRARY SYSTEM DEVELOPMENT

One reproduces a timeline of system developments reported in the Victoria University Library Annual reports. The key characteristics are the burgeoning system development post 1995, as well as the noticeable commitment to adding features to the current ILMS. Additional systems are incorporated but do not dominate development. For the sake of clarity, non-ILMS developments are bolded to indicate differentiation.

Timeline of System Development:

* *1990*:
  – Acquired Innopac (ILMS)
* *1994*:
  – Acquired BISAC ordering feature
* *1995*:
  – CDROM Network operational via DOS based menu
* *1996*:
  – Patron self requests and renewals
  – Library website launched with hours, telnet catalogue
* 1997
  – Major installations of 3M self service equipment with Innopac circulation
  – 70% of loans now done via selfcheck
* 1999
  – Serial invoices paid electronically

- Five years of Higher Education Exam papers digitised using Ereserve module
- Major launch of Web OPAC
- Library acquires ERL server to mount databases and allow access outside the library.

* 2001
  - EReserve explodes as a major service.
  - MARC invoices accepted from book suppliers for invoice payment and order creation as required.
  - Advanced Search implemented on Library Web Catalogue and integrated Encyclopaedia Britannica in catalogue search results.
  - Implementation of Ezproxy.
  - WebCT adopted as University online learning platform. Library under pressure to participate. Currently assists via help desk, modules on adding library resources.
  - ADT – participation in Australian digital theses. Very small number of theses added.
* 2002
  - EDIFACT orders
  - LIDDAS – implementation project (ILL). Not yet functional.
  - AARLINi – participate in this CAUL pilot portal development
* 2003
  - WAM – install new authentication system which unifies all library required authentication into uniform ID and PIN.
  - Library Ereserve becomes digital repository for all University copyright material offered online to the academic community.
  - Implement Serials Solutions as primary search interface to Ejournal Materials

STAFFING PROFILE

The steady build up of staff to support these system developments is illustrated in table. It is worth noting not only the steady increase in staffing but also the co-option of staff to systems support roles. This co-option is expressed in the addition of bits of staff to systems duties. This staffing addition is also reflected in the responses to the CAUL survey.

Table 5.1. Two System Staffing Growth.

1995		Manager with part responsibility for systems + 1 day per week Cataloguer for additional Innopac support
+	1999	Systems Librarian full time for the acquisition of computer equipment as well Innopac support + 1 day per week circulation system coordinator from Lending
+	2000	Network Information Services Librarian: web coordination, databases, Web Opac

This case study illustrates the key characteristics further reinforced in the later survey responses. These key characteristics are the increasing need to adjust to digital information requirements, a steady investment in self-service features and additional investment in staffing resources. These key characteristics do not support H1, as the ILMS is not being bypassed but is still a dominant part of the Library's system development. H2 is neither supported nor disproved, as there is both continued investment in the ILMS and increased complexity in range of services provided and staffing.

SURVEY OF ACADEMIC LIBRARIES

In October 2003, via the CAUL network, the authors sent out a survey via the CAUL list to all Australian University libraries. Twenty-six responses were received. In addition, a response was received from a university library in the United States. This response was not sufficiently different to cause this case to be singled out for any differentiation in the reported results.

Survey responses are grouped into three main areas. Firstly there are responses in terms of ILMS - brand, age, staffing support. Secondly questions on systems used to support EServices are investigated, as is the integration with technical services workflow. Lastly responses are reported on the self-assessment given by respondents on their own system's capabilities.

THE ILMS

Responses to the survey indicated dominant library systems within academic libraries – basically Innopac was the most commonly reported in these responses.

The systems used were:

Systems	Numbers
Advance	1
Advance	1
Aleph	3
Aleph	3
Dynix	2
Dynix	2
Horizon	1
Horizon	1
Innopac	11
Innopac	11
Spydus	1
Spydus	1
Virtua	4
Virtua	4
Voyager	4
Voyager	4
Total	27
Total	27

On the whole the ILMS were not new. Only five libraries had new systems acquired post 2001. The majority had systems acquired between 1995 and 2000. Seven respondents indicated they had acquired their systems between the years 1990 to 1994 and 2 had systems dated pre 1990. Fifteen respondents indicated however that they were on new releases of their ILMS so libraries are upgrading systems purchased. These responses indicate coherence with the findings of Breeding and Roddy's ILMS survey article in 2003 with the library system market being dominated by a small number of vendors and vendors working hard to ensure they migrate clients to new versions of systems.

Support staff for library systems within the libraries clearly relate to the size of the libraries with some respondents indicating "nil" to "10 full time staff". Of note is the number of 'parts' of staff used for the library management system. For example ".2 of a cataloguer", "50% Innopac Coordinator", Module Coordinators for each functional module – 5%.

The job titles ascribed to these positions indicate some staff are dedicated to the library management system, for example, "Innopac Coordinator" but others have broader system responsibilities, for example, job titles like "Systems Officer", "Information Systems Librarian", "Library IT Coordinator", "Systems and Electronic Resources Manager". The range of job titles partially supports H2 and the increasing complexity of managing library systems developments.

E-SERVICES SUPPORT SYSTEMS

A series of questions were asked to see if the ILMS incorporated some of the basic features seen as required in the new electronic information environment, *i.e.* URL access via the OPAC; handling of digital data; learning system interfaces, self service features, and portal developments. Twenty-six of the 27 libraries included URLS in their catalogues. URL's included can be characterised as coming from: "online journals, web sites, image online, online books. If a URL is useful we include it in the record".

Twenty-one respondents indicated they include digitised documents in their catalogue. These digitised objects largely consist of "ereserve, lecture and tutorial notes, electronic course readings, exam papers, theses". As well as these standard, almost to be expected inclusions, a small minority of libraries mentioned exceptional inclusions such as "exhibition catalogues", "video, sound" and one library indicated plans "to add photos, sound and moving files". Twelve respondents indicated the numbers of digital objects included in their catalogues. Some libraries have sizeable collections of digital documents included Table 5.2.

Table 5.2

Number of Digitised Objects	Respondents
120-250	4
1,600 – 4,000	4
5,100 – 12,500	4

Seven respondents indicated they handled digitised objects *outside* of the ILMS. This was an early indication of where ILMS were being bypassed by add-on systems. It should be pointed out that some libraries chose add-on systems even though their ILMS appears capable of this implementation. The bypassing of the ILMS may be a time, local requirement specification rather than an ILMS weakness.

Some of the responses are reproduced below as they indicate the size and scope of these add-on systems:

* Access to approx. 4,000 documents is provided via various links in the catalogue
* Separate locally-developed system for exam papers
* Separate websites accessible from XXX Library Website
* We also have digital documents available on our archives rare books website

Another requirement of the changed information environment is the requirement to interface with teaching tools such as WebCT and Blackboard. In common with the case study it appears to be a functionality that is either not currently available within the ILMS or has not been activated or tested. Seven respondents indicated they had *"canned"* or *"precanned"* searches or links from the online learning platform to the catalogue. This is clearly an area that will need to develop in the future if library resources are to be integrated into flexible delivery teaching systems.

Libraries are keen implementers of ILMS Self Service Features. All respondents had selfservice features on their catalogue. At the most basic these catalogues offered "Place holds, view patron record." Most also offered "Patrons can check the status of their record, place holds, cancel holds, and renew loans. Users can also e-mail search results to the e-mail address of their choosing." A smaller number of respondents allowed for "PIN maintenance"; "messages to patron", "request ILL" "Book audiovisual item; Book study carrel", "Webcomments for queries", "build cart bibliography/ e-mail cart/ save search sessions; broadcast searches to linked Z39.50 library catalogues". A much publicised future direction is the requirement for libraries to act as portals to other information sources.

As many as 10 libraries either did not answer this question or indicated that their system currently had no portal features. Other respondents indicated that they were using products developed by ILMS suppliers had a *"user driven customisable interface"* or were involved in the AARLIN project. In terms of electronic information services requirements, ILMS are being used to incorporate URLs and self-service features. The inclusion of digital data is less popular although undertaken by a majority of respondents.

Digital data are being either mounted via the ILMS or on separate systems. The decision on technology pathway does not seem to be related to specific ILMS but to specific local requirements. This therefore does not support H1 as the ILMS itself seems to be able to adjust in these areas but is not being used by libraries due to local requirements. In terms of portal and learning system interface – these areas are clearly under developed in terms of the ILMS and these libraries' implementation of their systems. This indicates a gap between the requirements of the new information environment as perceived in the literature and the actual implementation process within academic libraries. It also points to an area where systems vendors may need to take note.

INTEGRATION WITH WORKFLOWS

This series of questions was to do with the use of ILMS as strategic infrastructure support. The questions were around the cataloguing of electronic aggregations, and integration of acquisition and serials workflows

Cataloguing

In terms of the cataloguing of aggregated electronic resources, several Libraries indicated they were still working on procedures/practices and 4 had no response. To characterise response received – cataloguing efforts fell into three main categories. There was in house – via standard cataloguing practices, for example "We follow a philosophy of "format" integration and therefore try to use a single record for print and electronic titles.

We therefore manually update records to include URL, rather than bulk load MARC records from aggregator/ publishers". The creation inhouse of MARC Records via own programmes, for example, "Brief records created from spreadsheet data using AUTOCAT and MARCMAKER". Lastly there was the acquisition of bulk records from vendors. Of note is that Serial Solutions is mentioned as a source by 5 libraries.

Others bulk purchase from vendors and Kinetica "Through loading of:

* Purchased records from Kinetica
* Purchased record sets from Kinetica
* Purchased record sets from vendors
* Purchased records from Serials Solutions.

Remaining material is originally catalogued to at least CONSER level".

Acquisitions

All respondents indicated a level of integration with vendor systems although some did not send orders electronically, with one using *"e-order using vendor systems"* and another still trialling electronic orders. For the other 26 respondents, most commonly send e-mail orders. Twelve respondents mentioned the downloading of MARC records for the creation of order and bibliographic records from approval plans. In terms of further connectivity of the library system, only one mentioned *"ordering outputs to central finance"*. Electronic invoicing was indicated by 12 respondents, so was also a popular feature.

Acquisitions linkages to book supply vendors seem strong, with commonly used invoice and order interfaces as well as bibliographic record generation. Linkages however to other internal administrative systems, such as the University Finance Departments do not feature. The strategic potential of this workflow feature could be further developed by libraries and ILMS vendors.

Serials

Many more libraries indicated *no* interfacing with serial vendors or that interfacing was under investigation. Seventeen libraries indicated some level of interfacing with serial vendors. Twelve respondents indicated electronic invoicing, 1 the use of SICI barcodes, 1 the downloading of accessioning data from serial vendors, 7 sent claims electronically. Serials interfacing with vendors is not as well-supported as those with acquisitions. Given the strategic value of workflow integration, this should be an area for closer investigation by libraries and system vendors.

SELF ASSESSMENT OF SYSTEM PERFORMANCE

To further investigate areas of strategic gap, respondents were asked to indicate how they rated their current systems' performance and the relative value of this service. They were asked to nominate a figure in terms of Importance and Performance of several features on their library systems. In addition they were given an opportunity to comment on their assessment.

Cross Tabulation of Data

A statistical analysis was done on respondents' ratings of various features of their systems performance and importance. A gap was identified between perceived performance and importance. This gap is the standard deviation calculated between High Performance and High Importance. The greater the standard deviation between these two variables, the greater the strategic gap between perceived importance and actual performance.

Note the key critical areas investigated, in terms of electronic information services offered, were not necessarily part of the ILMS. The strategic gap analysis indicated a perceived gap, greatest in terms of the importance and performance of the Eprint Server, EReserve and Portal Developments. Figure illustrates these results.

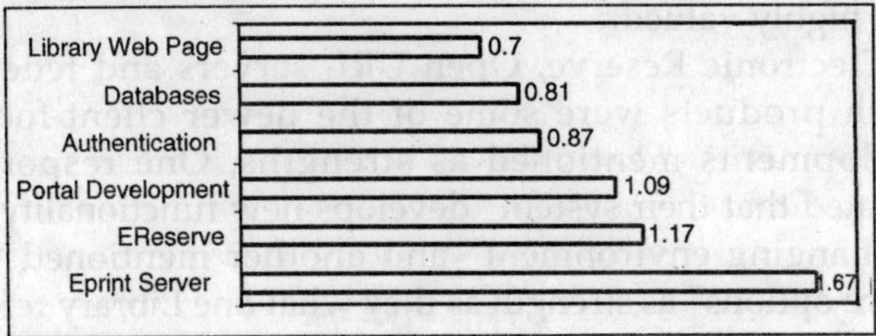

Fig 5.1. Strategic Gap between Performance and Importance.

Comments on ILMS and E-Services

In order to get a general impression of participants' overall view on their ILMS and EServices current performance and areas for future development, matching questions were asked:

* In your opinion what are the main strengths and weakness of the current functionality of the ILMS/ E-Services?
* What features are you hoping will be developed in the next 2-3 years?

ILMS

Strengths

Standards, reliability, stability and integration were four areas of strength that were mentioned in various forms by a number of respondents in relation to their ILMS. The standards in MARC, AACR2 and Z39.50 were seen by a number of participants as providing a foundation for their system. For one library the AACR2/MARC combination created "an environment supporting interoperability". The reliability of the ILMS and its ability to allow staff to perform core functions was also emphasised. "The strength of our current ILMS is its maturity in handling traditional core functionality".

Individual systems were variously described as "robust", "reliable", "stable". Many of the strengths nominated were related to traditional staff functions such as cataloguing, acquisitions, course reserves and serials. Integrated functionality across these areas was seen as important and the "ability to move records between modules from a central point "was highly valued.

Electronic Reserve, Open URL servers and federated search products were some of the newer client-focused developments mentioned as strengths. One respondent indicated that their system "develops new functionality with the changing environment" and another mentioned "self-service options" as strength as they what one Library referred to as "patron empowerment".

Weaknesses

While some respondents view the traditional standards of MARC and AACR2 positively, some libraries also mentioned them as a weakness. *'Basic system and products robust, but limited by MARC format"* and for one library, the ILMS' foundation on these traditions means their system is *"Somewhat rooted in the card catalogue"*. The need for accurate reporting was an area that at least 4 respondents nominated as a weakness of current systems. These include financial and collection reports and statistics. For one respondent, current reporting is *"unreliable"*, while another indicated that some report functions within their system are *"not working"*.

The importance of accommodating new online developments was also touched on. While noting the strengths of their systems in *"traditional"* functions, some respondents noted that there was *"no portal/meta search development path"* or that their ILMS *"does not cope well with online developments"*. These developments also include interfacing with online learning platforms such as Blackboard or WebCT.

Opportunities over the Next 2-3 Years

The majority of the respondents indicated that at worst their systems are acceptably functional, despite weaknesses and raised issues for development. A number of development areas nominated by respondents involved interfacing or integration with other systems. One respondent referred to this as *"seamless integration with other systems"* and another mentioned *"integration with e-learning platforms such as Blackboard"*. There was also discussion of interacting with other *"University"* or vendor systems.

Related to this is the importance of portal developments, open URL technology and enhancement of the client interface. One respondent would like to see their OPAC able to present results more like "Google", while another mentioned more features like "Amazon".

Copyright and *"electronic resources management"* were suggested as definite areas for development, but there was almost no mention of metadata. It would appear, based on this survey, that while there is much discussion on metadata within the library and information industry, its adoption and incorporation within traditional library systems has not been readily seen by librarians as a development need.

E-Services

Strengths

Strengths of E-Services were seen as the range of materials offered as well as access. Several libraries placed value on *"comprehensive"*, *"integrated"* or *"seamless"* access to these EServices from within the catalogue. Other responses nominated the idea of the catalogue as the main point of access and discovery for materials of any type *"All materials accessible from library catalogue"* and, not surprisingly, with particular emphasis on *"Integration of both print and electronic resources"*. Keeping interfaces and systems *"simple"*, *"easy to use"* and *"user friendly"* was suggested by a number of libraries as a strength of their e-services, and authentication was a related area that was important. Maintaining a *"good authentication environment"* was seen by one library.

Weaknesses

Integration and increased staffing and resources pressures were reported as weaknesses. Respondents noted the lack of integration between e-services and student/University portals and e-learning environments - "links from WebCT to online articles not developed". One respondent saw "potential difficulties in integrating a range of different software applications" and "integrating with University systems".

A high number of respondents expressed concerns regarding the resourcing of services, whether it be staff or financial. The "Inability to devote financial or staff resources to development" was referred to by one Library, and this sentiment was echoed by a number of others. "There's not enough money to buy what we need", "lack of infrastructure resources" were just two of the suggested weaknesses of current e-services. Despite this "innovative" staff and their ability to "do a lot with not much" were mentioned.

Opportunities Over the Next 2-3 Years

Areas for development are not unlike those nominated in the responses regarding ILMS developments. Integration with other systems, portal features "we need a strong portal" and federated searching was seen as important. "We look forward to integrating the library into the campus portal". Again the growing emphasis on online learning platforms was mentioned "Integration of library resources within courseware of increasing importance". At least 3 libraries made some reference to licence administration "better control of licences" and digital rights management as an area that requires development over the next 2-3 years.

Authentication was also raised, as an issue with one library suggesting there is a need for a "more granular and flexible authentication and access rights management system". Eprint servers and the need for development in the area of digital repositories were raised by at least 2 respondents. It would appear to be an area requiring development and is perceived by some respondents as a gap in their current service provision.

In reviewing the responses to both questions, it becomes clear that there are a number of issues that are common. The need to integrate the ILMS and E-Services with other systems such as e-learning platforms and portal products is of concern to librarians. There is also an ongoing tension between the demand for increasing development of these services and an ongoing lack of resources to sustain this.

The E-Services question elicited slightly more emphasis on end-user functionality than the one focusing on the ILMS. This may be explained by a number of factors including the traditional place of the ILMS in not only providing access to clients but as the main framework around which staff workflows have been structured. Overall the survey indicates that in terms of the present ILMS, and possible add-on systems, academic libraries are searching for developments in portals, EPrint server functions, linkages to teaching systems and assistance with license administration.

Present ILMS systems offer but need to consider strengthening the functionality of their services in terms of Ereserve and integration with other administrative systems such as University Finance systems. There needs to be consideration by both libraries and vendors of why existing ILMS facilities such as serials' integration with supplier's systems appear to be underutilised.

The context of all these developments needs to be sensitive to cost and staffing pressures. There is a sense throughout the responses of the need to increasingly integrate the ILMS within the broad range of electronic services. Despite this desire to achieve integration it still appears to many respondents that the ILMS is a distinct entity somewhat removed from electronic service provision.

The commonality of issues raised however suggests maximising the effectiveness of the library's ILMS performance would go some way to addressing broader questions regarding E-Services functionality. Libraries need to refocus on what they are trying to achieve via the use of the ILMS. The emphasis on staff functionality in the ILMS related survey responses indicates that there is a need to place significant effort into ensuring that its role as a discovery and access tool for clients is emphasised and developed. This is vital if the current level of investment of these systems is to remain and for the associated workflows to continue to be efficient and relevant.

CONCLUSION

In many ways the ILMS is being overlooked rather than "bypassed" (H1). Some libraries appear to be choosing to look for solutions in other systems, even when their ILMS can accommodate the function they are attempting to implement. It would take an additional study to determine the reasons for this, but it may be possible to speculate that they include local specifications and integration, cost and ability to interface with other systems. For the future, and particularly for end users, the ILMS will need to offer more than the presentation of the library catalogue.

ILMS vendors and developments must continue to incorporate more of an ability to customise, to allow client-centred development to reflect new learning styles and expectations. H2 is supported by the survey results. Libraries are using a range of solutions to meet their overall E-Service needs and do not appear to be completely satisfied with the patchwork of systems that results.

Areas for future developments must allow for new areas of services such as portals, EPrint repositories and linkages to teaching systems, but cannot be too staff intensive, as there is a general agreement that increasing financial constraints are creating a tension for resourcing of this area.

Based on the survey results and this study, the following issues will be important for the future of the ILMS, E-Services and their strategic position in the service infrastructure of the library. For libraries, the key questions relate to the place of the ILMS in the broader context of their E-Service environment and looking critically at what functions and services it can enable.

The ILMS is a large investment in human and financial resources and maximising the usefulness of the system for both workflow and as a client centred interface to a "collection", whether physical or virtual, will continue to be an important challenge. For ILMS vendors, there is another set of challenges relating to the pace of development, interoperability and customisation of systems.

Technology is more accessible than it has ever been, and there is no reason to believe that the proliferation of "add-on" or "third party" systems will disappear. Vendors need to look at this technological landscape for how they can integrate or enhance their ILMS to work with the best aspects of these systems. They also need to continue observing developments in client expectation and learning styles. These need to be reflected in any ILMS of the future so that it is not "bypassed".

6

Financial Management

BUDGET

DEFINITION

A budget is a plan of financial operations embodying an estimate of proposed expenditures for a given period and the proposed means of financing them. In the State of Michigan, all general and special revenue funds are required by law to be budgeted annually. Revisions to the Uniform Budgeting and Accounting Act in 2000 removed Debt Service Funds from the type of funds required to adopt a budget.

PURPOSE

Under Michigan Public Act 621 of 1978, a budget appropriation must be in place before a governmental unit may commit to spending money in their General Fund or Special Revenue Funds. However, there are other reasons for developing a budget. An important reason is to ensure that libraries establish a plan on how to allocate resources in order to meet the goals and service expectations of the library.

For that reason, although an official budget is not required for debt service or capital project funds, it is prudent to develop a financial plan for those activities. The plan could be prepared on an annual basis, or on a project basis. A budget also allows for easy evaluation of whether the goals and service expectations are being met.

BUDGET PROCESS

Regardless of the type of library, the annual budgetary process involves the following three generic phases.

Preparation

The preparation phase is usually the responsibility of the library director. It is accomplished by analysing past financial data and allocating the anticipated library resources to provide the various services and activities for library patrons.

Adoption

Once the budget has been prepared, it is presented to the library's legislative body for consideration, possible modification and final approval. Typically, the public is invited to participate in this phase via public hearings on proposed budgets.

Execution

Budgetary accounts are set up to record the estimated revenue and expenditures for the appropriate funds. As economic conditions and circumstances change, budget amounts can be amended by a process determined by the library's legislative body. Typically, the process is very similar to that of the original budget. The budgetary amounts are then compared with actual amounts periodically. This allows the library's management team to effectively operate the library. The comparison of budget to actual results can be accomplished using a variety of formats.

TYPES OF BUDGETS

Types of budgets available to libraries are:

* *Line Item*: A line item budget shows a library's budget by account type
* *Cost Centre*: A cost center budget shows a library's budget by groupings

* *Fund Total*: A fund total budget shows a library's budget in fund totals

All of the above budget types are acceptable methods of budgeting. Typically, the line item or cost center budgets are used. The use of either of these not only meets legal requirements but also provides management and the board with an effective tool to help operate and manage the library.

BUDGET REQUIREMENTS

Budget Questionnaire	Yes/No
1. Has a budget been adopted (General and Special Revenue Funds)?	______
2. Was a public hearing held on the budget?	______
3. Was all the necessary information included in the budget document for the budgetary funds:	
A. Actual prior year (both revenue and expenditures)?	______
B. Estimate of current year (both revenue and expenditures)?	______
C. Proposed budget (both revenue and expenditures)?	______
D. Amounts for contingencies if appropriate?	______
E. Amount of fund balance (deficit) accumulated from prior years and the estimated surplus or deficit expected in the current year?	______
4. Is the budget balanced (budgeted fund balance is zero or positive)?	______
5. Has the budget been amended when necessary if actual revenue is less than the budget estimated?	______
6. Has the budget been amended to allow expenditures in excess of the original appropriation?	______
7. Are expenditures equal to or less than amounts appropriated?	______
8. Are all expenditures authorized in the budget?	______

In order to comply with the Michigan Public Act 621 of 1978, certain requirements must be met. The following questionnaire is a general guide to the specific requirements. All questions should be answered "yes" to comply with the Budget Act.

BUDGET CALENDAR

The following is an example of a budget calendar for a library with a fiscal year of January 1 through December 31.

Timeline	Process
July	Library director begins process – concludes on format, sets management team's workshop sessions and submits data request to management team
August	Data request forms collected and summarized in workshop sessions – initial budget is formed
September	Proposed budget submitted for board review
October	Board reviews and provides input on proposed budget
November	Public hearing and budget adoption

LEWIS AND CLARK LIBRARY SYSTEM: FINANCIAL POLICY

GOAL

The goal of this policy is to ensure that Lewis and Clark Library System (LCLS) has internal fiscal controls in place to provide reasonable assurances regarding:

* Effective and efficient operation,
* Reliable financial reporting,
* Compliance with applicable Illinois state and federal laws and regulations
* Compliance with the Illinois Library System Act: Administrative Rules, and
* Compliance with the Bylaws and other policies of the LCLS.

SCOPE

Financial Format and Reporting:

* The fiscal year for LCLS shall begin on July 1 and end on June 30.
* The funds, accounts, and descriptions of accounts shall be consistent with generally accepted

accounting principles and the Uniform Accounting and Reporting Manual for the Illinois Library System Headquarters. The funds shall be brought together per the Governmental Accounting Standards Board Statement No. 34–Basic Financial Statements—Management's Discussion and Analysis—for State and Local Governments. Budgeted versus actual comparisons shall be included in financial reports submitted to the Board of Directors and the Illinois State Library.

* The Board of Directors shall adopt and then submit an annual budget prior to the beginning of each fiscal year to the Illinois State Library. The accounting system shall provide the basis for comparison of actual expenditures to this budget. Any revisions to the budget shall be approved by the Board of Directors and reported to the Illinois State Library for approval.
* A six-month cumulative report is due to the Illinois State Library on February 15 of each year for the period July 1 through December 31. The format of the report shall be in compliance with the form contained in the Uniform Accounting and Reporting Manual for the Illinois Library System Headquarters.
* An annual audit of LCLS for the preceding fiscal year shall be filed with the Illinois State Library on or before September 30 following the end of the fiscal year. The audit shall be conducted in accordance with the most recent Government Auditing Standards.

Control Environment:

* Meetings of the Board of Directors shall be held at least nine times a year to review financial reports, approve LCLS bills for payment, discuss any governance issues, and to be advised of and/or discuss key operational information.
* An annual audit for the preceding year shall be conducted by an independent certified public accountant. The Board of Directors shall meet with

the independent certified public accountant to discuss the annual audit and any material management findings.

* Every employee at LCLS shall have some responsibility to ensure a well functioning financial system. However, responsibility for the financial reporting and controls, as well as ensuring a culture of integrity and ethics shall be delegated to the Executive Director.
* LCLS Financial Procedures and Practices, which provide the day-to-day guidelines for financial reporting and controls, shall be developed and shall be approved by the Executive Director. The Financial Procedures and Practices shall be reviewed annually and updated as necessary.
* LCLS shall maintain policies and procedures which include a comprehensive code of conduct, policies addressing good business practices, conflicts of interest, and standards of ethical and moral behaviour.
* Any violations or deviations from established policies shall be investigated, documented, and brought to the attention of the Board of Directors.

Risk Assessment:

* The LCLS Board of Directors shall periodically review the financial health of LCLS. The Board shall receive assurances of the completeness, accuracy, and validity of the information provided and the systems and processes used to generate such information.
* LCLS management will periodically assess risks from both external and internal sources. Such assessments should include the potential impact of economic conditions, political actions, financing availability, retention and succession of key employees, and information system security and backup.
* LCLS shall consider the risks associated with misstatements of financial information and shall take steps to mitigate such risk.

Control Activities:

* LCLS shall have a process to ensure that appropriate policies and procedures are in place, adhered to, periodically reviewed, and updated.
* Financial practices shall include authority and responsibility for approvals, authorizations, verifications, reconciliations, reviews of operating performance, security of assets, and segregation of duties.
* The Board Secretary shall be responsible for the retention of LCLS Board of Directors Meeting Agenda, Minutes, and other such Board related documents which must be maintained at LCLS.
* The Business Office shall be the official repository of all financial and human resource records. This includes financial reports and information; original copies of all contracts, agreements, and memoranda of understanding; fixed asset information; and official employee files and payroll information. Retention and disposal of such records shall be based on the requirements as established by the State of Illinois—Local Records Commission, and other applicable state and federal rules, regulations, and guidelines.

Information and Communications:

* Periodically, information shall be collected from the library industry, political entities, member libraries, and other external sources to ascertain the potential impact on LCLS, the services it provides, its business, and financial reporting.
* Milestones to achieve programmatic and financial goals and objectives shall be monitored and reported to the Board of Directors to ensure that deadlines are met.
* Accurate operational and financial information shall be clearly communicated to management and other LCLS employees in a timely manner.
* A process shall be in place to document, analyse,

and eliminate operational and financial problems, errors, complaints, and new information which may require a change in operations.

* A process shall be in place for directors, employees, and others to communicate suspected wrongdoing by LCLS or LCLS employees. Such process shall ensure that anyone making such a report is protected from retaliation for making such a report.

Monitoring:

* The LCLS Board of Directors and employees shall be obligated to communicate to management any known weaknesses in the internal controls of the LCLS.
* LCLS employees shall acknowledge that they have read and understand the Employee Handbook which includes LCLS's policies on conduct and ethics.
* Reconciliations and other control activities shall be followed as identified in the LCLS Financial Procedures and Practices.
* LCLS shall follow-up on any recommendations made by the external auditors.

POLICY MANAGEMENT LIBRARY

The *Policy Management Library* (PML) implements key components of a well-known policy management architecture, and provides a generalized policy model able to support arbitrary policy languages. The library fully supports the Java binding for CIM-SPL policies, a recently approved standard from the Distributed Management Task Force. PML provides conflict, coverage, and dominance analysis building on the Apache Imperius project, which provides the parser, Java-binding, and policy evaluation engine. Finally, policies written in Groovy are also supported, although without the policy analysis feature that is available for those written in CIM-SPL.

HOW DOES IT WORK

The Policy Management Library builds on a common model for policy run-times and includes the following components and capabilities:

* *Managed Environment*: A platform that requires the dynamic configuration and deployment of decision making. This might include the ability to change how a network fire wall is configured, who has access to a file system, or to downgrade information for a specific user. This is the application into which this library is deployed.
* *Policy*: A condition specification and an optional action to execute when the condition evaluates to true. The condition is defined over a set of run-time data provided to the policy at evaluation time by the managed environment. The decision is defined over a set of run-time data also provide at evaluation time.
* *Policy Enforcement Point* (PEP): A point in the Managed Environment that needs to have a decision made, for example, to decide whether access to a secured resource should be granted. It requests the answer to this decision from the Policy Decision Point. One implements such points tin the Managed Environment as PEP instead of a hard-coded decision so that the decisions can be configured with policy. There may be any number of PEP in the Managed Environment.
* *Policy Decision Point* (PDP): Provides for the execution of policies and provides results of the execution are returned to the PEP for action based on the decision. It decides which policies in the Policy Repository apply to the decision request.
* *Policy Repository*: Holds the policies that are available for execution by the PDP. Policies may be activated or deactivated within the repository.
* *Policy Analysis*: Provides a set of specialized algorithms that supports policy authors in assessing the interaction between policies. The operations supported by the policy analysis component are dominance checks, coverage checks, simultaneous applicability check and conflict detection/ resolution.

* *Policy Transformation*: Enables rule-based transformation of abstract policies to concrete managed environment resource models.

In addition to the base library and architecture a number of key components are provided and described here:

* The *Policy Authoring and Management Tool* (PAMNT) is a Web-based tool used to author, negotiate, analyse and manage policies within the management environment. The policies are authored in a controlled natural language format based on templates. The templates are defined by an administrator prior to authoring of the policies. The analysis operations check whether there are any conflicts, uncovered regions or dominated policies among the set of authored policies. Once authored and analysed, policies can be deployed or removed from the managed environment. Policies may also be deactivated and left deployed within the environment.
* The Policy Negotiation Tool is part of the PAMNT tool and enables two or more parties to negotiate a single agreed upon set of policies. Each party brings their own polices to the negotiation and each party alternates making proposals. Goal based negoti-ation to remove conflicts between the policies is provided.
* The *Policy Enabled Network Gateway* (PENG) enables policy controls over MQTT messages flowing between two or more networks.
* *Distributed Policy Repository* (DPR) provides redundancy and resilience of policies storage within an unreliable, distributed network of Policy Decision Points. Support for policy supercession and rollback in support of network topology changes is provided.

RESOURCE MOBILIZATION

UNDERSTANDING RESOURCE MOBILIZATION

Looking Beyond Just Raising Funds

Most development research organizations have had, up until recently, a comfortable, sheltered life. In order to access funding for an applied research project, a board member, executive director, programme officer or some other staff member would write up a grant application addressed to one, two, or a handful of institutional donors. They would get part or all of the funding required; implement the research; then submit midterm and final reports to the donor, documenting results, and meeting financial reporting requirements. Projects would have to meet donor requirements, and their successful implementation could mean more money for another project cycle.

In some cases, the grant application is just a token gesture because funds are assured anyway. A few organizations may have other, smaller sources of income: training and consulting services, sale of organic products and traditional medicines produced by local communities, a random rummage sale or participation in a bazaar. But the income generated from such activities is rarely substantial.

The bulk of the organization's funding would still be from one or two funders. Now that funding from aid agencies has become less reliable due to shifting donor trends and preferences, many research organizations are left with unfunded programmes, and may even begin to wonder about their survival. More grant making institutions require counterpart funding, and token grant proposals just to meet paper trail requirements don't work anymore.

Non-profits actually have to earn their keep! As the non-profit sector comes face-to-face with the reality of declining funds from the international donor community, non-profit leaders are left with two options: close shop, or aggressively and creatively look for alternative funding sources to fill the gap. The latter poses as a challenge for non-profits that have been used to writing up grant proposals to secure funding. Board members, executive directors and non-profit managers must now learn to diversify funding sources and come up with creative resource mobilization strategies to ensure survival.

The Importance of Diversifying Funding Sources

A diversity of funding sources provides protection against fickle donor trends. Other than grants, income sources include gifts and earned income.

The characteristics of each are found in Table 6.1:

Tabel 6.1. Different Funding Sources.

Sources	Characteristics	Examples
Grants	Usually restricted, project-based, time-bound, short-to-medium-term funding	Governments, foundations, associations, multilateral and bilateral agreements
Gifts	Unrestricted, can lead to endowments, medium-to-long term funding	Individuals, groups
Earned Income	Unrestricted, short-to-long term funding, for-profit operation, needing different management skills	Sale of products, fee for service, interest income

Rather than focusing all energies towards bagging large grant amounts from big funders, there is value to develop a following made up of individual donors, corporations and groups with various degrees of affinity for the organization's programmes. Their support may come in the form of large or small gifts, could be unrestricted, could be one-time donations, or could lead to long-term funding.

An organization in search of unrestricted funding would do well to expand their base of individual givers. There is also value in professionalizing existing earned income activities to the point where they could significantly impact an organization's financial viability. This alternative approach encourages a healthy mix of funding sources, thereby spreading the risk in the event that one source dries up.

Building Constituents

The call now for development research organizations is to make the shift from dependence on grants to building their own constituencies and mobilizing local support through other strategies. Raising resources from a local base has direct implications on the relevance of an organization's reason for being. A community willing to support the organization's research efforts, financially or otherwise, suggests that it shares the objectives of the programme, understands them, and aspires to see them realised.

This becomes an endorsement of the organization's mission, and serves as an indicator of how wide and deep the organization's impact is on its constituents. In addition, more grant giving institutions, foundations and corporations are using the level of community support as a criterion for funding. Developing a base of support should thus be a part of an organization's resource development plan.

The task then falls on the organization to identify who these people are in the community, find a way of talking to these people, offer them opportunities for support, and have systems in place that assure these supporters, or donors, that their donations are directed towards the projects for which they were intended. To accomplish the above requires more than just the technical skills of resource mobilization. It involves the complex and delicate task of building relationships with other people who share similar values and goals, and upon whom the organization can rely for support.

Defining Resource Mobilisation

Thus resource mobilisation may be defined as:

* A management process that involves identifying people who share the same values as your organisation, and taking steps to manage that relationship.

Looking closely at this definition, one can see that resource mobilization is actually a process that involves three integrated concepts:

The key concepts are:

* Organizational management and development,
* Communicating and prospecting, and
* Relationship building.

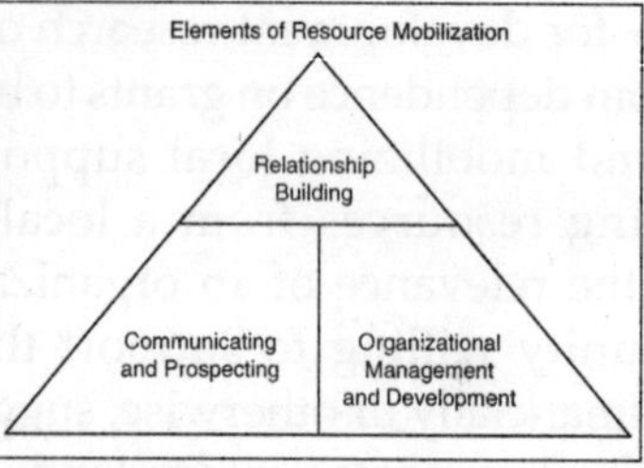

Fig. 6.1

Organizational Management and Development

Organizational management and development involves establishing and strengthening organizations for the resource mobilization process. It involves identifying the organization's vision, mission, and goals, and putting in place internal systems and processes that enable the resource mobilization efforts, such as: identifying the roles of board and staff; effectively and efficiently managing human, material, and financial resources; creating and implementing a strategic plan that addresses the proper stewardship and use of existing funds on the one hand, and identifies and seeks out diversified sources of future funding on the other.

This concept covers the following principles, elaborated throughout the practical guidebook:

* Resource mobilization is just a means to the end, the end being the fulfillment of the organization's vision
* Resource mobilization is a team effort, and involves the institution's commitment to resource mobilization; acceptance for the need to raise resources; and institutionalizing resource mobilization priorities, policies and budget allocation
* The responsibility for the resource mobilization effort is shared by the board, the president or the executive director, and the resource mobilization unit
* An organization needs money in order to raise money
* There are no quick fixes in resource mobilization

Communicating and Prospecting

Once an organization has achieved a certain readiness for resource mobilization, it must then take on another challenge: ensuring its longterm sustainability by acquiring new donors and maintaining a sizeable constituency base. The art of resource mobilization entails learning how to connect with prospective donors in a manner and language they understand, and finding common ground through shared values and interests. It also entails discerning the right prospect to approach, and matching the appropriate resource mobilization strategy to the prospect.

This concept is governed by two principles:

* Resource mobilization is really FRIEND raising. Financial support comes as a result of a relationship, and not as the goal in and of itself.
* People don't give money to causes, they give to PEOPLE with causes. People give to organizations to which they have personal affiliation, in some shape or form.

Relationship Building

And thus the courtship begins: once you identify your donors, the objective then is to get closer to them, get to know them better, very much the same way as developing a casual acquaintance into a trusted friend and confidante. As the relationship deepens, this increases the chance of donors giving higher levels of support over time, intensifying commitment and enlarging investment.

As cultivation techniques become more targeted and personal, a donor may become more involved in the organization. Initiating new relationships, nurturing existing ones, and building an everexpanding network of committed partners is an ongoing activity, embedded as a core function of the organization.

This requires the dedication of board members, staff and volunteers, and in order to build enduring relationships, the following principles should be remembered:

* Donor cultivation means bringing the prospect to a closer relationship with the organization, increasing interest and involvement
* Start at the bottom of the resource mobilization pyramid to get to the top

The Resource Mobilization Pyramid and the 80–20 Rule

The resource mobilization pyramid is a graphic depiction of the proportion of an organization's supporters *vis-a-vis* their level of involvement in its activities:

* Major Donors make up only 10% of an organization's support base, but contribute 70% of total donations received.

* Repeat Donors make up 20% of an organization's support base, and contribute 20% of total donations received.

* First-time Donors make up 70% of an organization's support base, but contribute only 10% of total donations received.

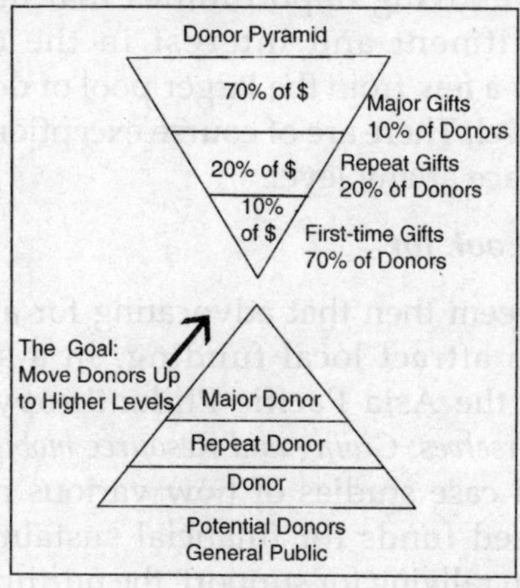

Fig. 6.2

The pyramid reflects a concept called the Pareto Principle, also known as the 80-20 Rule, which states that a small number of causes is responsible for a large percentage of the effect. In one business application, it can mean that 20% of the customers generate 80% of the sales, or that 80% of merchandise comes from 20% of the vendors. In the non-profit application of the Pareto Principle, it can mean that 20% of an organization's funding comes from 80% of its donors, forming the base of the pyramid.

Majority of the supporters are involved in a smaller capacity. Further up the pyramid, individuals with greater involvement become fewer, and the apex is the smallest group of supporters who contribute the most. The percentages per se are not as important as understanding that the higher the gift or donation, the smaller the number of donors who have the capacity or interest to give it. The donor pyramid serves as a model to envision the resource mobilization strategies that are appropriate for each level. An entry-level strategy such as a special event or a direct mail campaign can be used to draw in donors to an organization.

As a donor's capacity to give increases over time, other strategies, such as face-to-face solicitation, are then implemented to draw them up the pyramid, providing them with successive giving opportunities that may cultivate a deeper commitment and interest in the organization. Generally, only a few from the larger pool of donors move up into the next level. There are of course exceptions, and a major donor can surface at any level.

What Donors Look for

It would seem then that advocating for a good cause is not enough to attract local funding. In a seminal study conducted by the Asia Pacific Philanthropy Consortium, *Investing in Ourselves: Giving and Resource mobilization in Asia,* which covered case studies of how various nonprofits and NGOs mobilized funds for financial sustainability, it was observed that in rallying for support, the nurturing of personal and community relationships was more critical than the espoused cause itself. It further stated that these relationships were based on three major characteristics that an organization needed to have in order to attract support: legitimacy, transparency, and accountability.

Legitimacy

Different countries have different terms and requirements for recognizing the legal existence of organizations. But however diverse these requirements are across the region, each state still exercises a degree of control over the incorporation of non-profit organizations. Only those that have been established according to their country's civil laws and traditions are considered to be legitimate. Such organizations are more likely to gain donor support because they have achieved some level of compliance with government standards, and are less likely to be suspected of being fronts for underground political movements or "fly-by-night" operations.

Transparency

This refers to open communication with internal and external stakeholders regarding an organization's financial and management health, and is a characteristic of organizations that disclose information ab0ut their programmes, activities, and even financial transactions and investments to stakeholders and anyone who wishes to know more about the organization. It is a criterion that is highly regarded by prospective donors and partners, as transparency assures them of an organization's trustworthiness and commitment to its constituents.

Accountability

This refers to an organization's ability to stand up for its mission, and to be guided by sound management and financial principles. An accountable organization is one that responsibly services its community, properly manages its resources, and is able to report back to donors regarding the use of donated funds. Such organizations are also likely to gain public support, as quite a number of donors now expect to be updated on how their funds have been used by their beneficiary organizations.

Moreover, it is not uncommon for donors to request visits to project sites to be sure that their monies are being used in the best way possible. If there is only one message to take home from this chapter it is this: In building a base of donors, the focus is less on resource mobilization, more on friend raising. The funds come as a by-product of the relationship, and not so much as an end in itself.

DEVELOPMENT AND MANAGEMENT OF A RESOURCE MOBILIZATION PROGRAMME

This part discusses the major steps in resource mobilization planning:

* Reviewing the organizational strategic plan

* Determining resource mobilization targets
* Identifying constituencies and broadening stakeholders
* Developing key messages
* Reviewing and selecting resource mobilization strategies
* Gearing up for resource mobilization

Ideally, these steps are to be performed in successive order, and you will notice that they build upon each other to create a full understanding and appreciation of the resource mobilization planning process. Throughout the succeeding chapters, we have provided case stories, studies, tools and exercises you can use in your own planning exercise.

Reviewing the Organizational Strategic Plan

This part starts with the importance of revisiting your Organization's Vision, Mission and Goal statements, accompanied with an exercise that can be used in reviewing or refining existing statements. The part on Situational Analysis discusses the merits of going through this exercise, and how this can be used to determine the strengths and weaknesses of your resource mobilization capacity, as well as the opportunities and threats to the organization. Accompanying this part are guidelines to Planning for a Situational Analysis, and an excerpt from the SWOT analysis of eHomemakers. Also included are case stories of FRLHT, ANSAB and KADO, as well as excerpts from a Donor Scoping Study commissioned by the IDRC.

Bringing the Future into the Present

Linking Resource Mobilization with the Vision and Mission

Most established non-profit organizations possess an articulated Vision and Mission and engage in a regular strategic planning exercise. Ideally, at the end of each Strategic Plan cycle, the members of the organization engage in a review of its collective achievements, challenges faced, and current realities *vis-à-vis* its Vision, Mission and goals, in order to plan for the next cycle. A similar process is employed when developing a Resource Mobilization Plan, since your organization's Vision, Mission and Strategic Plan are the bases for its formulation.

The nature of a non-profit is to fill its funding gaps from sources other than its beneficiaries. In an organization's constant quest for resources, it can be tempting to develop a project just to match a donor's requirements and criteria. In some cases, an organization's good intentions can lead it to decide to serve this or that beneficiary, without taking into consideration its financial limitations and available resources. Many non-profits are born out of the fiery goodwill and intentions of an individual or a group of individuals who identify social needs that are unmet and seek to find solutions to those needs.

In the early years of the non-profit, operations run informally, almost intuitively, and the initiator or prime advocate sets the direction of the organization. However, as your organization grows, more complex programmes will require more formal systems, and stakeholders would like to have greater influence in the running of your organization, it is easy to lose sight of why the organization was formed in the first place. The vision and mission statements are what keep an organization on track. A non-profit without a vision statement is like being on a boat with no compass, flailing at the changing winds of a funder's, or a founder's, preferences.

The Vision

There are as many definitions of a "Vision" as there are organizational development consultants, but in the simplest of words, an organization's vision is the "shared hopes, dreams and images of the future." Much more than a statement of identity, your vision is a proactive, public declaration of how your organization sees the ideal future in the area in which it works.

The forward motion of your organization depends on the clarity of your vision. Your vision statement is your prescription for pointing you in the right direction. All other documents and tools – your mission statement, strategic plan, marketing plan, business plan, and even your fundraising campaigns-are the means to reach your destination. When your vision is internalized by all the members of your organization, all of your work leads you towards accomplishing this. Because you know your vision, you believe in it, and you all live it. As you begin to plan for resource mobilization, it is time to put on a resource mobilization lens and analyse your existing vision statement using the following criteria:

* Is your vision powerful?
* Does it capture the organization's image of the future?
* Can members of the organization relate to it and be motivated to achieve it?
* Do they live the vision in their daily lives and passionately share this vision with others — with potential donors and with the community?

The International Center for Integrated Mountain Development (ICIMOD) has a clear, to-the-point vision statement:

* ... ICIMOD is committed to a shared vision of prosperous and secure mountain communities committed to peace, equity, and environmental sustainability.

The Foundation for Revitalization of Local Health Traditions (FRLHT) has an even shorter one:

* . . . to revitalize Indian medical heritage.

When clearly crafted, an organization's vision is unchanging, and timeless. A well-thought out vision statement attracts donors that share common aspirations. It discourages your organization from force-fitting programme elements that have nothing to do with your vision, which may have only been created to meet the requirements of a particular donor. Staying focused on vision-driven vs. donor-driven programmes will address real, and not perceived needs within beneficiary communities. Conversely, it helps your organization determine the prospective donors to approach and as a result, moves you forward to its achievement.

The Mission

An organization's mission statement is a brief expression of why it exists-its reason for being. It states your organization's purpose, with and for whom your organization works, how your organization will go about fulfilling its vision, and the values that your organization adheres to.

A mission statement:

* Is clear, concise and understandable
* Expresses why the organization does its work or the organization's ultimate purpose
* Is broad enough for flexibility but not too broad to lack focus
* States with and for whom the organization works
* States the organization's distinctive competence or the difference the organization will make for those it serves
* Serves as an energy source and a rallying point for the organization

The following example of the mission statement of FRLHT captures the organization's focus.

To demonstrate the contemporary relevance of Indian Medical Heritage by designing and implementing innovative programmes related to:

* Exposition of the theory and practice of traditional systems of medicine;
* Conservation of the natural resources used by Indian systems of medicine; and
* Revitalization of social processes for transmission of the heritage on a size and scale that will have societal impact.

The mission statement of the Indian Institute of Forest Management clearly states its intended outcome, as well as its particular area of focus:

* To provide leadership in professional forestry management aimed at environmental conservation and sustainable development of ecosystems.

Such mission statements provide a guiding star to help an organization stay on track and keep its activities well-focused. When applied to resource mobilization planning, your organization's mission becomes the anchor by which you will communicate your cause to your potential donors, why you are deserving of support, and how you will prioritize your limited resources. As a result, your mission statement also gives you a sense of your organization's resource gaps.Which, ultimately becomes a major component of your resource mobilization plan.

Goals

When the vision or dreams for the future have been defined, those who will benefit from that vision have been identified, and how to go about making that a reality has been fleshed out through a mission, your organization's goals now shape the targets towards which plans and actions are directed.

A framework that is most useful for setting goals is the S-M-A-R-T goal framework:

* Specific - what is required is clearly stated
* Measurable - results are quantifiable
* Attainable - targets are realistic but challenging
* Relevant - goals have an impact on intended communities
* Time bound - a clear timeframe is defined

SMART goals ground the vision and mission, and help your organization carve out a niche for the services you render. The goals distinguish your organization from others within the sector. Vision, mission and goal statements have the power to hold your organization together, and thus, present a consistent image to your publics. These keep your organization on track with what you would like to accomplish, and provide a yardstick to measure your present performance against your future plans. The example illustrates the link between ANSAB's Vision, mission and goals, and how these direct its resource mobilization efforts. Resource mobilization for a Clear Purpose:

The ANSAB Story:

* The *Asia Network for Sustainable Agriculture and Bioresources* (ANSAB) was founded in 1992 by Enterprise Works, the Government of Nepal — Ministry of Agriculture and Asian country representatives to help improve peoples' livelihoods. According to Bhishma Subedi, Executive Director, ANSAB is committed to enterprise oriented solutions to biodiversity conservation and economic development. ANSAB has a vision of rich and productive biodiversity for prosperous communities. Rich, healthy, and productive ecosystems are actively managed and used by local communities who are capable of addressing threats to biodiversity and advancing sustainable resource management. Focusing its services at the grassroots, national, and regional levels and collaborating with key stakeholders and clients, ANSAB integrates and builds on local and scientific knowledge systems, innovations, perspectives, and opportunities for ground level tangible impacts and wider replications. The organization started with a US$200,000 project budget with three staff members, and now has grown to over 60 staff members and 200 partner organizations implementing seven to eight projects per year. Dr. Subedi cites the following strengths of ANSAB–the capacity to design projects well, credibility, having unique tools, and persistence, which he further explained to mean not always following what the donor wants. "We always want to stay in the practical level, and what want us to do may not always be in the general direction." He adds, "ANSAB has various types of donors, those who support environmental conservation and those interested in livelihood improvements and community development. This twin focus helps to increase the pool of interested donors. However, it is still a challenge to find donors who are interested

in both." In ANSAB, the Executive Director leads the resource mobilization. Board members, a loose committee and programme managers are also involved in identifying project opportunities and proposal writing.When asked about what others can learn from ANSAB's experience, Dr. Subedi says, "My tips to other organizations are:

- To choose a focus and to stay focused; and
- To choose good programmes first before looking for funding opportunities."

Your vision and mission statements are your organization's guides in creating programmes. In the process of identifying possible funding for your programmes, you will come across those that fund activities in your area of work, but do not match your existing programmes. This does not mean that your organization develops a programme because there is available funding. Rather, you need to look at how your project can be modified to meet the donor's requirements. If there really is no fit, there is no need to force the issue!

Crafting Vision-Mission-Goal Statements

How do you go about crafting your vision-mission-goal statements?

There are a number of ways:

* Choose representatives from all the units of your organization to form the Vision-Mission team. They then draft the statements, which are then presented to the general body for feedback.
* Have an individual draft the statement, then present to general body for feedback.
* Contract an organizational development consultant to facilitate the process within a workshop setting.

The key is to use a participatory process involving all the stakeholders of your organization, including your beneficiaries. Especially for non-profit organizations, the days for top-down dictation of vision, mission and goal statements are long gone.

Developing Your Organization's Vision and Mission Statements: Vision Statement Exercise

In a vision-mission planning process:

* Individually, have each participant list ideas of the ideal future vision for the organization five years from now:
* Have each participant share their individual list with either a subgroup, or directly with the entire planning team.
* After all have shared their statements, have each group create a bullet list of common concepts from all the statements.
* Have each sub-group share common concepts with the larger group. On behalf of the entire group, one person writes down the list of common concepts.
* As a unified group, create a short, positive, and inspiring vision statement that has the consensus of all.

Mission Statement Exercise

Individually, answer each question below:

* Why does our organization exist? What is our purpose?
* Whom do we serve?
* How do we achieve our purpose?

Procedure for Revising Your Vision and Mission Statements

When board, staff and volunteer leaders take the time to regularly examine and measure organizational achievements and its current challenges and realities in relation to its vision, long-lasting benefits can be realised. The organization's Vision and Mission electrifies and directs its efforts. On some occasions, there will be a need to revise the organization's Vision and Mission statements, in light of major shifts in its environment, a need to change the organizations programmes due to increased demand for specific services which fall within its expertise, or decreased support for existing programmes.

There is one crucial question that will spur the need to revisit your Vision- Mission statements:

* Are the current vision and mission statements clear and on-target in today's operating environment?

If the answer to this question is a "No", the following procedure can be adopted:

* Define your organization. What is the end result of your efforts? Of what value is this end result to your stakeholders?
* Solicit the opinions and impressions of your external stakeholders on why your organization exists, what it has achieved, the quality of your programmes and what are the emerging needs, if any, of these external stakeholders. These inputs can be used to help define your organization's reason for being.

Knowing Where you are before Getting to Where you are Going: Situational Analysis

Development organizations come up with methodologies and technologies that contribute to the viability and sustainability of the communities with which they work. But does your organization "walk the talk" of sustainability? Do you have enough funding to see your own projects through? Is there a strategic plan in place that allows you to see resource gaps, and create action plans to close the gap? Who decides on funding targets and priority projects? What are the targets and timelines? Is there a participatory system in place to elicit from various programme units their resource mobilization needs and concerns?

In short, what are the prevailing factors affecting your organization's ability to raise resources? The answers to these and many more questions stem from situational analysis tools. This chapter discusses the rationale of going through a situational analysis using a resource mobilization focus, and introduces a method often used in both for-profit and not-for-profit settings.

Why do a Situational Analysis?

A situational analysis is conducted for many different reasons, including assessing organizational performance, capacity in various skills and knowledge areas, motivation and environmental influences on its performance. This process can likewise be utilized to assess the resource mobilization capacity of your organization.

It is all very well to have high hopes and dreams for long -mid- and even short-term programmes, but if passion is not matched with the infrastructure to make dreams a reality, then at the end of the fiscal day, your organization will be staring at many unfunded proposals in the face. The process involves the undertaking of a SWOT Analysis to determine your organization's strengths and weaknesses to your resource mobilization capacity, as well as opportunities and threats to your resource mobilization efforts.

Revisiting this process while using a resource mobilization lens presents a clearer, realistic view of what particular programmes to generate resources for, the particular constituency groups you wish to target, what resource mobilization strategies will appeal to this targeted group, and what systems and structures must be present within your organization to be able to generate resources efficiently and effectively, and ultimately, fulfil your vision and mission.

What Information Can you Get From a Situational Analysis?

A situational analysis report has the potential to determine what are the internal factors, or factors within the control of your organization that contribute or hinder resource mobilization efforts. In addition, a situational analysis report can also identify the responses of your organization to external factors, those that are beyond your control, that similarly contribute to or hinder your resource mobilization efforts.

For the following internal factors, a situational analysis may:

* Affirm resource mobilization successes to date
* Provide a sense of history and present the organization's evolution in its responses to changes in the funding environment
* Present a "reality check" on where the organization is at currently *vis-a-vis* the achievement of its vision, mission and existing strategic plan goals

* Validate funding targets over a set period of time, identify available funding and resource gaps
* Indicate gaps in administrative systems such as Finance and Accounting
* Indicate gaps specific to resource mobilization skills and systems such as proposal writing, implementation of other strategies, donor acquisition and upgrade
* Establish ownership of resource mobilization functions
* Open new doors or widen perspectives on prospective resource providers
* Determine buy-in, or lack thereof, of various stakeholders to organization's funding priorities and resource mobilization strategies
* Establish resource mobilization policies and code of ethics anchored to the organization's core values
* Review the relevance of the organization's existing key messages
* Determine the organization's capacity to invest in a resource mobilization programme

A situational analysis may also reflect your organization's response to the following external factors:

* Funders' priorities and changing trends
* Demand for your organization's services
* Technological innovations related to your area of work
* Legislative and regulatory changes
* Competing grantees
* Prevailing political, social and economic conditions

The situational analysis therefore, is a powerful process that keeps you grounded in the current realities existing for your organization. When you are able to see things as they are, and have increased awareness about what is going on within and outside your organization, you are then able to set realistic resource mobilization targets. Knowing where you are in the present maps out a clearer direction for where you are going in the future.

How do you do a Situational Analysis?

One of the most popular frameworks used by organizational development consultants in conducting situational analysis is to determine the *Strengths, Weaknesses, Opportunities and Strengths* (SWOT) in the achievement of an organization's mission. Each area is defined as follows:

* *Strengths* – attributes/factors internal to the organization, which it can manage or control, that support or aid in the fulfillment of its mission
* *Weaknesses* – attributes/factors internal to the organization, which it can manage or control, that act as hindrances to the fulfillment of its mission
* *Opportunities* – conditions external to the organization, which it cannot control, that may contribute to the achievement of the organization's mission
* *Threats* – conditions external to the organization, which it cannot control, that may hinder the achievement of the organization's mission

During resource mobilization planning, these areas are examined once more in the context of their impact on the organization's resource mobilization performance, as well as its potential.

Some Things To Remember About SWOT:

* The SWOT tool does not exist in a vacuum or in the abstract. The tool is used towards achieving a holistic view of a current situation, with the intention of deciding what the next appropriate step is. A desired end result must first be determined. For example, your organization can use the tool to determine if it has the capacity to generate a total of US$50,000 from a minimum of four sources within the next three years.
* SWOT questions must be able to draw out answers that point to factors relevant to the desired end result, and not count aspects that do not have any connection to the desired end result.

* Opportunities are sometimes interpreted as strategies. However, opportunities are conditions, and strategies are actions.
* One organization's opportunity may be another's threat, and vice versa. This also applies to its strengths and weaknesses. A SWOT map is very specific to an organization: one size DOESN'T fit all!

Answers are then placed on a matrix like this:

INTERNAL			EXTERNAL
	Strengths	Opportunities	
	Weaknesses	Threats	

Fig. 6.3.

Once the matrix has been filled out, you can then formulate resource mobilization goals, and choose strategies that match your organizations resources and targeted constituency groups. It would be ideal if you consciously take into account your organizational Strengths to ward off or reduce vulnerability to Threats, or use Strengths to generate strategies to take advantage of Opportunities. Conversely, you see the Weaknesses that need to be overcome to pursue Opportunities and parry Threats.

The SWOT is constructed primarily through a series of questions specifically formulated to draw out answers that cover the four areas. There are various methodologies to conduct SWOT interviews, and once a methodology is decided, a list of interviewees or participants is drawn up, making sure that there is a mix of respondents to provide a multi-dimensional view of the organization.

Planning for Situational Analysis

Data Gathering Steps

* Determine the focus, goals and overview of the *Situational Analysis* (SA) Process.

- *Focus*: Desired end result as determined by the organization
- *Goals*: To assess systems, skills, personnel, resources in place in terms of effectiveness, relevance and usefulness in support of the desired end result
- *SA Process Overview*: Determine appropriate methodology for information gathering

* Identify who will be the sources of information or who will be interviewed.
* Decide whether the situational analysis is to be done by external reviewers or internal reviewers.
* Work on a common definition of terms to be used by all reviewers.
* Review existing relevant publications, documents, web sites, etc.
* Handle logistics: set time, date, venue of interviews.
* Prepare interview guide questions.
* During interview process, present objective of interview to participants.
* Conduct interviews.
* Review notes between interviews and check for accuracy.
* Transcribe interviews.

Determining Resource Mobilization Targets

This part focuses on the importance of Setting Realistic Targets as a part of a well-grounded resource mobilization plan. It starts off with key Considerations in Determining Targets. The part ends with a Resource Timeline tool, a grid that can be used to identify current resources, gaps, prospective funding sources, and projections.

Finding out how Much you Really Need

After assessing your organization's capabilities and peripheral factors affecting performance, it is time to find out how much money you really need to raise and what are the resources you need to mobilize in order to continue the work you do. Setting goals is one of the most essential factors in the success of your resource mobilization undertaking.

It cannot be overemphasized how crucial this step is as it requires that you:

* Make an inventory of your current resources, both financial and in-kind; and
* Project the needs that your activities may still require to achieve fundamental results.

Not only do determining resource mobilization targets allow you to plan for the future of your programmes, *i.e.*, where you want to be and what you want to accomplish given a specific timeframe, but it also gives you a clearer picture of what you can do here and now.

Advantages of Setting Resource Mobilization Targets

There are some scenarios common to development research non-profits. In some cases, an organization may seek resources only when the need arises, or when the end of the grant period draws nearer. In this scenario, there's a tendency to fall into the trap of being fund-driven: a programme exists only when there's funding. It often is the case that funding targets are set without consideration to real needs. For example, a non-profit may set a target of US$50,000 just because it is their 50th anniversary. They dream of building a training center to have a space of their own, without considering the costs of building maintenance. By determining realistic resource mobilization targets, you are able to check if the goals are actually linked with or rooted in your organization's strategic plan and your current programmes, and see if the time and effort you exert are well worth it.

Key Considerations in Planning

* A review of the organization's current resource situation is important to be able to plan resource mobilization activities realistically.
* The resource target should be based on the programmes you are implementing at present and the activities you are planning to execute. It is

pragmatic to always go back to the organization's strategic plan to determine which programmes or activities must be pursued that would make possible the realization of your organization's mission.

* Financial management and strategic budgeting are of high importance in planning your resource mobilization programme. These contribute to getting the most accurate and updated budgetary figures, as well as in helping determine the best strategy for closing the resource gaps.
* A Resource Timeline becomes a very important tool in determining targets as it provides you with sufficient lead time to ensure the sustainability of your programmes. If carefully laid out, it helps you visualize what your current resource situation is and enables you to see how long your resources can sustain your programmes.

Identifying Resource Needs Using the Resource Timeline

The resource timeline is a tool used to identify the existing resources, both financial and in-kind, that are currently available with your organization, as well as to project the programme requirements for the immediate future. This tool will help you identify the total amount of funds and resources that need to be mobilized in order to sustain the programmes of your organization. Essentially, information on funding targets and resource needs puts your resource mobilization programme in a proper perspective as it guides you in determining which strategies will work best in filling resource gaps.

Objectives

* Review current resource situation
* Determine programme areas in need of funding and resources throughout a three-year period by using a resource timeline
* Identify the funding gaps or resource needs

Mechanics

Table. 6.4.

1.Activity/ Programme	2. Resources		3.Resource Gaps/Needs	4.Resources Providers	5.Timeline			6.Resources Classification
	2.a. Requirement	2.b. Available			Yr1	Yr2	Yr3	
			Total RM Target					

- In column 1, list down programmes that your organization is implementing at present and the activities you intend to pursue over the next three years.
- In column 2a, indicate the funding and resource needs of your activities/programmes. This should reflect the sum of monies and the equipment your organization ought to have in order to achieve the programs' key results over a three-year period. It is best to consult with your finance unit so as to show the most realistic projections.
- Among the requirements presented in column 2a, specify the amount of funds and in-kind resources that already exist with your organization. Again, confer with your finance unit to get the most updated figures.
- Column 3 should be able to show the variance between column 2a and 2b in terms of funds needed, as well as present a listing of items and equipment. These are the resource gaps, which would be the resource mobilization targets and the basis of developing your resource mobilization programme.
- In column 4, indicate the sources of your available funds and resources. Include individual contributors, donor agencies and funding partners, other non-profit organizations, resource mobilization strategies, etc.
- Draw an arrow in column 5 to show until when the money and resources will be available.

* The last column must indicate if the available funds in column 2b are restricted, *i.e.* to be used only as proposed or how you have committed it to be spent/ utilized, or unrestricted, *i.e.* to be utilized freely, when you want to or whenever it's necessary.

Identifying and Broadening the Stakeholder Group

Building relationships with your community is at the core of resource mobilization planning. This part discusses how to Identify and Define your Community Using the Constituency or Stakeholder Map, and how you can use the 3Cs – Connection, Capability, Concern — in qualifying prospective donors and partners.

Also featured are insights from SEARICE as it engages its stakeholders. The Case Stories of the Govi Gnana Seva Project and GREEN Foundation show the wide network these organizations have used to implement their initiatives. Then you'll find a summary of the findings of the seven-country research project, *Investing in Ourselves: Giving and Fund Raising in Asia*.

The study affirms the belief that philanthropy is alive and well in Asia, and explores the giving attitudes of individual givers across Asia. The part closes with an exercise on Identifying your Stakeholders using the Stakeholder Map.

Looking Beyond the Usual Sources

Stakeholder Development in Resource Mobilization

While the tendency to pursue grants still prevails among nonprofits, more organizations are realizing the need to broaden their base of support beyond the usual sources of funds. Nearly every door in the global donor community now puts out a welcome mat only for organizations with selfsustainability and long-term viability of programmes and projects.

For several years now, counterpart funding and exit strategies have become necessary components in grant proposals. Exit strategies include activities and programmes that ensure a non-profit organization's sustainability beyond the grant period. A few grant-giving institutions have included resource mobilization training as part of their exit strategy. Donors want to ensure that their grantees know how to raise resources after the donors have pulled out of a country or programme. They need assurance that the organization they have funded will work to raise resources and not just be dependent on funds provided by them or by other funding institutions.

What Stakeholders Give:

* Money.
* Technical Assistance.
* Volunteer time.
* Seconded Staff.
* Goods/Products.
* Sponsorships.
* Assets.
* Joint promotions/ cause related marketing.
* Equipment.

Golden Lessons on Broadening Stakeholders

The first golden rule, then is that development research organizations need to move on from dependence on grants to diversifying funding sources. The second is that this can happen only when your organization seeks to build its own constituency by mobilizing local support through other strategies. Raising resources from a local base implies that an organization has the mandate from the community to continue its programmes.

Assuming that your organization has elected to work on a valid cause, what you do benefit more people than just the direct beneficiaries. Defining your "community", also known as constituents or stakeholders, helps you determine whether what you are doing is relevant or not, and helps you identify possible linkages and partnerships beyond the obvious. It makes sense then to begin by identifying who are the individuals or groups that are directly served or influenced by your organization's mission, and whose needs shape the strategies your organization undertakes.

These people have an intrinsic connection to your organization, and have a stake and interest in the continuing existence of your organization. Stakeholders could consist of members of your general assembly, past and present consultants and contributors, past and present participants of trainings or seminars or other projects that you've run, institutional donors, corporate donors, local NGOs, cooperatives, community leaders, local government units, academic institutions, your staff, their families, beneficiaries, and volunteers as well as other similarlyinclined people and institutions who have been involved with your work in various capacities.

The rationale behind focusing on these groups, as opposed to the more typical route of going after grantmaking foundations and large benefactors, is that if you're able to inspire people that are closest to you to give or give of themselves, then it may become that much easier to get those remotely connected at least interested in knowing more about your organization.

Developing a Stakeholder Map

To visualize the environment your organization finds itself in, you can use a tool called a constituency or stakeholder map. The map is a simple diagram made up of a series of concentric hexagons containing the people most connected to your organization. Each level indicates their degree of participation, with those at the core having the most involvement, and those in the outer levels with the least. People with similar interests and general donors are placed on the outer layer, while major donors, the board, staff, and loyal supporters, regarded as key movers, are in the inner circle.

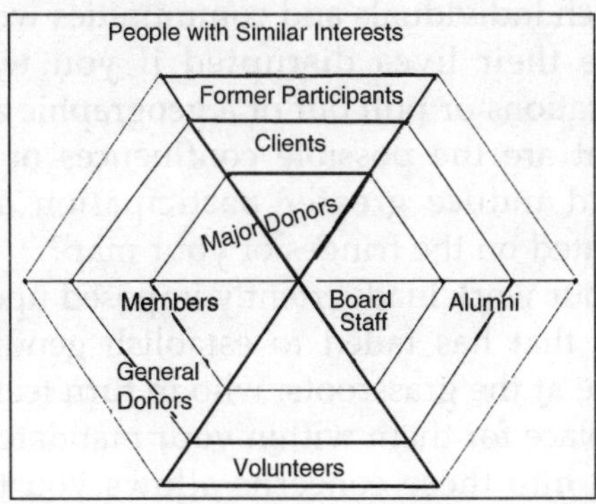

Fig 6.4. Stakeholder Map for a Training Organization.

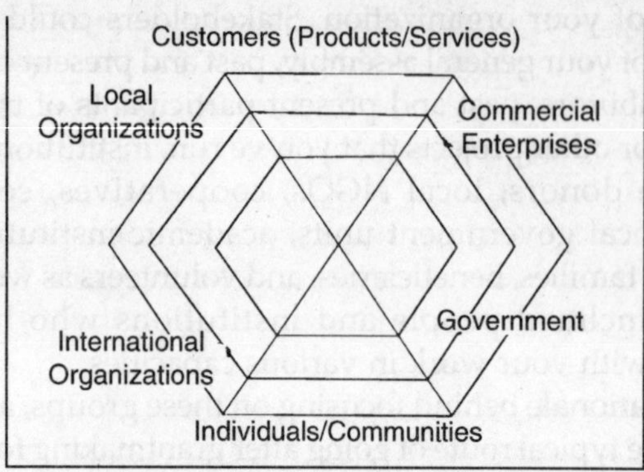

Fig 6.5. Stakeholder Map for a Development Organization.

As you go through the exercise of drawing your own constituency map and filling it with the names of individuals, organizations and other groups that matter most to your work, you will find that you can create a picture of the mix and degrees of commitment represented by your current set of constituents. The map not only provides baseline information from which you can assess the health of your organization, it more importantly allows you to qualitatively measure the impact of your work as it requires you to deliberately identify your constituency.

The map forces you to address core questions such as:

* What is the range of services you provide, and what types of people and organizations are both directly and indirectly serviced by what you do?
* Which individuals and communities would suffer or have their lives disrupted if you were to cease operations or pull out of a geographic area?
* What are the possible confluences of interest that could induce greater participation among those situated on the fringes of your map?
* Is your work inadvertently imposed upon by a small core that has failed to establish genuine ties with those at the grassroots, who in turn feel that there is no place for them within your mandate?

Looking into these concerns allows you to determine who may be receptive to your overtures for either fresh or higher degrees of support, who among your constituents you need to woo and which openings or leads you can explore as you seek to harness resources waiting to be tapped and mobilized. Over and above this, the stakeholder map helps you determine if you already have the right mix of supporters or if you need to bring in new people with other competencies.

The stakeholder map is a graphic device that not only serves as a barometer of your relationships but also helps you define your sphere of work in resource mobilization.While the map allows you to identify the types of individuals and organizations that you should target as you broaden your reach as an organization, it also helps you figure out how you can deepen the level of participation of those who are already close to the core, but not as close as they could, or should be.

Fund Raising is Friend Raising

The goals are then first, to draw in people from the larger universe to the periphery of your map; and second, to bring those at the outer levels of your map closer to the center, where a greater level of participation and commitment, financial and non-financial, can be expected. This is the primary objective of "friend raising", as opposed to mere fund raising. Friend raising emphasizes the development and nurturing of relationships both within and outside your immediate spheres of influence. Fund raising, on the other hand, may tend to be more like one-shot, take-themoney- and-see-you-around approach.

While drawing on old reserves of resources, you need to be constantly enriching and enhancing what you already have. This may entail your board members, staff and close volunteers examining even the most mundane of personal connections, and doing your homework as you research for prospects.

In order to determine whether a prospective individual or organization would make a good donor, ask yourself the following questions, based on the 3Cs:

* *Connection*: Do we have a connection to the donor? Do we know anyone who can introduce our organization to the prospect? Is there anyone among the board, management or staff, contributors, consultants or volunteers who would be received more warmly by the prospect than someone from the fund raising staff?
* *Capability*: Can the prospect afford to donate to the organization? If not, can the donor still be able to contribute to the organization in other ways? How small or large are the amounts that this prospect has contributed in the past? Is this a good time to ask, or has she just had a major expense recently? How's he doing at his job or business?
* *Concern*: Are the prospect's values and interests aligned with those of your organization? Is this donor someone who will genuinely care about the welfare of the organization and its beneficiaries, and not only worry about its impact on his personal reputation or standing in society? What are her pet causes? Who have been his beneficiaries in the past? Does she have roots in the community you serve?

Bringing stakeholders closer to your organization: What's in it for them?

* Personal sense of satisfaction
* Result/impact to which they are contributing
* Information, contacts, public recognition to enable them to maintain or expand their interests
* Economic returns on their social investment

Once you have satisfactorily answered the questions posed by the 3Cs, move on to learning more facts about the prospective donor, his donation pattern, and specific interests. This will help you see how your own programmes can match the prospect's needs, and vice versa. A good prospect is one who meets the criteria of all 3Cs. As the goal of resource mobilization is to cultivate lifelong relationships, you must ascertain that this relationship starts out on the right foot, and with both parties clearly understanding the responsibilities involved in a partnership.

Identifying Stakeholders Using the Stakeholder Map

The stakeholder map is a tool used to identify current and potential supporters and partners. These stakeholders are classified into six categories: customers, commercial enterprises, local organizations, international organizations, the government, and individuals and communities.

Activity Mechanics

Identify the different stakeholders, both current and potential, for your organization. Plot them on the map according to the three Cs — Connection, Capability and Concern. The higher their CCCs, the closer they should be to the center of the map. For example, if the prospects that you have identified have 3 of the 3 Cs, then they should be put in the core of the map. Create a pattern so that prospects with 2 Cs are placed in the outer layer next to the core of the map while those with just 1 C are placed in the outer layer of the stakeholder map.

The UPWARD is an Asian network of scientists and development specialists working to increase participation by farmers and other users of agricultural technology in research and development.

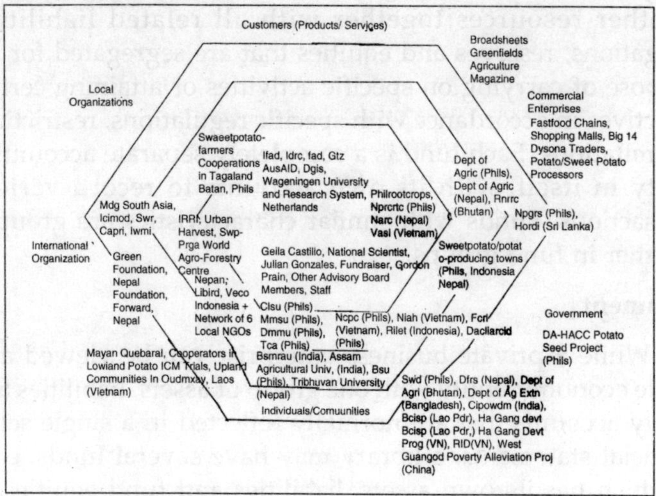

Fig. 6.6 User's Perspectives with Agricultural Research and Development (UPWARD)

The UPWARD used the stakeholder map to identify and plot their various stakeholders in the map based on the level of resource support and programme influence that they provide. Stakeholders with the highest involvement and contribution to UPWARD are placed in the core or inner part of the map while those in the outer layers of the map were perceived to have the least involvement with UPWARD.

ACCOUNTING

INTRODUCTION TO LIBRARY FUND ACCOUNTING

Purpose

The purpose of a library accounting system is:

* To show that all applicable legal provisions have been complied with; and
* To represent fairly and accurately the financial position and results of financial operations of the library's funds and account groups.

Definition of a Fund

A fund is defined as an independent fiscal and accounting entity with a self-balancing set of accounts recording cash and/or other resources together with all related liabilities, obligations, reserves and equities that are segregated for the purpose of carrying on specific activities or attaining certain objectives in accordance with specific regulations, restrictions or limitations. Each fund is a completely separate accounting entity in itself, with its own accounts to record various transactions. Funds with similar characteristics are grouped together in fund groups.

Comment

While a private business enterprise can be viewed as a single economic entity with one group of assets, liabilities and equity accounts that are normally reflected in a single set of financial statements, a library may have several funds, each of which has its own assets, liabilities and fund equities. A library may be a combination of several distinctly different operations, each of which functions, and must be reported on, independently from any other fund. The implementation of GASB Statement 34 will add a layer of financial reporting in addition to the distinct fund reporting. This new layer will consolidate the activity of governmental units into a single financial report, similar to the way private enterprise prepares financial reports. This new layer of financial reporting will be on the "full accrual" basis of accounting. It is important to realise that the day-to-day recordkeeping will not change substantially. The recording of receipts and disbursements and the preparation of budgets for most libraries will continue to be maintained on the "modified accrual" basis of accounting.

Users of Library Financial Information

* Taxpayers.
* State Treasurer/Oversight Bodies.
* Administrative/Finance.
* Bond Rating Agencies.
* Intergovernmental Grantors).
* Contributors/Creditors.
* Employees.

BASIS OF ACCOUNTING

There are two basic methods of accounting for funds: the modified-accrual basis and the accrual basis. Under the modified-accrual basis of accounting, revenue and expenditures are recorded. Under the accrual basis of accounting, revenue is recorded when earned and expenses are recorded when incurred. In general, governmental libraries will utilize the modified-accrual basis of accounting in the day to day accounting records and budgets. When preparing the year end financial report, they will also prepare government wide financial statements on the full accrual basis of accounting.

Characteristics of Modified-Accrual Basis of Accounting are as Follows

* Expenditures are recorded when incurred, not when cash is paid or when an invoice is received. Special rules are provided for the following:

- Prepaid expenses: Purchases that benefit more than one period may be prorated between periods.
- Interest on long-term debt should be counted on the due date of the debt.
- Employee compensated absences should be counted when the amount comes due for payment, *i.e.* time is taken off, or the employment is terminated.
- Contingent liabilities should also be recorded at the time they come due for payment.
- Capital assets should be counted as expenditures when purchased rather than capitalized and recognized over its useful life.

* Revenue is recorded when collected or collectible soon enough to be used to pay current liabilities. "Available" generally means collectible within 30 to 60 days. Special rules are provided for the following:

- Property taxes should be recorded in the fiscal period for which they were levied, provided the "available" criterion is met.
- Grants receivables for reimbursement of expenditures should be counted at the same time that the expenditure is recorded, however, GASB Statement number 33 requires that the corresponding revenue be recorded using the "measurable and available" rules. When a grant receivable will not be collected until a date beyond the "available" criterion, a deferred revenue should be recorded.
- Miscellaneous revenue such as fines and fees etc., are generally recognized when the cash is received.
- Proceeds of long-term debt are recorded as an "other financing source", rather than as liabilities of the fund.

Characteristics of Full Accrual Basis of Accounting are as Follows:

The full accrual basis is used to report the government wide financial information. After the accounting records of the individual funds have been completed on the modified accrual basis, then each government will also create government wide financial statements on the full accrual basis. This basis of accounting measures total economic resources, rather than just the current financial resources.

As a result:

* Revenue is recorded when earned, regardless of when it is received.
* Expenses are recorded as soon as a liability is incurred, and are allocated to the periods benefited.

Some of the more significant differences from modified accrual includes:

* Property tax revenue is recorded in the period levied, less an allowance for uncollectible amounts
* Unused vacation time is recorded as an expense when it is earned
* Capital purchases are not recorded as an expense at the time of purchase; instead, depreciation expense is recorded over the estimated useful life of capital assets. This means that purchases of library books would be capitalized as an asset and depreciated over an appropriate time period.

TYPES OF FUNDS

Following is a list of the typical funds which may be found in accounting for governmental libraries.

General Fund

The General Fund accounts for all revenue and expenditures that are not required to be accounted for elsewhere. This fund typically accounts for the daily revenue and expenditures necessary to operate and provide service of a library. Most revenue and expenses are recorded in this fund. In many cases, this may be the only fund the library maintains.

Special Revenue Funds

Special Revenue Funds are used to account for the proceeds of earmarked revenue or financing activities requiring separate accounting because of legal or regulatory provisions. In many cases, the use of the separate fund is mandatory. Typical special revenue activity might include accrued employee benefits and LSTA grants. This could potentially include endowment type situations, where the principle of the gift may be spent to support the Library's programmes.

Debt Service Funds

Debt Service Funds are used to account for the annual payment of principal, interest and expenses in connection with certain long-term debt. The proceeds from bond issues or other types of debt are typically recorded in the General or Capital Project Funds, depending on the stipulations of the debt instrument.

Debt service fund resources are typically received via special voted property tax levies or transfers from other funds. In many cases, the use of Debt Service Funds is optional.

Capital Projects Funds

Capital Projects Funds are used to account for the development of capital facilities, such as an addition to a building. Typically, this fund is established to account for the construction of fixed assets or to set aside money for future capital needs. In many cases, the use of Capital Projects Funds is optional.

Endowment Funds/Permanent Funds

Prior to GASB (Government Accouting Standards Board) Statement number 34, Endowment Funds were established to account for gifts and bequests that may be either expendable or nonexpendable, depending on legal restrictions that apply. While recording activity under a separate fund is common, it is not mandatory. In many instances, gifts and bequests may be accounted for under the General Fund. GASB Statement number 34 created a new fund type called Permanent Funds that are used to report resources that are legally restricted to the extent that only earnings, and not principal, may be used for purposes that support the reporting government's programmes. Permanent funds report trust arrangements in which the reporting government is the beneficiary, including public-purpose funds previously classified as nonexpendable trust funds.

Account Groups

Prior to the implementation of GASB Statement number 34, there are also two self-balancing account groups:

* *General Fixed Assets Account Group*: The General Fixed Assets Account Group is set up to account for long-lived assets. The assets are always acquired through a fund, usually the general fund or a capital project fund. The acquisition is accounted for as an expenditure and, therefore, no depreciation is applied against the asset. However, beyond the date of acquisition, the assets are accounted for in the general fixed assets account group. Essentially, the account group is a summary of all the long-lived assets. When recording assets in this account group, consideration should be given to materiality and useful life of the item. Only material items need to be accounted for as fixed assets. Libraries should establish a dollar threshold for items to be capitalized. The objective is to establish a limit high enough to avoid too much detailed record keeping yet low enough to record material fixed assets. In the event the items are sold or retired, the cost of the item should be deleted from the account group. Prior to GASB Statement number 34, books, periodicals, recordings and film were often recorded at one dollar per item. When GASB Statement 34 is implemented, assets including books, periodicals, recordings, etc should be reported at their historical cost, net of accumulated depreciation. Replacement value is often estimated based on trade publication average costs adjusted for discounts and processing costs applicable to a library's purchases. Periodically, a library should compare its insurance coverage to replacement value.

* *General Long-term Debt Account Group*: The General Long-term Debt Account Group is set up to account for the unmatured principal of bonds, warrants, notes and other forms of long-term indebtedness that is secured by the full faith and credit of the library. The proceeds from issuing general long-term debt are recorded as revenue, typically in a capital projects fund or the general fund as "other financing sources." The debt service fund typically records the expenditure of the debt payments. However, beyond the date of issue, the outstanding principal amounts are accounted for in the general long-term debt account group. Essentially, the account group is a summary of all long-term debt owed by the library. As debt is retired, the account group is reduced.

Effective with the implementation of GASB Statement 34, reporting of the account groups will no longer be required, however, fixed assets and long term liabilities will be reported on the Statement of Net Assets. It will be necessary for each governmental unit to maintain the records regarding the historical cost of assets, along with the related accumulated depreciation expense and the long term debt. Although there are several alternatives to maintaining this information, libraries should consider continuing to track the information in a manner equivalent to the current techniques used for the General Fixed Asset Account Group and the General Long-tem Debt Account Group, with the added emphasis on recognizing annual depreciation expense and accumulated depreciation.

COMPARISON OF GOVERNMENTAL FUNDS AND COMMERCIAL ACCOUNTING

Similarities

* Periodic balance sheets or statements of net assets, income statements and statements of changes in equity balances are prepared by both The double entry system of accounts is utilized by both.

* The historical cost principle, consistency principle and, for the most part, generally accepted accounting principles are used by both.
* Fund accounting and commercial accounting use the same accounting terminology. However, fund accounting has some terminology unique to it.

Differences

* A profit motive is absent from all the funds. Libraries are service and responsibility oriented.
* Most libraries use a "modified-accrual" basis of accounting, where commercial accounting uses accrual basis. Under the requirements of GASB Statement number 34, the day-to-day recordkeeping will continue to be done on a modified accrual basis. The new statement will, however, add a layer of financial reporting to the current modified accrual basis of reporting. The new layer will bring together the financial information of the Library as a complete entity using the full accrual basis of reporting in a manner similar to most commercial accounting.
* The fund accounting emphasis is on "budgetary accounting."
* In the fund level "modified-accrual basis" of accounting, capital expenditures are treated the same as operating expenses. Accordingly, governmental libraries typically do not compute depreciation expense at the fund level of financial reporting. This practice differs from commercial accounting where capital purchases are accounted for in asset accounts and charged to expense over time through the depreciation account.
* Some accounting systems record purchase orders on the books as encumbrances in the library funds. Generally accepted accounting principles do not record these as expenditures, however the accounting rules do allow encumbrances to be included in the comparison of actual results of

operations to budget. Although not a common practice, encumbrance accounting may provide a superior form of budget control during the year.

* A library may be a combination of several distinctly different financial operations, each having its own set of accounts or funds.
* Governmental accounting is concerned more with a comparison of actual results to budgeted amounts, rather than a maximization of net income or working capital, as in commercial accounting.

GOVERNMENTAL ACCOUNTING STANDARDS BOARD (GASB)

The GASB was established as an arm of the Financial Accounting Foundation in April 1984 to promulgate standards of financial accounting and reporting with respect to activities and transactions of state and local governmental entities. The GASB is the successor organization to the *National Council on Governmental Accounting* (NCGA). The GASB Concepts Statement 1 states: "Governmental financial" reporting should provide information to assist users in

* Assessing accountability and
* Making economic, social and political decisions."

In order to meet these overall objectives, GASB issued the following guidelines regarding financial reporting:

Accountability

Financial reporting should assist in fulfilling government's duty to be publicly accountable and should enable users to assess that accountability.

To accomplish this goal, financial reporting should meet the following criteria:

* Provide information to determine whether current year revenue was sufficient to pay for current year services.
* Demonstrate whether resources were obtained and used in accordance with the entity's legally adopted budget; it should also demonstrate compliance with

other finance related legal or contractual requirements.

* Provide information to assist users in assessing the service efforts, costs and accomplishments of the governmental entity.

Decision-Making

Financial reporting should assist users in evaluating the operating results of the governmental entity for the year.

To accomplish this objective, financial reporting should also meet these criteria:

* Provide information about sources and uses of financial resources.
* Provide information about how the governmental entity financed its activities and met its cash requirements.
* Provide information necessary to determine whether the entity's financial position improved or deteriorated as a result of the year's operations.

MISCELLANEOUS ITEMS

Library Types

There are a variety of library types and sizes. State laws governing how a library is established, levies taxes, issues and pays for debt, qualifies for state-funded revenue and performs other business functions vary depending on the type and size of a library. Refer to the Library Laws Handbook from the Library of Michigan, the State Laws Relating to Michigan Libraries, or consult legal counsel for detailed information concerning legal matters for the type and size of your library.

Users of Governmental Financial Statements

The public is vitally concerned with the cost of public services, the adequacy of revenue in meeting such costs and the stewardship and efficiency of both elected and appointed officials. Contributors and bankers are also interested in the financial status and operating results. With the development of extensive and complex intergovernmental fiscal relationships in the form of grants-in-aid, shared revenue and administrative supervision, governments must be provided with adequate financial data on the operations of other governmental jurisdictions with which these relations exist. In addition, educational and research organizations, statistical reporting agencies and such individuals as accountants, financial analysts and economists whose professional activities embrace the study and improvement of financial administration and, of course, public management whose responsibility it is to evaluate past performance in daily decision-making and in planning future operations are also users.

Grants

In recent years, many libraries have received grants and other revenue from various federal and state agencies. In connection with these, recipients agree to comply with various statutes and regulations that accompany the grants. The various statutes and regulations may vary among libraries, thus every library should follow its own agreement accordingly. Typically, most agreements are pass-through monies. These types of grants are usually reimbursement in nature and as expenditures are incurred, revenues are accrued. In addition, some statutes and regulations require that certified public accountants perform audits of libraries to test the compliance with these statutes and regulations in addition to performing financial audits.

Chart of Accounts

A chart of accounts is an organized listing of all accounts used by a library to record financial information in its general ledger. The chart of accounts is to the accounting function what the Dewey Decimal System is to a library. It provides a foundation for arranging financial data into useful information. To provide reliable and consistent financial information, it is imperative that the chart of accounts be simple and functional. Accordingly, a "Uniform Chart of Accounts" has been developed by the State of Michigan under Public Act 2 of 1968, as amended, for all Michigan units of government.

Record Retention

Under MCL 399.5 and 750.491, government agencies must keep official books, papers or records unless it has received approval by filing a MH-38, Certificate of Records Disposal, with the State Archives of Michigan. However, a library may adopt its own record retention and disposal plan.

Tax Exempt Status

The General Sales Tax Act and Michigan Sales and Use Tax Administrative Rule, generally provides that governmental and not-for-profit library purchases are not subject to sales and use tax. Michigan Department of Treasury Revenue Administrative Bulletin 1996-6 illustrates the recommended sales and use tax exemption claim formats. Typically, a library will provide its vendors with a blanket certificate of exemption at the time of purchase.

Selection of Accounting Software

There are a number of factors to consider when selecting accounting software. This is true for both large and small library organizations.

Key steps involved in selecting accounting software include the following:

* *Assess Existing Resources*: Determine current resources in terms of software, hardware and funding.
* *Assess User Requirements*: Survey individuals that will be using the software to determine needs/desires over the near-, medium- and long-term, volumes of transactions in the near- and long-term and expectations concerning the potential benefits to be gained from use of the software.
* *Identify Available Software*: Identify available software by surveying similar organizations, reading articles and software directories, attending trade shows or

contacting consultants. Make an initial determination of potential vendors.

* *Evaluate Vendors*: For entry or mid-level "off-the-shelf" software packages, evaluation of vendors may be accomplished by identifying the perceived strengths and weaknesses of the different packages based on research conducted before making a final determination. For other software packages, a more formal selection process may be undertaken. This could include developing detailed software specifications, soliciting bids from potential qualified bidders, evaluating bid responses and attending vendor demonstrations prior to making a final determination. Factors to evaluate include, but are not limited to the following: ease of use; vendor knowledge, stability and support; flexibility; expandability; security; ability to track needed information and ability to access needed information.
* *Implementation*: Once software has been selected and purchased, a strategy should be developed for how to implement the software. Establish dates for accomplishing specific tasks. Regularly review progress of implementation. A rule of- thumb is to run both the old and new systems for a month or two to ensure that a back up exists if problems occur with the new system. This is typically time-consuming and, therefore, should be taken into account when planning the implementation.

7

Emerging Initiatives in Library Management Systems (LMS)

INTRODUCTION

Library Management Systems (LMS) or computer based systems that automate one or all functional areas of a typical library have had a history of evolution going back to the mid 1950s. LMS have also been referred to as *Integrated Library Systems* (ILS) in later years to reflect the fact that all functions are managed via a central database with processes that transparently exchange data between functional components such as catalogue records and circulation transactions. This chapter examines current initiatives that will determine the future of LMS. To understand and appreciate these initiatives it is important to briefly look at the past and recount the influences that have played a role in the evolution and how new influences both within libraries and outside have made it necessary to rethink the design of LMS. The chapter discusses the drawbacks of current commercial and open source LMS and the need for new design principles that take advantage of new software and interoperability paradigms such as *services-*

oriented architecture (SOA) and web services that have arisen from the distributed nature of the web, changing user behaviours and the need to manage both core functions of a traditional LMS, new electronic resources plus the capability for interoperating with external applications, *e.g.*, course management systems, personnel directory systems, that are now becoming an integral part of institutions. Initiatives of the OLE Project, the eXtensible Catalog Project, the proposals of the *Digital Library Foundation* (DLF), the *National Information Standards Organization's* (NISO) proposals for best practices and OCLCs recent proposal to use cloud computing paradigms to move the traditional LMS to becoming a fully web-spaced one are discussed as pointers to the emerging future of LMS.

A SNAPSHOT OF THE EVOLUTION OF LMS

The evolution of LMS since the mid 1950s till the present day is seen to have taken place in five different phases.

This division is more for convenience and obviously there are overlaps in the phases:

* *First generation systems*
  - Stand-alone un-integrated applications beginning with circulation;
  - No standard metadata in use;
  - The emphasis was on library housekeeping efficiencies, little or no concern for user access;
  - Most applications were home grown;
  - Very little vendor interest in LMS; and
  - Mostly main-frame computer based and batch processed systems.
* *Middle generation systems*
  - Metadata standard for bibliographic records (MARC) became available;
  - Emphasis was on exchanging bibliographic data, centralized cataloguing and distribution of catalogue cards;
  - Systems were developed by vendors which leveraged the catalogue data in other modules
  - Circulation, acquisitions;

- First generation integrated LMS came into being;
- These were targeted to single libraries;
- Proprietary backend designs were common; and
- Mostly mini-computer based; character-based interfaces; some systems were still homegrown.
- Pre-Internet generation
- Networking via LANs and WANs became possible and libraries began to ask for networking of closely related libraries;
- Micro-computer-based systems with richer interfaces;
- Client-server LAN systems became the norm;
- Interactive applications became possible with GUIs;
- Vendor systems with networking capabilities became available;
- Marketplace soon made home grown systems unnecessary and not cost effective;
- Most integrated systems had similar functionality with small differences;
- First generation OPACs made their experience. The OPACs were heavily librarian-centric in design; and
- Federated searching became possible via the z39.50 Information Retrieval protocol; and
- Movement away from proprietary to RDBMSbased backend systems and SQL-based search systems.

* *Internet generation*
  - Initial move was to host the OPAC on a web server; other functional modules were still locally administered;
  - Rich GUI front ends using tools like Visual Basic, Visual C++ became available;
  - When reliable Internet connectivity became widely and cheaply available in the 1990s, new client server systems that used the web for data storage and transaction processing became available;

- Platforms like JAVA and .NET became the development options for web applications;
- Open source OS platforms like Linux made an entry. Few applications and quite geeky; and
- Backends were still predominantly RDBMSbased and search systems were SQL-based.

* *Post 2000 – the Web 2.0 Era*

- The Web became the platform of choice for software. Development philosophies changed from finished product to work-in-progress and frequent updates delivered over the web;
- The web has become from an information delivery only platform to a participative platform. Ordinary individuals contributed via blogs, wikis, podcasts and social networks. This has impacted the expectations that library users have from libraries and LMS;
- Web services via protocols and APIs resulting in information reuse, greater interoperability, RSS/ Atomfeeds, mashups enhanced user experience in discovery applications, *e.g.*, Amazon, Library Thing;
- Open source offerings make a serious entry into the marketplace;
- Dissatisfaction with the monolithic nature of the LMS and the OPACs is increasingly voiced;
- The consolidations and mergers in the commercial market place is evidence of upheavals in the industry;
- New kinds of enterprise applications have become available to institutions and there is demand for better integration of LMS with such systems.

The snapshot overview of the evolution can also be seen from the point of developments in technology, *e.g.* changes from using mainframe to mini-computers to microcomputers; from software for un-integrated systems to integrated systems; from single library systems to multi-library and networked systems; from using proprietary to relational database backends; and from LAN-based systems to web-based systems. Developments in both hardware and software technology and the use of new paradigms such as the relational model, object-oriented analysis and design, client-server architectures and languages particularly well-suited to the world wide web have had an influence on the evolution. A major technological influence has been the growth of the web and its distributed environment under different platforms, formats, languages and data models requiring that the LMS supports interoperability Equally important influencing factors that have challenged LMS with new demands from librarians as well as users have been.

CHANGES IN THE INFORMATION ENVIRONMENT

The emergence of new forms of information, *e.g.*, the web page, electronic forms of conventional information objects such as audio and video, fulltext, e-serials. The plethora of formats in which information objects could occur have also required that LMS should be able to deal with new information objects.

CHANGES IN USER BEHAVIOURS AND DEMANDS

This has probably been most challenging of all influences on the evolution of the discovery interface or OPAC built into LMS.

Some of the searching and use behaviours that have challenged LMS are:

* Users want greater freedom in managing their access to information.
* Users want access not only to just library-held information but to other material types and on the web in general.
* Users seek a simple search interface that is not only easy to use but also retrieves items ranked by relevance and points to related items, reviews, recommendations, and allows a degree of faceted searching
* Users want access to full-text and other digital content and expect the library to assist them in

obtaining the full text or other digital content via the LMS;

* The Google generation demand the freedom to tag items of their interest, access to information by their own tags or those of peers in a social network. They also value access to reviews, recommendations, and peer ratings of materials that may be useful to them.

Development of New Metadata Standards and Protocols

Although the MARC metadata standard has been a long-standing one for bibliographic records, its complexity and the need for a high level of training for its use to create metadata records is a shortcoming in its use by non-librarians, *e.g.*, authors, painters, musicians, social activists who are today also generators of information. These require to be described in institutional and webbased search systems including generic search engines. This has led to the development of simpler and more generic metadata schemas such as Dublin Core. Other information objects, *e.g.*, courseware and learning objects require metadata that is not covered well enough by bibliographic standards. It is important to recognize that today's users, particularly in the academic world, require access to other materials as well and they expect that the LMS should be able to inter-operate with such systems in meaningful ways. The open access movement and the development of the OAI-PMH has enabled the development of institutional archives of scholarly contributions. These are valued by researchers and faculty and there is demand for the interoperability of such resources with the LMS.

Emergence of Related Application Streams Leading to Pressures from Librarians, end-users as well as Institutions

Database producers, e-journal publishers, providers of data, audio and video feeds and content, subject portals, learning management systems, enterprise-wide information systems have their own workflows, search interfaces, applications and metadata standards. There is a growing demand from librarians, users and institutional heads that libraries should interoperate their systems with these related applications to permit access to a wider information base and to avoid unnecessary duplication of similar data across applications and avoidable errors in transactions that may take place between LMS and other applications, *e.g.*, between a LMS's acquisitions system and the Institution's Purchase Management System.

LIMITATIONS OF CURRENT CROP OF LMS IN TODAY'S CONTEXT

One of the advantages of current offerings of LMS is that it tightly integrated all functions within a common application as a means of increasing efficiencies. However, what was once considered to be a virtue, has many drawbacks in the changed times of today.

Some of the drawbacks are:

* The LMS is a complex, closed system, the software uses proprietary code and is expensive to license and difficult to customise even if the software is open source. The complexity of the code militates against customization by a third party. Even if this is theoretically possible, it is expensive in terms of development costs.
* The LMS imposes rigid workflows. These are suitable for conventional materials. The management of electronic resources requires different workflows, *e.g.* management of: digital rights, management of access rights to e-journals, implementing consortial borrowing, document delivery and access to full text via applications and protocols. Libraries are faced with two options: either to use the inefficient workflows to manage e-resources with their LMS or to implement a parallel system for the management of electronic resources. Parallel systems are obviously an additional burden in terms of costs and maintenance.
* New enterprise-wide information systems, personnel directory systems and purchase management systems are being implemented. Current LMS do not integrate with the new systems. Libraries create complicated processes for extracting data from the

enterprise systems, reprocess data inside the LMS, and then send data back to the enterprise systems, *e.g.* student or patron data; library acquisitions data.

* Lack of integration with widely used tools, *e.g.* database search systems, institutional repositories is a serious deficiency. Libraries cope with these problems by developing add-on components or by purchasing new LMS components and writing programmes to connect them to them to the LMS
* It is nearly impossible for a library to integrate its commercial ILS with tools outside the LMS, such as a course/learning management system or social-networking tools.
* Current OPAC offerings of LMS, most of which are librarian-centric do not provide the discovery experience that many users are accustomed to in collateral systems such as Amazon.com, eBay, Google, LibraryThing, social network applications.
* New OPAC offerings in the commercial space, *e.g.* Endeca, Primo, Aquabrowser, improve user experience, but purchasing and implementing a second OPAC is an extra expense and an extra support burden on top of costs and support for the LMS. New open source OPAC offerings such as Scriblio, VuFind have also become available, but use of these requires programming effort on the part of libraries and the need for the vendor of the LMS to expose ways in which third party applications can use the data embedded in their application.
* The work done and experience gained to add-on new workflows in existing LMS to cater to the management of newer resources is not easily transferable to other LMS products or to other libraries trying to solve the same problems.

NEW INITIATIVES IN THE REDESIGN OF LMS

The drawbacks of current LMS products have simmered in the discussions,, in the past few years now. Librarians and vendors; bodies such as the NISO, DLF and associations such as the ALA; and active web forums have discussed these in several live meetings, online forums and webinars. In the last two years there have been very proactive initiatives. Among these, the following initiatives have made significant progress and their findings will undoubtedly have a great impact on the future shape of LMS.

Significantly, all the initiatives, except the OCLC proposal are predicated on open source principles and on using open standards:

* The OLE Project under the leadership of the Duke University, USA
* The DLF Discovery Interface Task Force
* The NISO Best Practices for Designing Web Services in the Library Context
* The eXtensible Catalog project of the University of Rochester, USA
* The OCLC proposal for a web-scale, cooperative library management service

Of the above initiatives, the OLE Project has had the widest participation and must therefore be considered as representing a broad spectrum of views and concerns.

THE OLE PROJECT

The project is an initiative of the Duke University in the USA. The Project, begun in 2008 with funding from the Andrew Mellon Foundation and has involved a multinational group of libraries in the USA, Canada, Australia and UK with the objective of developing the design for an *Open Library Environment* (OLE), an alternative to the current model of an Integrated Library System. The goal is to produce a design document to inform open source library system development efforts, to guide future library system implementations, and to influence current Integrated Library System vendor products.

The aims of the Project are to:

* Adopt a transformational design approach to create a flexible, interoperable system that goes beyond replicating the concepts that underlie legacy LMS.

* Develop and use open, flexible technology to produce a community-sourced alternative to current LMS and *electronic resource management* (ERM) systems.
* Automate core library functions in a way suited to modern workflows and one that interoperates with business and content applications beyond the library.

OLE is a framework and platform that goes beyond the monolithic LMS through its ability to utilize other systems and deliver valuable new services. At the same time, OLE allows institutions to avoid redundancy of data, and reduce purchase and integration of add-on components to their current ILS in order to carry out library business. The OLE places the library's business in context within the fabric of the institution and the research process, rather than keeping it a separate, siloed operation. The Australian National Library, one of the partners in the OLE Project, articulated a service framework based on a *services oriented architecture* (SOA). In the SOA sense of the word, a service is a set of capabilities offered by a service provider through a service definition that makes the capabilities discoverable by a service consumer. The implementation of the service is "opaque" to the consumer, and the invocation of a service itself may seek out the SOA-defined capabilities of another service provider. Importantly, the services may be locally owned or those under the control of others,. The articulation of SOA requires service definitions and agreed protocols and schemas. Thus standards, in this case, web services-based, will be required to be defined. This is where bodies such as the DLF and NISO have made their presence felt.

The OLE framework has also suggested a predominantly SOA-based model and has the following characteristics:

* *Flexibility:* Supports a wide range of resources; accessed by a wide range of customers in a variety of contexts; provides structures for extending and adding new types of resources, customers and contexts.
* *Community Ownership:* Designed, built, owned, and governed by and for the library community on an

open source licensing basis; sustained by the community with the assistance of a thriving vendor marketplace; evolves over time through transparent processes that enable and respond to input and innovation from the community.

* *Service Orientation:* Developed using the methods of *Service Oriented Architecture* (SOA) and implemented with web services to be a modular and technology-neutral framework that ensures the interoperability of library business systems and accommodates a diversity of solutions without the risks posed by single-source providers. Further, it can be customised to support local needs.
* *Enterprise-Level Integration*: Designed to adapt to and integrate with other enterprise systems such as research support, student information, human resources, identity management, fiscal control, and repository and content management.
* *Efficiency:* Provides a modular application infrastructure that integrates with new and existing academic and research technologies and business processes for improved efficiency and effectiveness of the institution; meets current and future business needs of the community.
* *Sustainability:* Creates a reliable and robust framework to identify, document, innovate, develop, maintain, and review the software necessary to further the operation and mission of libraries.

The OLE Project draft final report provides an open source reference implementation of a set of technology services that that allow libraries to carry out their backend business operations, and therefore to replace their current ILS. However, OLE will also support functional capabilities that go beyond the existing ILS core. Each OLE component will be highly modular and use standards-based interfaces, allowing an institution to mix-and-match OLE components with other, existing campus and library systems if desired—including both open source and commercial systems.

This will allow institutions to install only selected portions of OLE, or to adopt a phased replacement strategy. The OLE will not build the front-end or resource-discovery functionality of today's ILS's, but will instead provide support for several open source front-end projects, as well as any commercial alternative that is willing to use OLE's standards based interfaces. OLE also expects its services to be delivered through non-library interfaces such as smart phones, learning management systems, campus portals, and other institutional products that involve resources and/or support from the library. The Abstract Reference Model for OLE shows the relationship between OLE middleware, OLE components, entities acted on by OLE, and third-party components, such as Identity Management, Institutional Repositories, and Course Management Systems.

The OLE Reference Model is an abstract representation of the OLE framework. As such, it describes the high-level *functional components* that will form OLE. Each of these components is made up of a number of workflows and/ or processes. A workflow is a series of activities that involve people, business processes, and software that achieve a library business goal. For example, the OLE component *Describe Entity* is comprised of the processes *Obtain Metadata, Create Metadata, Modify Metadata, Delete Metadata* and *Expose Metadata*. Additionally, the reference model shows examples of *third-party components* with which OLE will interoperate. These are reusable services, not developed or supplied by OLE, that fulfill an OLE business process.

The components that straddle the boundary between OLE and third-party components represent the functions that will be provided partly by OLE and partly by third-party components. The reference model also includes the *entities* that have so far been identified as belonging in the OLE framework. These are resources, collections, persons, organizations, and services. Finally, the bottom portion of the Reference Model illustrates the software that will manage and connect OLE components. It is this *middleware* that will provide interoperability with third-party applications. An important point to note here is that the OLE Project used the ideas of the Australian NLA and also aligned its framework with a higher level framework such as the framework for Education and Research or e-Framework.

Similarly the OLE project aligns itself also with one or more services defined by the DLF. In other words, OLE will use the results of parallel activities both within the public domain as well as those of commercial vendors which conform to the principles of web services SOA is an architecture philosophy or framework that breaks down business processes into several generic services. Business processes or workflows, a *service usage model* (SUM) and protocols and schemas are defined. The framework also assumes that there is a Workflow Engine and a Rules/Policy Engine.

The Workflow Engine manages the modeled business processes whereas the Rules Engine modifies the workflows based on local policies. In other words a library using the OLE framework can customise the Rules Engine to suit its policy, which then modifies the Workflow Engine suitably for its purpose. This way, there will be no need for a library to reinvent commonly used workflows via a service layer but at the same time have the possibility of modifying the workflow with an appropriate change in the Rules Engine. The fact that workflows are defined within generic services, allows that two or more tasks may use the same service layer to accomplish different tasks.

This will ensure reusability of software and re-purposing of software, two key advantages of SOA. For instance, the Deliver Entity component describes processes that track the request and supply of a resource. It includes processes that initiate and receive the request, identify the user requesting the resource, check and verify the user's credentials, and determine availability and terms of use of the resource requested. A message is sent to the user whenever a condition is not met. The resource is supplied if all conditions are met. Another important feature of the OLE Project is that a Build Project is proposed following the planning phase which was completed in July 2009.

The Build Project will be a Community Sourced Project. It means a project that will be funded by a consortium of institutions that will sign an agreement and contribute financial/human resources in the building and testing of the The OLE planners have recommended becoming a project within the Kuali Foundation.

The Kuali Foundation, which directly supports administrative community source software projects in the higher education sector, was designed as a lightweight administrative organization and can provide administrative functions for OLE at a fraction of the cost of building an entirely new entity. In addition, the SOA middleware that Kuali has developed will play an important role in the OLE Build Project. The Build phase of the project is expected to begin soon after the funding proposal is given to and approved by the Andrew Mellon Foundation.

The advantages of building the software as a community sourced project are that it will:

* Provide sustainability over the course of product development
* Promote innovation and shared knowledge
* Allow Interaction with the broader academic and research library community to ensure that the delivered software is matched to as wide a set of needs as possible.
* Provide the ongoing support needed once the software is ready for use.

Assuming that funding is approved by the donor and contributions by Build partners, the first full release to partners, consisting of the full infrastructure and basic set of services needed for ILS replacement, as well as for the enhanced functionality specified by the OLE design, and accompanied by workflow/ customization templates for research universities and liberal arts colleges is expected by Jan 2012.

The Build Project will leverage the results of other initiatives:

* Existing systems, *e.g.* shared database feeds, open ERM data from e-publishers.

* Existing Discovery Tools
  - WorldCat Local
  - LibraryFind
  - VuFind
  - extensible Catalog toolkits

The Project will also outsource the coding to organizations in Bulgaria and India.

When complete, OLE will allow libraries to:

* Discontinue their current ILS and several ancillary systems necessary today to manage scholarly content, and to continue their business functions through OLE or through the enterprise integration of OLE with Identity Management, Enterprise Resource Planning systems and Virtual Learning Environment systems.
* Provide interoperability with institution-wide applications. This will allow the library to leverage rather than duplicate enterprise functions.

The OLE will also be format-agnostic for collection and resource management thereby dissolving differences between physical and electronic resources. What makes OLE different from current monolithic LMS products is that libraries take on only the services and workflows they need through workflow managers and engines.

Libraries that don't need certain services can turn them off or adapt them to the workflows that better fit their needs. It is not as if only OLE is alone in choosing to go the SOA route. As already pointed out, the Education and Research Framework and the Kuali Foundation have already used SOA based software and paradigms in their projects. What makes the OLE approach different from the model used in current offerings of LMS products is that the latter emphasize internal functional integration while the former advocates the freeing of the LMS via use of external services and tools using commonly agreed business processes, protocols and data models so that a library can choose to use those services, processes, etc., that it requires rather than committing itself to a complex internally integrated product. Since the release of the final draft report, some vendors have criticized the approach spelt out by the OLE project for contradicting itself: first by stating that the OLE Project was to . . . "guide further library and to influence current Integrated Library System vendor products" and second by stating that . . . "a proposal to carry the project forward into the next phase of building the software".

The criticism is that the project has not spelt out the business model that will support development based on the demand, market share expected, the existing competition, risks that institutions would be willing to take in investing in the build project. In spite of the criticism, the support OLE has received, the meticulousness with which the OLE Project's planning phase has been conceived and implemented and the fact that over 300 libraries in four countries participated in the exercise is indicative of the importance that was attached to the project and the consensus on using a totally different approach to designing and implementing LMS functions and beyond. The impact of OLE is bound to change the face of LMS, whether via the OLE Build Project or via vendor's adopting the principles and ideas that are undoubtedly sound.

The DLF Discovery Interface Task Force Recommendations

The DLF in 2007 created a ILS Discovery Interface Task Group to:

* Analyse issues involved in integrating *integrated Library systems* (ILS's) and discovery applications, and
* Create a technical proposal for accomplishing such integration.

A set of revised recommendations was released in December 2008. The task force recommendations were preceded by a careful analysis of the premises that should drive the task force's work.

The premises include the following:

* OPAC interfaces currently provided by most LMS's cannot by themselves meet the demands of users in a world where the availability and sophistication of

digital resources and web applications has increased significantly.

* This does not reflect on badly designed interfaces; it reflects the fact that users now need a wider variety of capabilities than any one software package can be expected to provide.
* These trends imply that the ILS needs to become a platform that supports appropriate interfaces for discovery applications living on top of it instead of trying to do everything on its own.
* Some ILS vendors provide proprietary methods for accessing their underlying data stores, *e.g.* API tools accessible only for a special fee to trained users, or direct SQL queries against the ILS's database
* These methods do provide the hooks into the ILS but making library resources more widely usable requires a larger, standards-based API.
* To enable outward integration ILS's should adopt a more standardized method for providing API access to the data store
* There is need to move away from traditional library centric protocols like Z39.50 towards an XML based web services API model.
* Such a model will enable developers outside of the library community to more easily access the information stored within the ILS, creating opportunities for greater integration with non-library applications, *e.g.*, course management tools.

The task force recommendations comprise a set of Abstract functions and bindings that should be satisfied by APIs and/or protocols at different levels of interoperability. The work of the DLF task force is for the benefit of developers of open source and commercial LMS vendors and will no doubt be used by the OLE Project in its build project. The future of LMS discovery interfaces will be bound by the standards and protocols that have been articulated by the DLF and a national standards body such as the NISO.

THE NISO BEST PRACTICES FOR DESIGNING WEB SERVICES IN THE LIBRARY CONTEXT

In a parallel move but not confined to discovery interfaces, the NISO too has come up with broad principles which may guide the design of web services of the following categories:

Discovery Services

Web services to discover metadata, full text or a service; web service to create and maintain a directory.

Locate Services

Web services to communicate requests and circulation transactions between peer circulation systems, *e.g.*, between members of a consortium of libraries.

Requesting Services; Delivery Services; Common Services

Like the DLF-DI task force recommendations, NISO guidelines are targeted to developers of LMS products. The OLE build project, no doubt, will take notice of the NISO guidelines and to that extent there is a common thread that will bind these apparently independent initiatives in the years to come. Both the DLF and NISO speak of 'Services', clearly indicating that the future of library applications will be firmly founded on the principles of SOA.

THE EXTENSIBLE CATALAOG (XC) PROJECT OF THE UNIVERSITY OF ROCHESTER

The XC Project is to design/develop a set of open source applications that will:

* Provide libraries with an alternative way to reveal their collections to library users.
* Provide easy access to all resources across a variety of databases, metadata schemas and standards
* Enable library content to be revealed through other services that libraries may already be using, such as content management systems and learning management systems.
* Make library collections more web-accessible by revealing them through web search engines.

As can be seen the objectives of the XC as indeed the OLE initiatives spoken of earlier are similar. However, the XC's uniqueness lies in the fact that it has developed and released various Tool Kits as open source implementations.

The following tool kits have been released:

* OAI. This will allow integration of XC with an existing ILS and digital repositories.
* NCIP. This tool kit will allow RFID functionality to be enabled within An existing LMS
* Learning Management.

The following tool kits are under development:

* *Metadata services* - four types of metadata will be available to XC: bibliographic, holding, item and authority data. The tool kit will also have live access to circulation status, authentication mechanisms, and native ILS circulation request functionality.
* *Drupal Tool Kit* - XC will offer a number of user interfaces including one that is embedded into the Drupal CMS
* A tool kit that will be embedded into the Blackboard Learning Management System

Toolkits will incorporate unanimously agreed-upon standards for searching through library resources including faceted browsing interface and compliance with the *Functional Requirements for Bibliographic Records* (FRBR) which lays stress on the usefulness of bibliographic displays rather than just the matching of search terms with catalogue records.

The fact that XC is open source will provide possibilities for customization, although this may be a theoretical advantage since the cost of such customization is not known. The XC Project and its tool kits are already recognized by the OLE Project as resources that can be leveraged in its Build Project plan. To this extent the work will contribute to the future of LMS and open source initiatives in this area.

Web-Scale Service Proposal of OCLC

In an announcement made by OCLC in 2009, they have proposed to offer "the first Web-scale, cooperative library management service." This will ultimately, it is hoped, bring into WorldCat Local the full complement of functions traditionally performed by a locally installed *integrated library system* (ILS) via the web.

In this, the OCLC will be using the WorldCat database, undoubtedly the world's largest bibliographic database of over a billion records plus OCLC's "cloud", or bank of servers and communications infrastructure. OCLC's vision involves shifting increasing portions of activity managed library-by-library through locally or consortially implemented automation to the network level, under its global WorldCat infrastructure. OCLC plans to work with the more than 1,000 libraries and partners that are currently using OCLC library management systems in Europe and Asia Pacific to help build the new service.

Like in the full version of WorldCat, WorldCat Local users search against the massive WorldCat.org database, with their local library's holdings presented first in result lists. The proposal envisages the use OCLCs' enriched WorldCat Local with article-level content including the material from its Article First service plus a vast body of articles from EBSCO to those who subscribe to First Search and EBSCO host. Other providers may be added in course of time. WorldCat's meta search enhancement will allow search also of a library's licensed content. The WorldCat Navigator will enable consortial borrowing.

OCLC plans to move circulation and acquisitions functions in time:

* Circulation is planned to be implemented via a web-based client
* Acquisitions through WorldCat Local will include functionality of the ILS print acquisitions module and an *electronic resource management* (ERM) system.

These moves could bring the local ILS in use at the libraries which may use this web-scale service, redundant. Since the users of OCLC are among the biggest libraries in the world, their influence on the rest is bound to be significant.

However, there are also concerns about the OCLC proposal:

* A library using the OCLC cloud services route, will

be exposing themselves to the risk of giving away to OCLC control of how all their data is used and shared

* The planned OCLC system would probably appeal mainly to smaller- to medium- sized institutions. Large libraries may not like to compromise on functionality and customization to be "web scale," as OCLC is describes it.
* Developing country libraries, many of whom are not members of OCLC will not find the option appealing
* The plan is presently confined as being applicable to a few ILS vendor systems

CONCLUSIONS

The LMS industry is going through a profound transition thanks to the initiatives presented here. The end of an era and the beginning of a new one in the evolution of LMS is seen - from that of a library-specific one to that of an enterprise-wide one. Vendors are evaluating how to respond. They will not become redundant if they adapt. Commercial and open source offerings incorporating the ideas and work of the initiatives among others will, no doubt, become available. Open source initiatives, particularly the Community-Sourced ones, are likely to significantly expand the options for libraries, worldwide. Services to libraries will probably be the next big opportunity rather than products.

8

Library Management System Using Association Rule Mining

INTRODUCTION

Data Mining, also popularly known as *Knowledge Discovery in Databases* (KDD), refers to the nontrivial extraction of implicit, previously unknown and potentially useful information from data in databases. While data mining and are frequently treated as synonyms, data mining is actually part of the knowledge discovery process.

Data Mining software is one of a number of analytical tools for analysing data. It allows users to analyse data from many different dimensions or angles, categorize it, and summarize the relationships identified. Technically, Data Mining is the process of finding correlations or patterns among dozens of fields in large relational databases.

The data mining is actually a step in a larger KDD process. The KDD process employs data mining methods or algorithms to extract or identify knowledge according to some criteria or measure of interestingness, but it also includes steps that prepare the data, such as preprocessing, sub-sampling, and transformations of the database.

Figure 7.1 shows data mining as a step in an iterative knowledge discovery process.

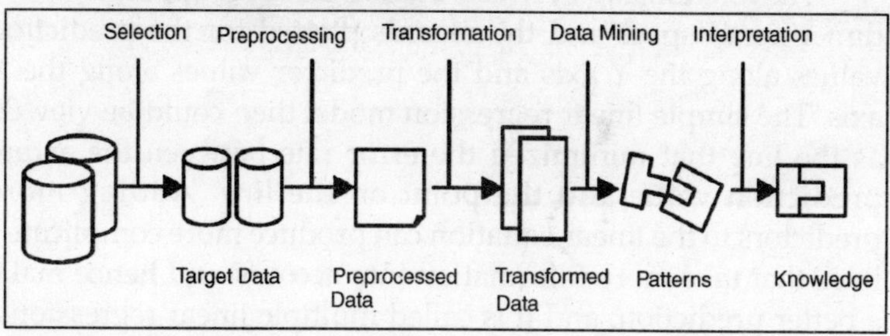

Fig 8.1. Data Mining is the Core of Knowledge Discovery Process

The first step in the KDD process is to select data to be analysed from the set of all available data. In many cases, the data is stored in transaction databases. These databases are quite large and extremely dynamic. Therefore a subset of the data must be selected from those databases, since it is unnecessary in the early stages to attempt to analyse all data. The KDD is an iterative process. Once the discovered knowledge is presented to the user, the evaluation measures can be enhanced, the mining can be further refined, new data can be selected or further transformed, or new data sources can be integrated, in order to get different, more appropriate results.

EXISTING WORK

STATISTICAL TECHNIQUE

Statistical techniques were being used long before the term data mining was coined. However, statistical techniques are driven by the data and are used to discover patterns and build predictive models.

Today people have to deal with up to terabytes of data and have to make sense of it and glean the important patterns from it. In statistics, prediction is usually synonymous with regression of some form. There are a variety of different types of regression in statistics but the basic idea is that a model is created that maps values from predictors in such a way that the lowest error occurs in making a prediction. The simplest form of regression is Simple Linear Regression that just contains one predictor and a prediction.

The relationship between the two can be mapped on a two dimensional space and the records plotted for the prediction values along the Y axis and the predictor values along the X axis. The simple linear regression model then could be viewed as the line that minimized the error rate between the actual prediction value and the point on the line. Adding more predictors to the linear equation can produce more complicated lines that take more information into account and hence make a better prediction, and it is called multiple linear regressions.

The Disadvantages of Statistical Technique

Certainly statistics can do more than answer questions about the data but for most people today these are the questions that statistics cannot help answer. Consider that a large part of data the statistics is concerned with summarizing data, and more often than not, the problem that the summarization has to do with counting. Statistical Techniques cannot be useful without certain assumptions about data.

CLUSTERING TECHNIQUE

Clustering is concerned with grouping together objects that are similar to each other and dissimilar to the objects belonging to other clusters. Clustering techniques is used by the end user to tag the customers in their database. Once this is done the business user can get a quick high level view of what is happening within the cluster. Clustering can be used for discovery or prediction. There are two main types of clustering techniques, those that create a hierarchy of clusters and those that do not. Those techniques are: *Hierarchical Clustering Techniques and Partitional Clustering Techniques.*

The Disadvantages of Clustering Technique

The interpretation of how interesting a clustering is will inevitably be application-dependent and subjective to some degree. Clustering techniques suffer from the fact that once a merge or a split is committed, it cannot be undone or refined. Sometimes clustering is performed not so much to keep records together as to make it easier to see when one record sticks out from the rest.

PROPOSED WORK

ASSOCIATION RULE

An association rule tells us about the association between two or more items. For example, If we are given a set of items where items can be referred as books and a large collection of transactions which are subsets of these items/books. The task is to find relationship between the presence of various items within these baskets.

In order for the rules to be useful there are two pieces of information that must be supplied as well as the actual rule: *Support* is how often does the rule apply? and *Confidence* is How often is the rule is correct. In fact association rule mining is a two-step process: Find all frequent itemsets/ booksets - by definition, each of these itemsets will occur at least as frequently as a predetermined minimum support count, and then generate strong association rules from the frequent itemsets – by definition, these rules must satisfy minimum support and minimum confidence.

Advantages of Association Rule Technique

Association rule algorithms can be formulated to look for sequential patterns. The methods of data acquisition and integration, and integrity checks are the most relevant to association rules.

MODULES

The following modules in this project are:

* Administrator
* Librarian
* User

Administrator

Administrator has the full authority to modify the library database like creating an account for a new user, deleting the account, adding a new book and deleting the book. Administrator monitors the library database updations (Figure. 8.2).

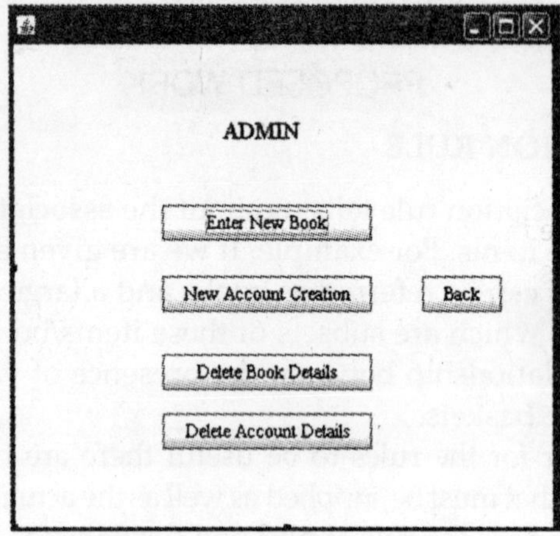

Fig. 8.2

Enter New Book Details

The book id is a automatically generated whenever a new book is entered in the library. The various entries should be entered such as the book name, ISBN, author name, cost, and date (Fig. 8.3).

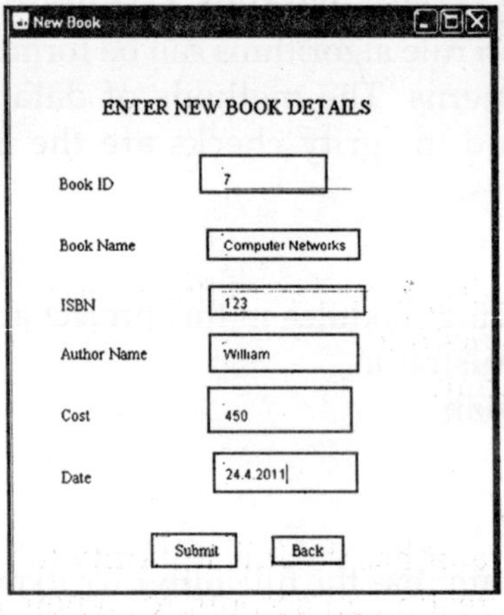

New Book

ENTER NEW BOOK DETAILS

Book ID 7

Book Name Computer Networks

ISBN 123

Author Name William

Cost 450

Date 24.4.2011

Submit Back

Fig. 8.3

New Account Creation

The user is classified into two types (Fig. 8.4 and 8.5)

New Account
NEW ACCOUNT CREATION
ID
U6
Name
Sheeba
Address
Annanagar
E-Mail
sheeba@ygmail.com
Phone Number
984201723
Status
User
Save
Back

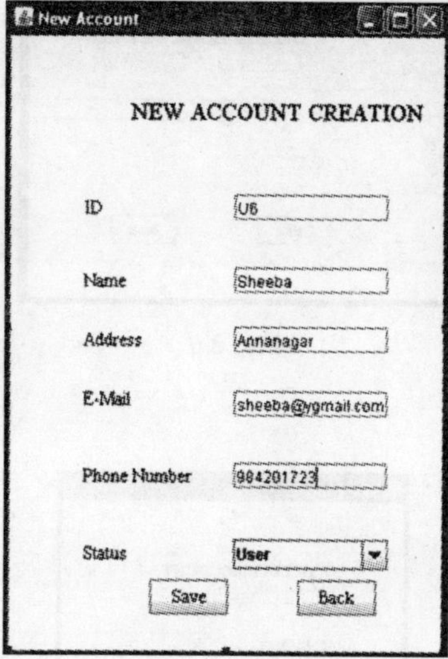

Fig 8.4. Other user

New Account
NEW ACCOUNT CREATION
ID
S6
Name
Hannah
Address
Adyar
E-Mail
hannah@yahoo.com
Phone Number
9597230493
Status
Staff
Save
Back

Fig 8.5. Staff user

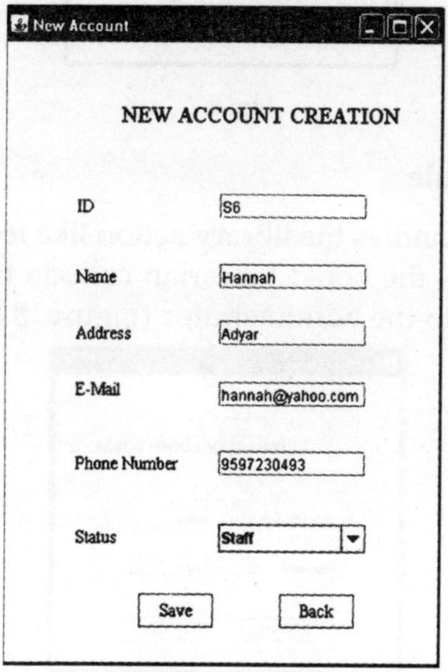

Delete Book Details

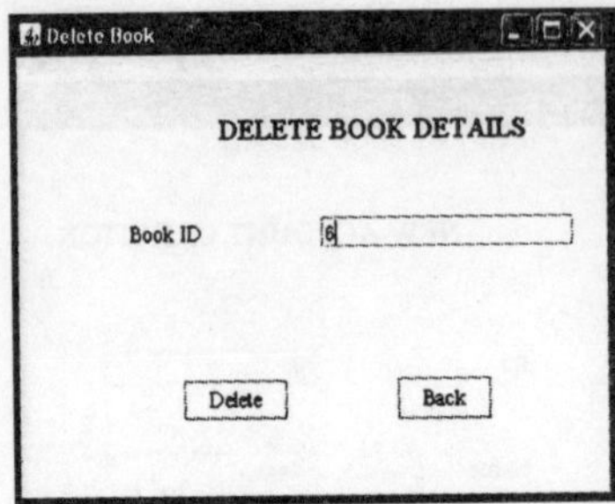

Fig. 8.6

Delete Account

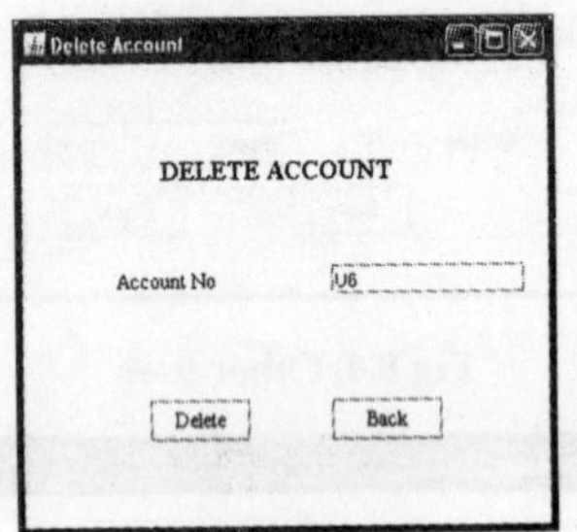

Fig. 8.7

Librarian Module

Librarian handles the library action like to issue the book and return back the book. Librarian collects the daily report and submits it to the administrator (Figure. 8.8).

Fig. 8.8

Issue & Return
LIBRARIAN
Book Issue
Book Return

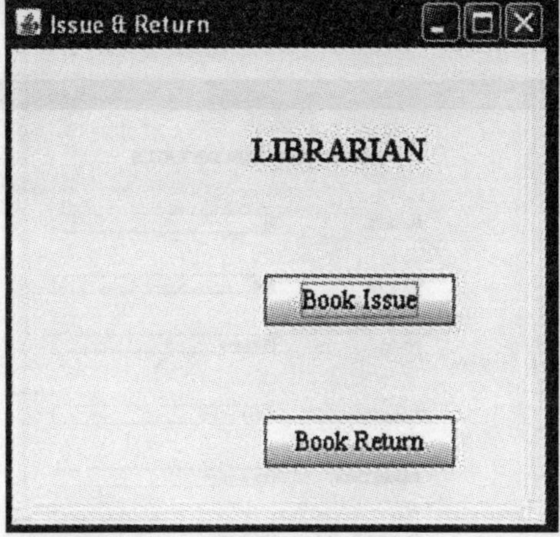

Fig. 8.9

Book Issue Details

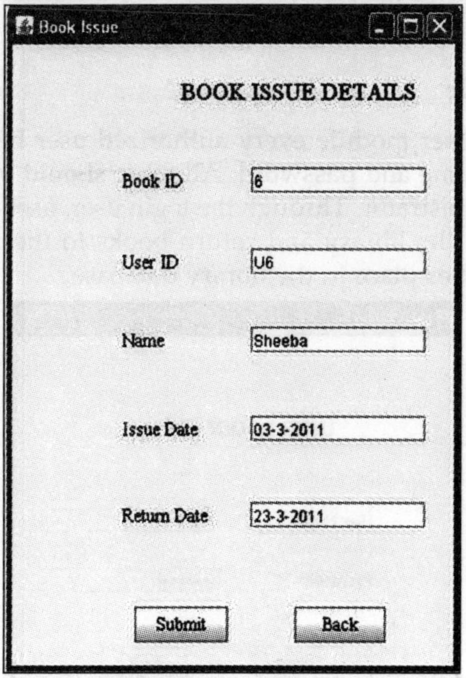

Book Issue
BOOK ISSUE DETAILS
Book ID
6
User ID
U6
Name
Sheeba
Issue Date
03-3-2011
Return Date
23-3-2011
Submit
Back

Fig. 8.10

Book Return Details

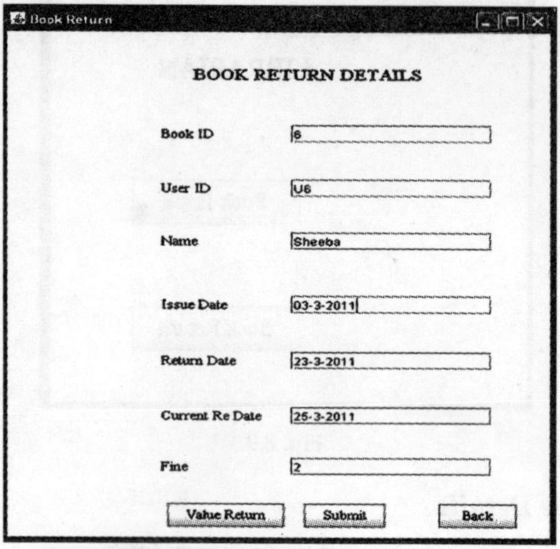

Fig. 8.11

User Module

In the user module every authorized user has a unique login username and password. All these should be provided by the administrator. Through the login user, user can receive books from the library and return books to the library. All updation takes place in the library database.

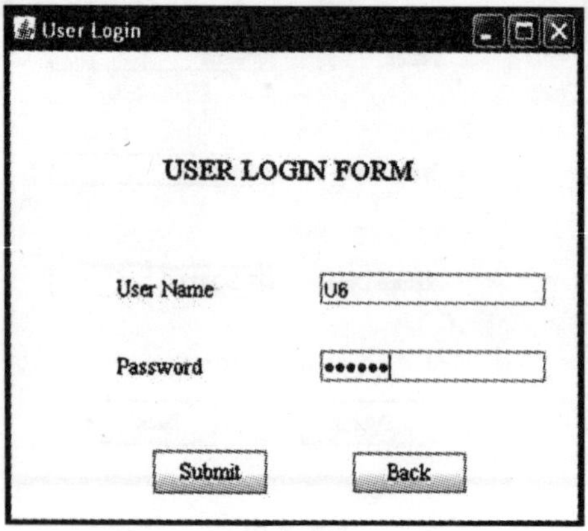

Fig. 8.12

Staff Module

All the staff have a unique login username and password. Staff have some additional feature compare to other user likewise they can take two more books and time extension compare to other user.

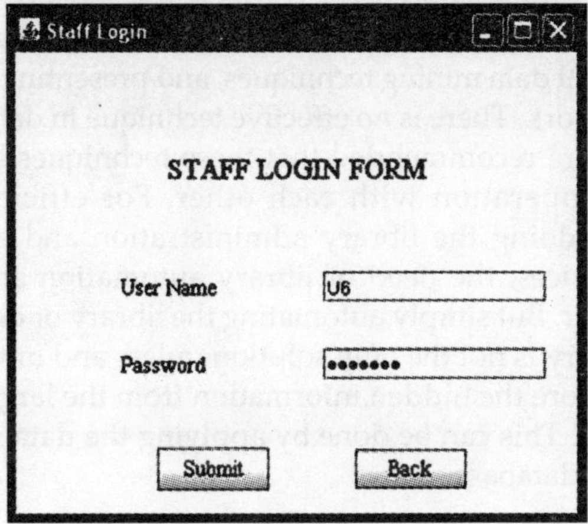

Fig. 8.13

RESULT

Association rules can be implemented in a two-step process: find all frequent item sets: by definition, each of these item sets will represent the transaction, and then generate strong association rules from the frequent item sets: by definition, these rules must satisfy minimum support and minimum confidence.

Table 8.1. Association Rule Mining

Rule	Support	Confidence
In a semester if a book "Mobile Computing" was issued to a member then a book ".Net" also issued to the same member.	5%	75%
In a semester if Issue- Count of a book is between 20 to 30	2%	90%

CONCLUSION

This chapter describes the processes of selected techniques using association rule mining. It has been realised that all association mining techniques accomplish its goals perfectly, but this technique has its own characteristics and specifications that demonstrate its accuracy, proficiency and preference. It claims that new research solutions are needed for the problem of categorical data mining techniques, and presenting our ideas for future work. There is no effective technique in data mining. It is therefore recommended that these techniques should be used in cooperation with each other. For efficiently and effectively doing the library administration and extending library services, the need of library automation and digital library occur. But simply automating the library or developing digital library is not the only solution unless and until it is not able to explore the hidden information from the large amount of database. This can be done by applying the data mining in the library database.

9

Managing Library Technology: Planning for the Future

INTRODUCTION

Whether public, private, or corporate, libraries are experiencing rapid changes as technology increasingly permeates their methodology and functionality. These technological changes affect all levels of librarianship, and management of new library resources and new expectations of staff must adapt accordingly.

As suggested, discuss management of resources and staff in today's fluctuating technological environment. In the first part, as suggested, use a systems development model to organize the discussion of resource management. In the second part, as suggested, turn our attention to issues that arise in the intersection between staff and technology by focusing on barriers to learning, online learning alternatives, and changes in staff development practices.

MANAGING RESOURCES

Librarians may be called upon to manage public and staff hardware, software, networks, digital products such as commercially owned databases and other online services, and output such as websites and social networking. In short, managing library technology may initially feel like herding cats.

Fortunately, several frameworks exist for organizing technology management. The work system life cycle, suggested by S. Alter is an example of such a framework. However, it should be noted that there are many other methodologies used by systems analysts, developers, and project managers that are equally adaptable to library technology purposes.

Alter's model is cyclical – it begins with initiation, followed by development, implementation, and operation and maintenance. During the operation and maintenance phase, if a given resource no longer adequately meets the needs of the institution, the cycle moves back into initiation, and the process begins again.

PHASE I: INITIATION - MAKING A PLAN

Alter describes initiation as an evaluation of goals, scope, and resources. For libraries, initiation begins with the drafting of a technology plan. Rachel Gordon writes, "since technology is now so tightly interwoven with all library functions, planning for the future of technology means planning for the future of the library itself". A good technology plan includes the following: a vision statement, background, goals and objectives, funding, training, and evaluation. Technology advances rapidly, and the key to crafting a good technology plan lies in forming objectives and goals that will not only withstand the onslaught of new products and services, but will also allow librarians to make decisions based on the library's needs rather than the perceived popularity of new services.

At this stage, in addition to clearly defined institutional goals, it is necessary to evaluate existing resources, both technological and financial. Evans, Ward, and Rugaas observed that the life span of technology is growing increasingly short, while library budgets are not accommodating the necessary expenditures needed to keep pace. They suggest a rolling budget to accommodate necessary upgrades, migration, support and training. M. Breeding mentions trends towards open source software and shared resources within library consortia as possible means of working with limited budgets.

PHASE II: DEVELOPMENT - FINDING/CREATING THE RIGHT RESOURCES

In Alter's model, development encompasses purchasing, licensing, and design of systems, as well as the research necessary to carry out each process. Librarians must make wise purchasing decisions regarding hardware, and must take into consideration the hidden costs lurking in maintenance, support, and staff training. Furthermore, most software and many digital services are provided not through purchasing, but instead through licensing.

A license to use a product must be understood and negotiated by the librarian in order to ensure that the product fulfills the library's goals. In addition to cost, librarians must pay careful attention to patron privacy considerations when negotiating contracts with vendors. Librarians designing web sites or social services, such as Facebook profiles and Twitter feeds, must follow a similar evaluation process, as they must design these services for patron usability. Particularly with library website design, standards compliance, privacy, and security must also be considered.

PHASE III: IMPLEMENTATION - PUTTING TECHNOLOGY TO WORK

During the implementation stage, librarians work to ensure that all goes smoothly through adequate testing and consistent deployment, whether they are rolling out a new website, a new ILS, new software, or new hardware. Librarians will need to be prepared for the headaches caused by data migration, resistance from both staff and users to new interfaces, and lengthy time commitments. The importance of adequate testing and familiarization with a new technology cannot be stressed enough.

PHASE IV: OPERATION AND MAINTENANCE - KEEPING OUR HEADS ABOVE THE WATER

Operation and maintenance is a critical stage of technology management; if this area is neglected, previous planning, research, and testing is worthless. Critical issues in this phase include security, upkeep, support, and evaluation.

Culp writes, "eternal vigilance is the price of security". Virus scans, testing, and continuing attention to developments in the nefarious world of security attacks is necessary to maintain a safe technological environment for both patrons and staff. This extends to public and staff machines, as well as stored patron and staff records. In addition to security, routine maintenance can greatly extend technology's lifespan. Basic tasks such as cleaning keyboards, defragmenting hard drives, changing printer cartridges, and downloading software updates should be performed by library staff, if at all possible.

When maintenance issues go beyond the reach of a librarian, the institution must have a tech support plan in place. Libraries rely on a variety of tech support systems. Bertot identifies seven broad categories of tech support: no tech support, internal library support without technology staff, internal library support with technology staff, library consortia, technology partners, city county or other agency IT support, and state library support. Regardless of a library's tech support plan, it is vital that all staff understand the procedures for troubleshooting and reporting problems.

Of course, during the operation and maintenance phase, it is important to constantly evaluate each piece of library technology in terms of its adherence to the library's goals. If it should fail that evaluation, then the librarian must move into the initiation phase and start again by planning upgrades or even entirely new systems.

MANAGING STAFF DEVELOPMENT

There can be no doubt that the need for professional development, continuing education, or workplace learning in regard to technology is vital for today's libraries. Never before have the profession's tools undergone such extreme and rapid transformations, and these transformations are not about to cease, as illustrated in the various thesis compiled in Core *Technology Competencies for Librarians and Library Staff*. It is, therefore, incumbent upon library administration to develop, implement, encourage, and support policies on staff competency and development.

It is, also, necessary for both professional librarians and paraprofessionals to—at the very least— be proficient in the current trends of technology, if not embracing the changes by keeping pace with them. In short, with a little innovative leadership, learning options are endless, as well as accessible, user-friendly, and exciting.

BARRIERS TO LEARNING

The "graying" of today's library is perhaps the most cited obstacle for staff development in technology. Long and Applegate, for instance, provide statistical data that reveals the willingness to learn of library staff according to their generation. Many professional librarians who received their degrees prior to 1995, or before the study of computers in Library Science programmes in the United States, understand the importance of keeping up with technology, yet a surprisingly large percentage of support staff is unwilling to adapt to the technical changes or to explore the possibilities that new technology brings.

Time constraints are another barrier to staff development. Workers who are given the time to develop skills are more apt to do so. However, many employees say there is little time to complete their usual tasks, much less learn new skills, regardless of whether employers allow the time for it. One thing is clear and that is that management needs to understand their employee's learning needs, as a number of investigations note the lack of managerial support in staff development. In fact, even professionals must often be self-motivated and seek out learning opportunities on their own.

E-LEARNING, WEBINARS, AND LEARNING 2.0

E-Learning, or learning delivered through electronic tools, is clearly the most popular form of staff development today.

Both professionals and paraprofessionals may choose from a myriad of sources for such learning. Among the many options are webinars from WebJunction, OCLC, EbscoHost, and Gale Cengage Learning, to name a few. However, Learning 2.0 has not only gained considerable attention, but it has also been implemented, studied, and documented, thereby, raising its stature and effectiveness.

Developed by Helen Blowers and based on Web 2.0 technology, Learning 2.0 is an incentive-based model programme for training library staff in new technologies. Students, who are self-directed, are asked to complete "23 Things," or online interactive projects on, for example, RSS feeds, flickr, wikis, podcasts, and LibraryThing. Kingsley and Jensen's paper on Learning 2.0's implementation at the University of Alaska Fairbanks Rasmuson Library stands as the most comprehensive study to date of the freely shared model, illustrating the programmes success rate and offering some concluding recommendations, such as making staff development mandatory.

ADMINISTRATION AND STAFF DEVELOPMENT

Not only are the tools with which library staff work changing, but so, too, are the philosophies and practices of management, especially in regard to staff competency and development. Mosley and Kaspar describe the challenges of hiring and retaining competent employees that can meet the ever-changing demands of library service. They suggest that management needs to look to the future by reconsidering job descriptions and job postings by avoiding the use of traditional library wording.

Management also must consider incentives when encouraging staff development. Incentives, such as the MP3s, PDAs, and laptops offered by Blower's pilot Learning 2.0 programme at the Public Library of Charlotte and Mecklenburg County, are not always possible, especially in the current economy. However, there are other methods of motivation. For instance, the University of Arizona Library restructured their monetary compensation, or wage, plans, which were based upon a traditional hierarchical scale. Their innovative and team-based "pay-for-skill" programme rewards employees for developing advanced capabilities, along with the willingness to learn and take on more responsibility.

CONCLUSION

Managing library technology is, indeed, an overwhelming aspect of contemporary librarianship because of its perpetually changing nature. Using cyclical management methods, like Alter's model, for library technology is essential because change is inherent in its foundation. Likewise, staff development must be an on-going practice that is not only encouraged by management, but included in library staffing policies. Our approach to technology is a mind-set: if we assume that change is inevitable, then planning for the future may be viewed as an exciting process, even for those who were not "born digital".

10

Competency Index for the Library Field

LIBRARY MANAGEMENT COMPETENCIES

A successful library involves leadership and careful management. The management perspective starts at the big picture level, establishing goals and objectives, planning for implementation, determining value and promoting community and stakeholder relationships.

There is so much overlap among the tasks related to managing a library that it is difficult to separate them into mutually exclusive buckets. If something seems to be missing in one of these competency parts, it's likely that it is covered in another part.

BUDGET AND FUNDING

While libraries face stagnant or reduced budgets, the demand for library services increases. The ability to prioritize assumes high importance and must be based on solid numbers and processes. Due to the wide variety of funding structures for libraries, these competencies are more general than specific. The Budget competencies are interrelated with most other competency areas.

Competency: Budget and Funding	**Understands and employs basic budget and finance concepts and terminology**
Associated Skills and Knowledge	* Understands and utilizes established accounting practices and procedures * Develops and evaluates the library budget in alignment with short and long range goals and objectives * Understands and applies federal, state and local financial laws and regulations * Works with the library board to develop members' understanding of the library finances, including the budget process
Competency: Budget and Funding	**Establishes effective financial management processes and services, using sound business and financial judgment**
Associated Skills and Knowledge	* Monitors economic trends and other fiscal issues for potential impact on the library * Conducts short-, medium- and long-range fiscal planning * Conducts financial analysis to identify costs, risks and alternatives, including cost-reduction and value enhancements * Monitors the progress of contracts for library materials and services * Promotes and justifies the library's needs to funding authorities * Assesses needs and develops plans for capital improvement projects
Competency: Budget and Funding	**Identifies and pursues multiple funding sources for the library**
Associated Skills and Knowledge	* Identifies sources for grant funding and writes effective grant applications * Conducts capital campaigns * Develops strategies for additional funding sources * Works with Library Foundation and

(*Contd...*)

	Friends of the Library groups to generate private-sector support and to cultivate and solicit private donors

COMMUNITY RELATIONS

Fundamentally, the library directors and leaders have to believe in the value of the library and its services in order to demonstrate its value to the community and form strategic relationships to promote the vitality of the library.

Competency: Community Relations	**Demonstrates the impact and value of the library to the community through zongoing evaluation and assessment of library services**
Associated Skills and Knowledge	* Employs evidence-based management and to demonstrate the value of the library * Uses appropriate business and management approaches to communi-cate the library's value to decision makers * Understands data collection, research and analysis methods * Identifies sources and tools for gathering the best available data, including systems to manage library data and generate reports * Performs outcome-based evaluations to measure the effect of the programmes and service on various user groups * Observes benchmarks and consults with comparable organizations
Competency: Community Relations	**Builds support for the library, using the most appropriate methods among a variety of groups**
Associated Skills and Knowledge	* Communicates the value of library services, products and policies to library management, library staff, key stakeholders, user groups and the community

(*Contd...*)

	* Leverages community to build support at the local, state and national levels, both for ongoing library services and special one-time campaigns * Leverages participation in organizations to promote library initiatives * Identifies and enlists strategic partners to obtain support for the library * Demonstrates strong communication skills to deliver a clear and coherent message * Promotes the library as a center of lifelong learning for the community
Competency: Community Relations	**Maintains positive public relations through communication and promotion of the library's values, services, accomplishments and needs to all stakeholders**
Associated Skills and Knowledge	* Understands the relationship of the library to others within the governmental organization * Sets policies and practices for clear communication of the library's message to staff, library users, the community, the library board, local and state government, and to funding agencies * Maintains visibility in the community by joining and networking with organizations that promote libraries and librarianship * Provides information about library services and products in multiple mediums, including print and electronic in accordance with the marketing plan * Enhances the library's message by speaking publicly at library programmes and throughout the community * Develops relationships with media

(*Contd...*)

	representatives, community leaders and decision makers
Competency: Community Relations	**Forms strategic partnerships with community organizations**
Associated Skills and Knowledge	* Identifies potential partners and opportunities and articulates the mutual advantages of partnership * Develops and leverages collaborative relationships to facilitate the accomplishment of the library's goals * Provides leadership to build effective relationships and coordinate efforts between internal and external stakeholders * Sustains partner relationships for future opportunities

FACILITIES

The significance of the library as "place" underscores the importance of atmosphere, usability and safety in the physical environment for your community.

Competency: Facilities	**Creates a welcoming and user-friendly physical environment that encourages all community members to use library services**
Associated Skills and Knowledge	* Understands space planning issues, including the application of ADA requirements to the physical space and equipment * Plans for new or updated facilities to meet current and future community needs * Understands the impact of the physical elements in the library on user satisfaction and emotional response

(*Contd...*)

	* Monitors the use of facilities and makes changes to improve the user's experience
Competency: Facilities	**Creates and maintains a healthy and safe environment for library personnel and users**
Associated Skills and Knowledge	* Understands the scope of building operations and addresses maintenance issues with appropriate inspections and upkeep * Addresses safety issues through appropriate maintenance and adequate information provided to staff

LAWS, POLICIES AND PROCEDURES

Well-written policies and procedures, based on sound legal footings, help all levels of staff to be consistent in their relationships with users, colleagues and other stakeholders.

Competency: Laws, Policies and Procedures	**Understands, applies and explains applicable laws**
Associated Skills and Knowledge	* Understands and applies state and federal laws that pertain directly to libraries and to public entities in general * Maintains awareness of current policy and legislative initiatives that may impact library services and administration * Understands and applies intellectual freedom and civil rights laws * Understands and applies copyright and intellectual property laws * Understands and applies laws and policies governing confidentiality and rights to privacy * Understands and implements the *American Disabilities Act* (ADA) and state and local regulations where appropriate

(*Contd...*)

Competency: Laws, Policies and Procedures	**Develops policies and procedures based on the library's mission and user needs to guide efficient and effective library operations**
Associated Skills	* Develops and updates policies in and Knowledge collaboration with other departments, institutions, regional systems and larger organizations, such as State Libraries * Understands liability and legal issues pertaining to policy and procedure development * Explains the rationale underlying library laws, policies and procedures and seeks staff and user feedback during policies and procedures development * Understands the relationship between library policies and customer service * Continuously evaluates the needs for new or revised policies and procedures
Competency: Laws, Policies and Procedures	**Creates policies and practices to ensure safety and security**
Associated Skills	* Creates and regularly evaluates and Knowledge emergency response policies and procedures and prepares staff to respond appropriately * Maintains up to date policies/ procedures for staff communication and crises communication * Creates and regularly evaluates disaster preparedness and recovery plans for library resources and equipment

MARKETING

Relying on past reputation and word-of-mouth appreciation from users may not be enough to ensure survival

(Contd...)

in the face of dwindling tax or government support. Effective marketing can overcome misconceptions, get the community involved and attract new audiences.

Competency: Marketing	**Understands and applies marketing theory and practices**
Associated Skills and Knowledge	* Understands the basic principles of marketing and how they apply to library services * Conducts research to assess marketing landscape and to determine current position among similar businesses and organizations * Conducts a SWOT analysis to determine the strengths, weaknesses, opportunities and threats * Conducts periodic review of the community for opportunities to align needs with library services * Identifies, analyses and prioritizes target markets and audiences, and determines how best to promote library services that can effectively serve them
Competency: Marketing	**Develops, implements and evaluates an ongoing marketing plan for the library**
Associated Skills and Knowledge	* Sets measurable market goals and objectives, including brand strategy * Highlights programming objectives that affect the overall marketing of the library * Develops consistent promotion and distribution strategies to meet the goals and objectives based on the analysis of target audiences * Creates graphics standards, style guide, and consistent print and electronic visual communication standards * Provides marketing training for all staff,

(*Contd...*)

	board members and other key stakeholders * Implements the marketing efforts, maintaining records and clear communication with staff and stakeholders * Evaluates the effectiveness of the strategies and revises as necessary

ORGANIZATIONAL LEADERSHIP

While library services involve many roles and staff members, the guidance and driving force originate with the director or manager. Examination of any dynamic and successful library will usually reveal an effective and energetic leader at the top.

Competency: Organizational Leadership	**Uses leadership skills to provide vision and guidance to library staff, board members and the community**
Associated Skills and Knowledge	* Articulates the mission, vision and values of the library organization * Aligns the library with, and is supportive of, the strategic directions and needs of the community * Defines and communicates the library's goals and objectives aligned with the library's mission and vision * Evaluates and revises if necessary the library's mission, vision, value statements and strategic plan * Understands the social, political and economic context in which the library exists * Models accountability for quality and timeliness of work and reliability in achieving excellent results
Competency: Organizational Leadership	**Contributes effective strategies and decisions regarding library services and resources**

(*Contd...*)

Associated Skills and Knowledge	* Understands the library's strengths, weaknesses, opportunities and challenges * Recommends adopting, modifying or eliminating services, based on the best available evidence * Prepares for and responds to crises and unanticipated events
Competency: Organizational Leadership	**Provides effective leadership of all stakeholders and teams**
Associated Skills and Knowledge	* Keeps current with new approaches to team behaviour and applies that knowledge to help achieve organizational goals and objectives * Builds trust relationships with all stakeholders and establishes appropriate procedures to keep informed of and respond to issues * Delegates decision-making authority and task allocation appropriately to maximize the effectiveness of organizational and individual efforts * Secures and allocates resources to assure stakeholders' accomplishment of tasks and responsibilities * Manages meetings and meeting participants effectively and practices consensus-building skills
Competency: Organizational Leadership	**Applies change management to assure effective implementation of change and acceptance by all stakeholders**
Associated Skills and Knowledge	* Remains open to new ideas, keeps current on trends and issues, and seeks and sponsors innovations * Recognizes the benefits of change and understands the principles, processes and responsibilities for managing organizational change

(*Contd...*)

	* Involves appropriate parties in planning, implementing and evaluating change * Prepares staff, Library Board, users and other stakeholders for change through effective communication to raise awareness, build commitment and ensure understanding * Anticipates change-resistant behaviour and applies strategies to address it

PERSONNEL MANAGEMENT

Productive performance by its personnel is the backbone of a successful library. Whether or not you prefer the term Human Resources Management, the strategic oversight of your workforce is key to achieving the library's mission and goals.

Competency: Personnel	Contributes to a productive workforce Management through effective recruitment and selection
Associated Skills and Knowledge	* Develops and applies consistent and effective interviewing techniques * Makes hiring decisions based on sound evaluation methods * Understands and complies with employment laws and regulations that impact recruiting and hiring * Understands and complies with library policies and procedures that impact recruiting and hiring * Values a diverse workforce and recruits for diversity
Competency: Personnel Management	**Leads and empowers employees to deliver effective, high-quality library service**
Associated Skills and Knowledge	* Fosters and facilitates a collaborative environment based on a shared vision * Models enthusiasm and commitment and energizes staff to meet defined goals

(Contd...)

	* Communicates clearly and regularly with staff about library, government or major community changes that may affect them * Promotes teamwork among staff and promotes team-building practices * Ensures that diversity needs are respected and supported in HR processes * Recognizes staff achievements through formal and informal methods
Competency: Personnel Management	**Establishes effective strategies for performance management**
Associated Skills and Knowledge	* Establishes clear performance expectations linked to the library's strategies and priorities, with appropriate levels of quantity and quality of work * Enables staff to strive for continuously higher standards of performance * Provides appropriate tools, resources and authority to support performance expectations * Establishes methods for review and evaluation of performance and holds all staff accountable to meet performance expectations * Provides constructive feedback and takes timely and consistent corrective/ disciplinary action when appropriate
Competency: Personnel Management	**Understands and applies legal standards and requirements for performance management**
Associated Skills and Knowledge	* Understands and complies with employment laws and regulations that impact performance management * Understands and ensures compliance with human resources policies and procedures

(Contd...)

	* Promotes effective labour relations and maintains a productive working relationship with employees and their representatives * Understands contract negotiation and administration * Understands a variety of problem-solving techniques and applies them to dispute resolution
Competency: Personnel Management	**Works appropriately with consultants and volunteers**
Associated Skills and Knowledge	* Develops and applies consistent practices for hiring consultants and recruiting volunteers * Articulates the need for consultants and/or volunteers and defines clear roles and responsibilities * Develops and administers contracts * Provides effective training and supervision of volunteers

PROJECT MANAGEMENT

The multiplicity of factors involved in managing any library project demands an organized approach. Basic project management skills enable the process for coordinating people, time, money and deliverables.

Competency: Project Management	**Employs sound project management principles and procedures in the planning and implementation of programmes and services**
Associated Skills and Knowledge	* Understands the basic principles and procedures of project management * Defines outcomes and expectations based on user requirements and needs * Develops support for projects that implement library goals and objectives * Uses resources efficiently and manages effectively within budget limits

(Contd...)

Competency: Project Management	Leads work teams with clear direction and effective communication
Associated Skills and Knowledge	* Conducts strategic selection of team members * Develops a work plan with tasks, timeframes, milestones, resources and realistic deadlines * Anticipates potential problems, sets controls and contingency plans, and responds effectively to resolve barriers

Competency: Project Management	Monitors and evaluates projects and uses the results for project improvement
Associated Skills and Knowledge	* Establishes processes for collecting, documenting and reporting data * Monitors project progress and evaluates performance to ensure quality and quantity standards are met * Fulfills legal or project requirements for compliance, record keeping and reporting * Analyses and identifies dissemination strategies, and reports project data and outcomes to stakeholders

STAFF TRAINING AND DEVELOPMENT

Staff development continues to be one of the most important needs in libraries. From the smallest library to the largest, training staff has become critical to meeting the library's mission within the changing landscape. Technically, this is a subset of Personnel (HR) Management, but it is called out separately due to the primary focus that WebJunction places on this set of competencies.

Competency: Staff Training	Establish strategies and long-range initiatives to create a learning environment within the library
Associated Skills and Knowledge	* Promotes the importance of continuing staff development and provides appropriate opportunities

(Contd...)

	* Understands how the learning function for library staff relates to the provision of quality library service * Creates a culture that enables both formal and informal learning processes in the workplace * Promotes a performance-based culture that aligns learning goals and objectives with desired outcomes * Fosters staff growth and opportunity through mentoring
Competency: Staff Training	**Plans for and supports staff career development opportunities**
Associated Skills and Knowledge	* Conducts assessment of staff to analyse training needs * Correlates training needs with identified internal and external changes that impact the library * Utilizes competency-based or other methods for assessing staff skills and supporting career development opportunities * Conducts and summarizes a job task analysis * Creates development plans for staff to gain necessary competencies
Competency: Staff Training	**Develops and implements appropriate training strategies**
Associated Skills and Knowledge	* Understands and applies knowledge of adult learning theory * Designs training activities to meet the needs of targeted audiences and to support specific results * Develops and implements training solutions that focus on the learner and accommodate different learning styles * Understands the variety of instructional

Table Contd...

	methods available, including e-learning and blended learning * Understands and applies instructional design concepts * Manages the learning environment for optimal participant experience and value
Competency: Staff Training	**Develops effective methods to evaluate learning initiatives**
Associated Skills and Knowledge	* Determines measures of success for all training strategies * Employs multiple evaluation techniques * Develops processes to evaluate transfer of learning to the workplace and achievement of targeted competencies * Provides time and procedures to review and reinforce learning

STRATEGIC PLANNING

A coherent overall plan that aligns with the library's goals and community needs will help the library provide successful programmes and services.

Competency: Strategic Planning	**Designs and implements an ongoing strategic planning process for the library**
Associated Skills and Knowledge	* Develops strategic plans to align with and fulfill organizational goals * Analyses and investigates the needs of the community and environment to anticipate and predict changing trends and influences * Involves stakeholder groups in the planning process and promotes the plan's value to the community * Creates appropriate mission statement, goals, objectives and activities that reflect analysis of community needs

Table Contd...

	* Ensures that long-term goals and objectives align with daily decisions and operations
Competency: Strategic Planning	Performs ongoing evaluation to gauge the success of the strategic plan
Associated Skills and Knowledge	* Develops and applies appropriate methods to continually measure and ensure the quality and value of library services * Modifies the strategic plan and redesigns processes as needed in response to ongoing analysis of community needs * Monitors progress of service planning and provides follow-up, educational and accountability measures

TRUSTEES AND FRIENDS

The Library Board plays a critical role in the governance of the library. Friends of the Library and Library Foundations provide vital support of the library, raising money and solidifying community relations. It is a primary responsibility of the director to enable the operation of these groups.

Competency: Trustees and Friends	**Manages the relationship and communication with the Library Board**
Associated Skills and Knowledge	* Understands the roles and relationships of the Library Board and the library administration * Practices strategic recruitment for new Board members * Provides orientation and ongoing training as needed for Board members * Provides timely and pertinent information and facilitates communication to support the Board's decision-making

Table Contd...

	* Motivates the Board to assess and adopt policies that meet user needs * Motivates the Board to plan for the future needs of the library * Motivates the Board to promote the library in the community
Competency: Trustees and Friends	Understands and sustains the library's roles and relationships with the Friends of the Library and the Library Foundation
Associated Skills and Knowledge	* Recognizes the benefits derived from a Friends group or Library Foundation * Develops and monitors operating agreements between the library and the Friends group * Maintains ongoing communication about the library's planning process and evolving goals and needs

PERSONAL/INTERPERSONAL COMPETENCIES

These competencies are foundational, most of them transferable to any workplace. In most situations in life, your effectiveness is enhanced by clear communication, strong relationships, ethical behaviour and the flexibility to be a leader, team player and lifelong learner. These competencies are the underpinning of all the other parts of the Competency Index. Librarians and library staff who possess all of these qualities will build a vibrant and relevant library.

COMMUNICATION

Clear and effective communication is the basis for success in your relations with co-workers, managers, users and all stakeholders. Communication competency is integral to customer service.

Competency: Communication	**Communicates effectively using a variety of methods**
Associated Skills and Knowledge	* Communicates openly and directly, both verbally and in writing * Identifies issues and ideas to be

Table Contd...

	communicated and provides information that is accurate and timely * Presents ideas in a manner that is clear and concise, with an appropriate level of enthusiasm * Demonstrates proficient writing skills * Demonstrates proficient public-speaking skills
Competency: Communication	**Communicates effectively with a variety of audiences and individuals from diverse backgrounds**
Associated Skills and Knowledge	* Speaks and writes in a manner that is professional, welcoming and appropriate for all audiences * Demonstrates understanding of the* Maintains ongoing communication about the library's planning process and evolving goals and needs erceptions, perspectives and communication styles of each audience * Fosters an inclusive, affirming and respectful climate for communication
Competency: Communication	**Selects and applies the most appropriate and effective communication means to meet situational needs**
Associated Skills and Knowledge	* Communicates effectively to obtain consensus, persuade, instruct and/or motivate * Understands and practices techniques of active listening and asking open-ended questions * Selects appropriate communication strategies to manage conflict constructively * Demonstrates negotiation skills to secure beneficial outcomes

CUSTOMER SERVICE

Table Contd...

Customer service is every bit as important in the library as it is in the marketplace. While there are fundamental differences between library services and commercial services, the behaviours and expectations of the people you serve are universal.

Competency: Customer Service	**Manages the library environment to enhance the user experience**
Associated Skills and Knowledge	* Organizes the library's collections and work areas to appeal to users and to meet their needs * Organizes physical elements in the library to create a positive and welcoming environment * Addresses the physical or mental barriers that could prevent people from using the library
Competency: Customer Service	**Develops and evaluates standards and practices for the delivery of quality customer service**
Associated Skills and Knowledge	* Creates a customer service plan * Anticipates and maintains awareness of users' needs and wants through customer service surveys, complaint logs and other means * Analyses input from users, evaluates the effectiveness of current services, and adjusts services and practices as applicable * Uses effective training strategies to teach staff good customer service techniques * Determines the relative needs of users, suppliers and library staff, and strives for balance in supporting them to achieve their goals
Competency: Customer Service	**Applies customer service skills to enhance the level of user satisfaction**
Associated Skills and	* Treats users in a welcoming, professional manner and provides other

Table Contd...

Knowledge	staff with an example of positive customer service * Acts as a goodwill ambassador for the library, promoting the library's values and services in all user interactions * Demonstrates thorough knowledge of all aspects of the organization that impact users * Recognizes, honours and responds appropriately to diversity and cultural differences
Competency: Customer Service	**Applies effective techniques to address difficult situations with users**
Associated Skills and Knowledge	* Encourages users to follow library policies; applies good judgment when deviating from official policies and procedures * Deals with users' concerns efficiently and effectively * Maintains a calm, professional manner in difficult situations and applies effective communication techniques

ETHICS AND VALUES

The library plays a crucial role in society and the community. Library ethics and values have been carefully formulated to fulfill the institution's commitments to the community and to guide the practice of everyone who works there.

Competency: Ethics and Values	**Understands and acts in accordance with the basic values and ethics of library service**
Associated Skills and Knowledge	* Understands the history of libraries and their role in society, both in general and in the particular community * Understands and adheres to the mission, values and vision of the library organization * Demonstrates familiarity with the

Table Contd...

	Library Bill of Rights and the ALA Code of Ethics, and articulates the relevance to library service * Understands privacy issues and protects user confidentially * Understands and promotes intellectual freedom and freedom of information * Provides equitable services to all users * Recognizes, respects and addresses the diverse nature of the library's users and community

INTERPERSONAL

Unless you work alone in a cave, you must interact productively with others in order to accomplish your own and your organization's goals. Master the interpersonal competencies and you have a recipe for success.

Competency: Interpersonal	**Develops and maintains effective relationships with others to achieve common goals**
Associated Skills and Knowledge	* Treats everyone with honesty, respect and fairness to build an environment of trust * Contributes to a collaborative, committed and collegial work environment * Pursues an understanding and embrace of individual and organizational diversity * Acknowledges own strengths and contributions, and recognizes the complementary strengths and contributions of others * Shares knowledge gained through professional discussions, conferences, formal courses and informal channels with colleagues * Gives and receives constructive

Table Contd...

	feedback from coworkers, supervisors and users
Competency: Interpersonal	**Works effectively in teams with strong team- building skills and attitudes**
Associated Skills and Knowledge	* Contributes constructively to the achievement of the team's goals and objectives * Contributes to a problem-solving environment and works towards mutually acceptable solutions, regardless of position or level * Participates actively in information-gathering and decision-making in order to promote the best interests of the team * Manages own and others' time effectively to deliver work on time * Finds opportunities to help others to develop new ideas and achieve their full potential * Gives or receives coaching or mentoring from team members as appropriate
Competency: Interpersonal	**Applies effective strategies to manage organizational politics, conflict and difficult co-worker behaviours**
Associated Skills and Knowledge	* Understands that organizations are inherently political and develops strategies to become an effective player * Understands a variety of difficult behaviour patterns and develops responses appropriate to each * Routinely examines own behaviour, accepts accountability for own actions and adjusts appropriately * Understands and applies strategies for conflict resolution

Table Contd...

LEADERSHIP AND PROJECT MANAGEMENT

It is not necessary to have "manager" in your title in order to exercise leadership or project management. There are many small to large opportunities to demonstrate leadership and build your skills through experience. Practicing good project management processes and approaches will score points with co-workers of all levels and positions.

Competency: Leadership and Project Management	**Aligns efforts with the vision and direction of the organization**
Associated Skills and Knowledge	* Demonstrates faith in the library's vision, works to achieve it and inspires others to do the same * Identifies the appropriate opportunities, resources and timing to act in support of the library's vision and mission * Works to meet or exceed goals by obtaining resources and support, and by eliminating obstacles

Competency: Leadership and Project Management	**Demonstrates an aptitude for leadership**
Associated Skills and Knowledge	* Actively pursues and accepts leadership roles and demonstrates ability to lead teams effectively * Takes initiative, seeks new opportunities and challenges, and applies creative and innovative thinking * Maintains a positive attitude and sets an example for others to follow, no matter what position is held in the library * Fosters an environment based on integrity and high ethical standards * Empowers others to take ownership in decision-making and problem-solving * Researches trends in leadership skills and styles and applies new knowledge effectively

Competency: Leadership and Project Management	Employs sound project management principles and procedures in the planning and implementation of programmes and services
Associated Skills and Knowledge	* Understands the basic principles and procedures of project management and the importance of applying them * Defines outcomes and expectations based on user requirements and needs * Develops support for projects that implement library goals and objectives * Uses resources efficiently, prioritizes workflows and manages effectively within budget limits * Demonstrates attention to detail * Establishes processes for evaluating the effectiveness of the project and implementing improvements as appropriate * Understands and fulfills legal or project requirements for compliance, record keeping and reporting
Competency: Leadership and Project Management	**Anticipates and adapts to change and challenges effectively**
Associated Skills and Knowledge	* Maintains the flexibility to accept change and to adapt with curiosity and enthusiasm * Maintains a positive attitude in the face of challenges and unanticipated changes * Anticipates future trends and recommends changes in priority or direction in alignment with organizational goals * Explores and adopts new technologies for their potential to deliver new ideas, products and services * Recommends and takes reasonable risks to test implementations of change

Table Contd...

LEARNING AND PERSONAL GROWTH

No matter what position you occupy or what your employment future holds, an embrace of lifelong learning and continual improvement will enrich your professional path and your life.

Competency: Learning and Personal Growth	**Manages the development of one's own career and ongoing improvement of skills and knowledge**
Associated Skills and Knowledge	* Understands the importance of lifelong learning for all levels of library work and actively pursues personal and professional growth through continuing education * Formulates personal career goals, identifies learning needs and creates a learning plan to achieve them * Recognizes the value of professional networking and actively participates in professional associations * Understands and uses resources and strategies for keeping up with new ideas and technologies * Seeks opportunities to apply new knowledge and to share best practices, research and experiences with colleagues
Competency: Learning and Personal Growth	Pursues a commitment to personal growth and lifelong learning
Associated Skills and Knowledge	* Practices ongoing self improvement in response to feedback * Hones critical thinking skills * Supports self and others in pursuit of a balanced lifestyle * Seeks exposure to new ideas, both within and beyond the library field, and stretches beyond one's comfort zone * Pursues learning in multiple formats and practices self-directed learning

PUBLIC SERVICES COMPETENCIES

All of the services that interface directly with the library's users come together under the heading of public services. These frontline staff anticipate and meet the needs of users in the most visible way. Fully supported by all the other sectors and departments, they work to provide the best possible programmes and services to the library community.

ACCESS SERVICES

Access Services is like the circulatory system of the library body—it keeps materials flowing in, out and around in a well-regulated manner, striving to deliver the right item at the right time.

Competency: Access Services	Understands and performs the basic operations of the circulation function
Associated Skills and Knowledge	* Demonstrates general knowledge of the library automation systems in use and specific knowledge of the operations that apply to circulation procedures * Performs circulation procedures for all library materials * Accesses the OPAC and uses a variety of tactics to locate items in the collection * Explains and performs intra- and interlibrary loan procedures, document delivery, resource sharing, reserves and other information retrieval options * Understands, explains and adheres to circulation and resource sharing policies and procedures, including copyright issues * Keeps current with changes in the automation systems and in circulation operations and policies * Performs procedures for shelving, shifting and shelf reading

ADULT AND OLDER ADULT SERVICES

Providing library services to the community is no trivial pursuit, given the diversity of needs and interests to be met. That door counts are up, circulation increasing and libraries thriving is a testament to the success of these services and programmes and the competency of the people who make it happen.

Adult Services and Outreach

Competency: Adult Services and Outreach	Designs and implements library services to meet the needs and interests of the community
Associated Skills and Knowledge	* Uses a variety of ongoing methods to determine the interests of adults in the community * Analyses demographic and other data collected about the community and develops a wide variety of services to meet the needs and interests of target audiences * Identifies potential partner organizations within the institution or in the community that have compatible goals and objectives to serve adults, and develops cooperative services and programmes to extend and enhance library service * Aligns all services and programmes with library policies and procedures * Evaluates all services, using appropriate evaluation strategies and uses the results to improve future services
Competency: Adult Services and Outreach	**Defines and implements outreach services for the library community to increase use of library services and to reach underserved populations**
Associated Skills and	* Identifies individuals and groups not adequately served

Knowledge	* Determines the particular needs of each target audience and designs a variety of programmes and services appropriate to them * Identifies individuals and groups not currently served by the library, determines needs, develops programmes and services, and promotes them to the non-users with targeted marketing * Aligns all outreach efforts with the library's overall goals and objectives * Determines the best means to deliver library services to remote users appropriate to library resources * Designs programmes and builds collections and information resources to meet the special language and literacy needs of the community * Collaborates with other community groups to meet the literacy needs of target audiences
Competency: Adult Services and Outreach	**Uses Web tools and social networking communities to engage with and provide services to users**
Associated Skills and Knowledge	* Understands and articulates the importance of engaging with users in non-traditional ways that extend beyond the physical library * Investigates and evaluates tools, and identifies those most applicable to the library's services and community needs * Determines objectives for enhancing library services and access, and acquires proficiency with selected tools to provide effective library services * Explores the potential of social networking to interact with users and meet their information needs

Table Contd...

	* Assists users with setting up and using Web tools and participating in social networking communities * Understands the unique opportunities, norms and limitations of online engagement with users * Devises strategies to keep up with emerging tools and techniques, and connects with professional communities to seek and share best practices

Adult Programming

Competency: Adult Programming	**Designs, implements and sponsors library programmes that offer information, special skills or entertainment**
Associated Skills and Knowledge	* Demonstrates ability to be creative, promote new ideas and identify a variety of tools and techniques to create interesting and engaging programmes * Aligns programmes with the library's goals and objectives and with the identified interests and needs of the community * Actively involves users in planning, implementing and evaluating programmes * Promotes the library's programmes to the community in coordination with marketing efforts * Develops programmes to acknowledge and celebrate the cultural diversity of the community * Identifies programme venues outside of the library * Coordinates with collection development efforts in support of programming

Table Contd...

	* Evaluates programmes, using appropriate evaluation strategies and uses results to improve future programming efforts
Competency: Adult Programming	**Develops and promotes gaming for adult programming**
Associated Skills and Knowledge	* Understands and promotes the value of games and gaming as part of library programming for adults * Investigates the options for gaming programmes and makes informed choices about games appropriate to the library's mission and means * Determines objectives of adult gaming programmes * Determines budget required to implement gaming programmes and seeks to integrate gaming into the library's budget * Coordinates with IT and other departments to address technology requirements for gaming * Identifies a variety of games, creates interesting and engaging game-based programmes, and invents creative ways to promote them to the target audiences * Evaluates the outcomes of adult gaming programmes and recommends improvements for future efforts

Older Adult Services and Programming

Given the large population of older adults, the extent of their leisure time, and their potential for contributing to library service, it only makes sense to provide a special focus on the competencies involved in serving this important audience.

Competency: Older Adult Services Programming	**Designs and implements library services to meet the needs and interests of older and adults in the community**
Associated Skills and Knowledge	* Analyses demographic and other data collected about older adults in the community and develops a wide variety of services to meet the needs and interests of older adults and their families and caregivers * Understands the range of older adults and identifies their particular needs and interests, acknowledging the range of skills, knowledge, strengths and limitations they bring to the library * Partners with organizations within the institution or in the community that have compatible goals and objectives to serve older adults, and develops cooperative services and programmes to extend and enhance older adult services * Identifies and maintains regular communication with agencies, institutions and organizations serving older adults in the community * Solicits and considers the opinions and requests of older adults when planning, implementing and evaluating programmes and services
Competency: Older Adult Services and	**Defines and implements outreach services to increase older adults' use of library services and to reach underserved Programming populations**
Associated Skills and Knowledge	* Ensures that older adult audiences are included in the target audiences for the library's outreach efforts * Identifies older adults who are unable to

Table Contd...

	visit the library, determines their special needs for library resources, and determines the best means to deliver library services to them * Understands and addresses specialized concerns of some older adult users
Competency: Older Adult Programming	**Designs, implements and sponsors library programmes for older adults that offer Services and information,special skills or entertainment**
Associated Skills and Knowledge	* Acknowledges the knowledge and experience of older adults and provides opportunities for them to volunteer with the library * Actively involves older adults in planning, Associated implementing and evaluating programmes * Promotes the library's programmes to the older adult community in coordination with marketing efforts * Understands the potential of games to address particular needs of older adults and identifies a variety of games and gaming programmes to meet those needs
Readers' Advisory	
Competency: Readers' Advisory	**Assists users with choosing popular and recreational reading, viewing and listening choices**
Associated Skills and Knowledge	* Demonstrates a broad knowledge of the library's collection and of a wide range of materials of interest to library readers * Demonstrates the ability to read widely, formulate connections between resources, and converse with users about the resources * Understands the theory of appeal,

Table Contd...

	listens carefully to information elicited from the user and bases recommendations on an interpretation of what appeals to the user * Identifies and recommends a selection of materials that align with what appeals to the user * Creates booklists, read-alikes, read-arounds, book-talks, displays, electronic documents and other special tools to increase access to library resources and promote their use * Uses Web tools to encourage participation and contributions from readers * Seeks feedback from readers on recommended materials and adjusts future recommendations accordingly
Competency: Readers' Advisory	**Develops strategies and sources to stay well-informed as a readers' advisor**
Associated Skills and Knowledge	* Identifies and uses a variety of online and print readers' advisory resources to identify materials * Maintains an ongoing knowledge of major new authors, fiction genres, nonfiction subjects and current releases * Keeps current with popular culture through a variety of channels * Connects with professional communities to seek and share best practices for readers' advisory
Reference	
Competency: Reference	**Develops and maintains a collection of reference resources to meet community needs**
Associated	* Demonstrates knowledge of the

Table Contd...

Skills and Knowledge	reference collection, encompassing print and electronic, and in-house as well as applicable external resources * Provides a variety of readily accessible reference resources that meet identified community needs * Prepares bibliographies, subject collections and other user guides to resources in a variety of formats, and creates tutorials to help users navigate information sources * Compiles and maintains information about community resources appropriate to users' needs * Performs ongoing evaluation of the currency and usefulness of the reference collection and makes recommendations for acquisition or deselection
Competency: Reference	**Facilitates library users' requests for information**
Associated Skills and Knowledge	* Practices effective reference interviewing skills to best fulfill a user's actual needs * Addresses the information-seeking behaviors and needs of users without bias across the spectrum of age, race, gender, ethnicity, ability or economic status * Demonstrates strong interpersonal communication skills, including welcoming manner, active listening and nonjudgmental response * Acknowledges users' knowledge and involves users as partners in seeking information and choosing resources * Answers questions knowledgeably, providing information of an appropriate scope and reading level * Evaluates the success of the reference

Table Contd...

	service through feedback from staff, users and other stakeholders * Identifies opportunities for instruction and empowers users to improve their own information-seeking ability
Competency: Reference	**Provides search and retrieval of requested information and presents results that are clear and of appropriate scope**
Associated Skills and Knowledge	* Identifies the best kind of resource to use to offer assistance * Understands and performs effective search queries, using multiple resources and search strategies * Continues the reference interview process with users to refine the search or topic as appropriate * Synthesizes information from a variety of resources and evaluates results for quality and accuracy * Customises the answer to meet the user's specific needs and characteristics and ensures that the user understands the results * Recognizes the limits of library resources and refers users or questions to other libraries, individuals or agencies as appropriate * Understands the advantages and limitations of federated search

CHILDREN'S SERVICES

The library plays a very significant role in the lives and development of children and in the interactions with their families, schools and caregivers. Covering the territory from infancy to tweens requires a robust set of skills and knowledge.

Children's Services and Outreach

Competency: Children's Services and Outreach	**Designs and implements library services to meet the needs and interests of children in the community**
Associated Skills and Knowledge	* Analyses demographic and other data collected about the community and develops a wide variety of services to meet the needs and interests of children and their families and caregivers * Ensures that policies and procedures for children's services are aligned with federal, state and local law and with the library's policies and procedures * Provides services and spaces appropriate to the developmental needs of children * Solicits and considers the opinions and requests of children when planning, implementing and evaluating programmes and services * Partners with organizations within the institution or in the community that have compatible goals and objectives to serve children, and develops cooperative services and programmes to extend and enhance children's and family programmes * Identifies and maintains regular communication with agencies, institutions and organizations serving children in the community
Competency: Children's Services and Outreach	**Articulates and communicates to stakeholders the needs of children to receive quality library service**
Associated Skills and	* Designs, implements and evaluates ongoing public relations directed

Table Contd...

Knowledge	towards children and their caregivers, with recognition of the diversity of the community * Models and promotes a welcoming, supportive and nonjudgmental attitude towards children and their families and caregivers * Promotes awareness of children's services to other staff members and contributes to their orientation and training in relation to the delivery of those services * Promotes awareness of children's services within the library governance structure and lobbies for inclusion in the library's plans and budget processes * Ensures that the needs of children are considered in overall library planning, including the application of ADA regulations and the appropriate access to resources and services
Competency: Children's Services and Outreach	**Defines and implements outreach services to increase children's and families' use of library services and to reach underserved populations**
Associated Skills and Knowledge	* Identifies children underserved or not yet served * Determines the particular needs of each target audience, designs a variety of programmes and services to match their needs, and promotes them with targeted marketing * Establishes an environment in which children receive courteous service and are encouraged to use the library and participate in library programmes
Competency:	**Works with parents, caregivers and other**

Table Contd...

Children's Services and Outreach	adults who serve children
Associated Skills and Knowledge	* Understands the importance of informing and coordinating with a variety of community members who work with children * Builds and updates knowledge of available resources that may serve the needs of children, families and caregivers * Identifies the need to educate adults who care for children and offers a variety of resources to help them provide improved care and guidance
Competency: Children's Services and Outreach	**Uses Web tools and social networking communities to engage with and provide age-appropriate services to children**
Associated Skills and Knowledge	* Understands and articulates the importance and of introducing children to age-appropriate online tools and environments * Investigates Web tools and social networking communities oriented towards children, and evaluates them for their potential to enhance learning and meet information needs of children * Understands the unique opportunities, norms and limitations of online engagement for children, and establishes guidelines for the use of social networking tools appropriate to the library setting and to the age groups * Assists children in accessing online children's programmes, using Web tools

Table Contd...

	and participating in social networking communities

Information Resources for Children

Competency: Information Resources for Children	**Builds a collection designed to meet the needs and interests of children**
Associated Skills and Knowledge	* Applies knowledge of the community and and solicited input from children, families and caregivers to build a children's collection that is diverse, current and relevant * Demonstrates comprehensive knowledge of the library's children's and other relevant collections and applies the knowledge to the decision-making process * Demonstrates broad knowledge and appreciation of children's literature, including authors and publishers * Establishes criteria for evaluation of children's materials in all genres and Skills formats * Evaluates, recommends and applies collection policies for children's materials consistent with the library's general collection development policies, including policies to handle challenges to materials * Ensures that community information resources address the needs of children and their families and caregivers * Displays and markets materials to be attractive and enjoyable to children, as well as convenient to use * Ensures that the collection reflects the diversity of the community, and helps to

Table Contd...

	familiarize children and their families with other perspectives
Competency: Information Resources for Children	**Establishes and pursues strategies to stay informed about current and relevant information resources to meet children's evolving needs**
Associated Skills and Knowledge	* Pursues a variety of information sources, including popular media, to keep current on topics relevant to children and families and to identify key changes in their needs and tastes * Connects with children, families and others who work with children to stay informed about new materials, resources and technologies * Maintains the quality and relevance of the collection through ongoing evaiuation of the currency and physical condition, and recommends materials for acquisition or deselection
Competency: Information Resources for Children	**Facilitates children's requests for information and provides accurate and appropriate answers**
Associated Skills and Knowledge	* Understands and practices effective reference interviewing skills particular to soliciting actual and unstated needs and protecting the confidentiality of children * Addresses the information-seeking behaviours and needs of children without bias across the spectrum of age, race, gender, ethnicity, ability or economic status; responds to questions regardless of their nature * Identifies opportunities for instruction and empowers children to improve their own information-seeking ability

Table Contd...

	* Establishes effective measures to manage Internet and other electronic resources that provide children with appropriate access
Competency: Information Resources for Children	**Connects children and their families and caregivers with resources that encourage reading**
Associated Skills and Knowledge	* Creates booklists, read-alikes, read-arounds, book-talks, displays, electronic documents and other special tools to appeal to children * Identifies and uses a variety of online and print children's readers' advisory resources to identify materials * Maintains an ongoing knowledge of major new authors, fiction genres, nonfiction subjects and current releases, including media and genres of particular interest to children * Seeks input from children, families and caregivers to inform future recommendations * Collaborates with families, schools and other community groups to promote reading and literacy to children * Understands the theories of reading development for children and the reading curriculum used by community schools

Children's Programming

Competency: Children's Programming	**Designs, implements and sponsors library programmes that offer information, special skills or entertainment for children and their families and caregivers**
Associated	* Uses a variety of methods to determine

Table Contd...

Skills and Knowledge	the and interests and needs of children, families, caregivers and others who work with Skills children in the community * Designs a wide variety of programmes appropriate to the identified interests and developmental needs of children, recognizing the breadth of needs from very early childhood to tweens * Demonstrates creativity, openness to new ideas, knowledge of a variety of tools and techniques, and a sense of humour * Identifies programme venues outside of the library that appeal to children * Evaluates all programmes, soliciting feedback from children and families, and uses those results to improve future programmes for children
Competency: Children's Programming	**Develops and promotes gaming programmes for children and families**
Associated Skills and Knowledge	* Understands and promotes the value of games for children * Investigates the options for gaming programmes and makes informed choices about age-appropriate games for children * Identifies a variety of games appropriate for children, creates interesting and engaging game-based programmes, and invents creative ways to promote them to the target audiences * Develops gaming programmes to accomplish specified objectives * Evaluates the outcomes of children's gaming programmes, involves families and caregivers in the evaluation process,

Table Contd...

	and recommends improvements for future efforts

COLLECTION DEVELOPMENT

A library's collection of materials is never static. New resources arrive continually; community needs and tastes change; obsolete materials must be purged. All of these decisions are deliberated, backed by thoughtful and coherent policy.

Competency: Collection Development	**Builds and maintains a collection of resources in many formats based on a determination of community needs**
Associated Skills and Knowledge	* Demonstrates comprehensive knowledge of the library's collection and applies the knowledge to the decision-making process * Demonstrates broad knowledge of authors, literature and publishers * Consults a wide variety of sources and connects with other professionals to stay informed about new materials, resources and technologies, and their potential to deliver improved services or reach new target audiences * Pursues a variety of information sources, including popular media, to keep current on topics relevant to library users * Strives to build a collection that is diverse, current and relevant, one that reflects the ethnic diversity of the community and promotes cross-cultural understanding * Assesses and responds to the community's changing needs and interests to inform the ongoing development of the collection
Competency:	**Establishes and applies selection an**

Table Contd...

Collection Development	**evaluation criteria to build a collection of high quality and relevant resources**
Associated Skills and Knowledge	* Understands the acquisition and collection and development processes and policies for the Knowledge library * Identifies and applies objective standards to evaluate the content of resources for accuracy and authority, and identifies any bias or point of view * Selects and evaluates resources to assure their quality, pertinence, authenticity and inclusiveness * Determines criteria for evaluating the Skills format, access and presentation aspects of resources to inform selections appropriate to a range of ages and developmental stages * Follows trends in traditional and digital publishing and gathers best practices of similar institutions * Consults a variety of review sources, in combination with informed judgment and knowledge of the community, to evaluate materials * Identifies and evaluates a variety of sources for materials, including commercial and non-commercial
Competency: Collection Development	**Researches and designs systems and services to provide optimal access to resources**
Associated Skills and Knowledge	* Organizes and effectively displays information so that it is meaningful and accessible to users * Determines and provides the appropriate mix of technologies, formats and delivery channels to meet the needs of a variety of users * Identifies any factors that impede the

Table Contd...

	use of resources and communicates with the information resource designers about usability improvements * Collaborates with IT and other departments, acting as a user advocate, to develop, implement and evaluate new systems and services that better meet users' needs * Recognizes the special information access needs of user groups, and provides them with the best possible access appropriate to the library * Researches and assesses emerging technologies for improved delivery of information resources * Identifies opportunities to cooperate with other libraries, departments or community organizations to share information resources
Competency: Collection Development	**Understands and establishes collection development policies and procedures**
Associated Skills and Knowledge	* Evaluates, recommends and applies policies and procedures for identifying and selecting library materials in all formats * Insures that collection policies are consistent with the mission and broader policies of the library and the ALA Library Bill of Rights * Develops policies and procedures for handling challenges to library materials * Develops policies for weeding the collection, handling donations and gifts, and disposing of obsolete materials

PATRON TRAINING

Depending on the size of library, there may be

management positions or whole departments responsible for development of patron training programmes. No matter where the responsibility resides, patron training and the advancement of information literacy are crucial ways in which the library serves its community.

Competency: Patron Training	**Develops training programmes to build information literacy skills and to meet other educational needs of users**
Associated Skills and Knowledge	* Understands the scope and the importance of information literacy and defines information literacy goals applicable to the institution * Defines desired outcomes for patron training programmes and builds a curriculum to meet those outcomes * Identifies topics of importance and interest to library users by a variety of ongoing means * Establishes a budget for patron training and promotes its value to the library's budget authorities * Identifies opportunities to partner with other departments or organizations to collaborate on training programmes * Identifies opportunities for combining training for staff and users; understands the advantages and disadvantages of doing so * Identifies resources for training and coordinates with appropriate departments to obtain them * Understands and applies basic instructional design principles to design training * Identifies and manages trainers and training materials; manages scheduling of classes

Table Contd...

	* Evaluates training programmes, using the appropriate evaluation strategies and uses results to improve future training content and delivery
Competency: Patron Training	**Delivers formal training to fulfill objectives of the patron training programmes**
Associated Skills and Knowledge	* Articulates the library's objectives for training users * Selects the appropriate style and presentation methods for delivery of training, based on an understanding of adult learning principles * Prepares the learning environment, including set-up of computer labs * Practices effective training techniques * Fosters a positive learning atmosphere, one that respects and values diversity * Accepts feedback on effectiveness of training and seeks opportunities to improve techniques and behaviour
Competency: Patron Training	**Provides informal instruction and assistance to build skills of library users**
Associated Skills and Knowledge	* Perceives needs of users for "just in time" and learning and demonstrates readiness to assist at the level of need * Identifies and makes available tutorials and other resources for users' self-paced learning * Assists library users with searching the Skills library's catalog and helps them develop the ability to recognize an information need, meet it and evaluate the results * Recognizes a user's need for formal learning and identifies appropriate

Table Contd...

	opportunities in the library's class schedule or through other ecommunity organizations
Competency: Patron Training	**Assists users on the public access computers with learning basic technology skills**
Associated Skills and Knowledge	* Instructs users in the use of the access, reservation, time and print management systems * Understands and explains the security restrictions of the public computers and the user's options for saving files and "bookmarks" both temporarily and permanently * Assists users in accessing and navigating the Internet, understanding common security protocols, locating resources, and downloading and saving files of all types * Assists users with Web-based e-mail programmes

YOUNG ADULT SERVICES

Providing services and programmes to young adults must be one of the most challenging and most rewarding efforts in the library. Working with teens involves flexibility, a solid sense of humour and the recognition that teens have valuable contributions to make to the library and to the community.

Young Adult Services and Outreach	
Competency: Young Adult Services and Outreach	**Designs and implements library services to meet the needs and interests of the young adult community**
Associated Skills and Knowledge	* Analyses demographic and other data collected about the community and develops a wide variety of services to

	meet the needs and interests of young adults * Ensures that policies and procedures for young adult services are aligned with federal, state and local law and with the library's policies and procedures * Provides services and spaces appropriate to the developmental needs of young adults * Involves young adults in planning, implementing and evaluating programmes and services * Partners with organizations within the institution or in the community that have compatible goals and objectives to serve young adults, and develops cooperative services and programmes to extend and enhance young adult programmes
Competency: Young Adult Services and Outreach	**Articulates and communicates to stakeholders the needs of young adults to receive quality library service**
Associated Skills and Knowledge	* Designs, implements and evaluates ongoing public relations directed towards and recognizing the diversity of young adults * Models and promotes a welcoming, supportive and nonjudgmental attitude towards young adults * Promotes awareness of young adult Skills and services to other staff members and contributes to their orientation and training in relation to the delivery of young adult services * Promotes awareness of young adult services within the library governance structure and lobbies for inclusion in the

Table Contd...

	library's plans and budget processes * Ensures that the needs of young adults are considered in overall library planning, including the application of ADA regulations and the full access to resources and services
Competency: Young Adult Services and Outreach	**Defines and implements outreach services to increase young adults' use of library services and to reach underserved populations**
Associated Skills and Knowledge	* Identifies young adult individuals and groups underserved or not yet served * Determines the particular needs of each target audience, designs a variety of programmes and services appropriate to them, and promotes them with targeted marketing * Establishes an environment in which young adults receive courteous service and are encouraged to use the library and participate in library programmes
Competency: Young Adult Services and Outreach	**Uses Web tools and social networking communities to engage with and provide services to young adults**
Associated Skills and Knowledge	* Understands and articulates the particular importance of engaging with young adults in nontraditional ways that extend beyond the physical library * Involves young adults in the investigation and evaluation of tools to identify those most applicable to the to the library's young adult services * Explores the potential of social networking to connect and interact with young adults and meet their information needs * Understands the unique opportunities,

Table Contd...

	norms and limitations of online engagement with young adults, and establishes guidelines for the use of social networking tools appropriate to the library setting * Assists young adults with setting up and using Web tools and participating in social networking communities

Information Resources for Young Adults

Competency: Information Resources for Young Adults	**Builds a collection designed to meet the needs and interests of young adults**
Associated Skills and Knowledge	* Applies knowledge of the community and solicited input from teens to build a young adult collection that is diverse, current and relevant * Demonstrates comprehensive knowledge of the library's young adult and other relevant collections and applies the knowledge to the decision-making process * Demonstrates broad knowledge and appreciation of authors, literature and publishers of young adult literature * Establishes criteria for evaluation of young adult materials in all genres and formats * Ensures that community information resources address the needs of young adults and their families * Displays and markets materials to be attractive and enjoyable to young adults, as well as convenient to use * Ensures that the collection reflects the diversity of the community, and helps to familiarize young adults with other

Table Contd...

	perspectives
Competency: Information Resources for Young Adults	**Establishes and pursues strategies to stay informed about current and relevant information resources to meet the young adult community's evolving needs**
Associated Skills and Knowledge	* Pursues a variety of information sources, including popular media, to keep current on topics relevant to young adults and to identify key changes in their needs and tastes * Connects with teens and others who work with teens to stay informed about new materials, resources and technologies * Maintains the quality and relevance of the collection through ongoing evaluation of the currency and physical condition, and recommends materials for acquisition or deselection
Competency: Information Resources for Young Adults	**Facilitates young adults' requests for information and provides accurate and appropriate answers**
Associated Skills and Knowledge	* Understands and practices effective reference interviewing skills particular to soliciting actual and unstated needs and protecting the confidentiality of young adults * Addresses the information-seeking behaviours and needs of young adults without bias across the spectrum of age, race, gender, ethnicity, ability or economic status; responds to questions regardless of their nature * Identifies opportunities for instruction and empowers young adults to improve their own information-seeking ability

Table Contd...

	* Establishes effective measures to manage Internet and other electronic resources that provide young adults with equal access
Competency: Information Resources for Young Adults	**Connects young adults and their families with resources that encourage reading**
Associated Skills and Knowledge	* Creates booklists, read-alikes, read-arounds, book-talks, displays, electronic documents and other special tools to appeal to young adults * Identifies and uses a variety of online and print young adult readers' advisory resources to identify materials * Maintains an ongoing knowledge of major new authors, fiction genres, nonfiction subjects and current releases, including media and genres of particular interest to young adults * Seeks input from young adults to inform future recommendations * Collaborates with families, schools and other community groups to promote reading and literacy to young adults * Understands the theories of reading development for young adults and the reading curriculum used by community schools

Young Adult Programming

Competency: Young Adult Programming	**Designs, implements and sponsors library programmes that offer information, special skills or entertainment for young adults**
Associated Skills and	* Uses a variety of methods to determine the interests and developmental needs

Knowledge	of young adults in the community * Involves teens in planning, implementing and evaluating programmes * Designs a wide variety of programmes appropriate to the identified interests and developmental needs of young adults * Demonstrates creativity, openness to new ideas, knowledge of a variety of tools and techniques, and a sense of humour * Identifies programme venues outside of the library that have young adult appeal * Evaluates all programmes and uses those results to improve future programmes for young adults
Competency: Young Adult Programming	**Develops and promotes gaming for young adult programming**
Associated Skills and Knowledge	* Understands and promotes the value of games and gaming for young adults * Investigates the options for gaming programmes and makes informed choices about games appropriate to the young adult audiences * Identifies a variety of games of particular interest to young adults, creates interesting and engaging game-based programmes, and invents creative ways to promote them to the target audiences * Develops gaming programmes to accomplish specified objectives * Evaluates the outcomes of young adult gaming programmes, involves teens in the evaluation process, and recommends improvements for future efforts

Table Contd..

TECHNICAL SERVICES COMPETENCIES

Those who work in Technical Services are involved in the full life cycle of information from its creation or acquisition through its destruction. This includes organizing, cataloging, dissemination and preservation. Because these functions interface with many other library operations, related competencies can be found in Public Services and Systems and IT.

ACQUISITION AND PROCESSING

Although this all happens behind the scenes, the more seamless the acquisition and processing of library materials is, the more satisfied the library user will be.

Competency: Acquisition and Processing	**Manages the processes by which library materials are ordered, received and tracked**
Associated Skills and Knowledge	* Establishes procedures for ordering and handling all library resources for expedient availability to library users * Establishes appropriate and consistent procedures for the physical processing of library materials; understands the marketing value of proper preparation of library materials * Understands how publishers, vendors and other sources involved in the purchasing process affect the quality, costs and efficiencies of the end result * Develops strategies for keeping up with changes in publishers, vendors and other sources for purchasing library materials * Establishes procedures for acquiring a variety of materials * Determines the most efficient, cost-effective and customer-centered means to acquire requested materials * Identifies and implements new

	technologies in processing * Establishes procedures for tracking materials and for negotiating resolutions for returns, incorrect orders, items not received and price discrepancies
Competency: Acquisition and Processing	**Manages the expenditures and accounting for acquisitions**
Associated Skills and Knowledge	* Manages the allocation of the materials budget and negotiates the purchase and licensing of materials * Maintains accurate budgets and accounts, including encumbered funds as well as expended funds * Demonstrates proficiency with software programmes appropriate for managing acquisitions accounts * Leverages partnerships with other libraries or organizations for discounted or cooperative purchasing options

CATALOGING

The efforts of catalogers enable users to locate what they need in the library collections. As the world of information evolved from physical materials occupying physical places to digital resources in a multiplicity of formats, catalogers have adapted with richer metadata sets, linking repositories and institutions, and delivering resources in-person and remotely.

Competency: Cataloging	**Catalogs all types of library materials according to relevant bibliographi control standards**
Associated Skills and Knowledge	* Understands the general structure, relationships and relative importance of library catalog systems and software * Applies relevant national and international bibliographic control standards to organize materials and

Table Contd...

	resources at a level appropriate for the library and the materials * Understands and uses the cataloging functions of integrated library systems * Understands and performs copy or original cataloging as needed, providing descriptive cataloging, classification and subject analysis appropriate to the content * Maintains authority control and provides appropriate references in the library's catalog * Applies in-depth knowledge of cataloging standards to assess bibliographic records for accuracy and completeness * Selects appropriate subject headings and call numbers for accurate identification and placement within the collection; understands the broader context in which collections function * Uses cataloging tools and services available from bibliographic utilities; assesses and learns new tools promoted by bibliographic utilities
Competency: Cataloging	**Manages the catalog to ensure that library users have optimal access to the collection**
Associated Skills and Knowledge	* Understands the core purpose of the catalog to provide library users with the best possible access to the collection * Pursues knowledge of current library trends and innovations; identifies how they may impact bibliographic control and resource management and how they may be adopted to advantage * Identifies and learns new tools and technical skills that will improve cataloging productivity and enhance

Table Contd...

	access to library resources * Articulates the need and works to provide bibliographic links in the catalog to electronic and other remote resources

COLLECTION MANAGEMENT

Although Technical Services personnel are seldom leading the selection of library materials, they play an intermediary role between collection development and the acquisition, dissemination and maintenance of resources.

Competency: Collection Management	**Establishes procedures and resources to facilitate collection development**
Associated Skills and Knowledge	* Understands the acquisition and collection development processes and policies for the library * Assists in the identification and selection of library materials to be added to the collection * Identifies special research and instructional needs and coordinates with teachers to provide access to materials * Evaluates data, including circulation statistics and requests, to determine the allotment of funds and to prioritize requests for formats and subject areas * Determines the availability of electronic resources through statewide contracts or through regional consortia * Follows trends in traditional and digital publishing and gathers best practices of similar institutions
Competency:	**Ensures that the collection is current,**
Collection Management	**useful and in good condition**
Associated	* Defines criteria and establishes

Table Contd...

Skills and Knowledge	procedures to evaluate library materials for retention, replacement, duplication or deselection * Conducts inventories of library materials, analyses usage and maintains appropriate records in support of maintenance procedures * Identifies items in need of repair and evaluates the cost effectiveness of repair, replacement and/or withdrawal * Manages gifts to the collection, including relations with donors, appraisals of value, record-keeping and arrangements for long term stewardship * Recognizes items of true historic value and recommends their preservation and conservation for this library or for another collection

E-RESOURCE MANAGEMENT

E-resources have assumed such prominence in the world of information that some libraries have reduced their physical collections to a mere sliver. The management of e-resources introduces new challenges in terms of "ownership," budget priorities, distribution, access and more.

Competency: E-Resource Management	**Develops and manages the library's collections of electronic resources and provides distributed access to them**
Associated Skills and Knowledge	* Understands the concepts behind e- and resource management systems and maintains awareness of available products * Selects, organizes and maintains the library's collection of e-resources * Gathers, maintains and provides reports on the library's subscriptions and/or purchases of e-resources * Interprets usage data for electronic

Table Contd...

	journal and database subscriptions and recommends adjustments to allocation of resources or renegotiation of license agreements * Evaluates, configures and maintains an OpenURL service for linking online resources to identifying services * Evaluates, implements and maintains metasearch tools for streamlined access to library resources * Understands and implements options for authenticated access to e-resources appropriate for the parent institution * Evaluates, configures and maintains services for restricting access to e-resources applicable within the institutional context

PRESERVATION

Preservation covers a wide range of activities: repairing the physical damage to well-used materials; transforming physical materials into digital format; or preserving the historic record or other notable resource collections.

Competency: Preservation	**Establishes and implements appropriate techniques for the preservation and conservation of library materials**
Associated Skills and Knowledge	* Understands preservation and conservation issues, including requirements for archival preservation and proper handling of materials * Identifies and applies appropriate methods and techniques for storage and conservation of all library materials * Applies timely and effective techniques for the repair and preservation of library materials in all formats * Identifies environmental factors that

Table Contd...

	impact the condition of library materials and provides guidelines for addressing these factors * Understands and adheres to library policies for disaster preparedness and recovery of library materials
Competency: Preservation	**Identifies, selects and maintains special collections**
Associated Skills and Knowledge	* Demonstrates broad knowledge of the history of the book, rare books and book arts * Identifies collections of historic value or special significance to the institution and articulates the value of building maintaining the collections * Identifies and applies special requirements for storage of materials that are of significant historic value * Establishes policies and procedures to ensure the security of rare and valuable items
Competency: Preservation	**Establishes and implements policies and procedures for digitization of librar resources**
Associated Skills and Knowledge	* Understands and articulates the value of providing digital access to the collections * Understands the theory, processes, standards and best practices of digital creation, management, storage and preservation * Identifies, procures and maintains digitization hardware and software and/ or determines reasons and vendors for outsourcing digitization processes· * Manages digitization projects, including scope, costs,

Table Contd...

	collaboration with other departments/institutions, timeline, delivery and promotion strategies

TECHNOLOGY COMPETENCIES: CORE SKILLS

Now that technology has permeated all levels of the library's operations and services, every position requires some level of comfort with computers. This part defines a core of technology competency that all staff need in order to contribute to the overall effectiveness of the organization, whether they are behind the scenes or interacting with the public.

CORE E-MAIL

Competency: Core E-mail	**Performs basic functions of e-mail applications**
Associated Skills and Knowledge	* Receives, opens, forwards as needed, or deletes e-mail messages * Composes or replies to, addresses and sends e-mail messages * Sends, receives and saves attachments * Manages addresses/contacts * Creates folders and files messages for retrieval as needed * Identifies and uses Web-based e-mail programmes as well as desktop e-mail applications
Competency: Core E-mail	**Performs basic calendar operations and task management**
Associated Skills and Knowledge	* Creates, accepts and sets recurring appointments * Sets reminders for calendar items * Plans and schedules meetings and invites attendees * Creates and manages task lists
CORE HARDWARE	
Competency:	**Understands and uses basic computer**

Core Hardware	hardware and peripherals
Associated Skills and Knowledge	* Understands basic technology terminology * Recognizes and understands the functions of basic computer components * Performs basic operations on computer hardware * Recognizes common removable storage devices and identifies the appropriate drives * Performs basic troubleshooting procedures for computer hardware and peripherals * Understands the set-up and use of data projectors and other audio-visual equipment used for library programming * Performs basic printer maintenance tasks

CORE INTERNET

Competency: Core Internet	**Understands and uses the Internet and the World Wide Web**
Associated Skills and Knowledge	* Understands the basic structure of the Internet and of the World Wide Web * Identifies and uses common browsers for accessing the Web; understands and uses URLs * Uses common functions of Web browsers * Downloads and saves files from the Internet, including image, audio and video * Downloads e-books and audiobooks
Competency: Core Internet	**Performs basic information searches**

Table Contd...

Associated Skills and Knowledge	* Identifies and uses search engines, Web directories and online databases * Evaluates information for quality and credibility * Demonstrates familiarity with a variety of search strategies * Utilizes the Find feature to locate information on a Web page
Competency: Core Interne	**Understands common security protocols related to Internet use**
Associated Skills and Knowledge	* Understands the purpose of anti-virus and anti-spam software * Identifies pop-up windows and blocks or allows them as necessary * Understands the function of cookies * Recognizes secure transaction sites and understands what type of activities are conducted there * Understands and applies the library's computer and Internet usage policies

CORE OPERATING SYSTEMS

Competency: Core Operating Systems	**Understands and performs basic operating system functions**
Associated Skills and Knowledge	* Performs basic operating system functions * Performs common file and folder management tasks and recognizes common file extensions * Performs basic computer maintenance tasks

CORE SOFTWARE APPLICATIONS

Competency: Core Software	**Understands and performs basic functions and tasks of common software programmes**

Table Contd...

Applications	
Associated Skills and Knowledge	* Identifies different types and uses of common software applications * Performs the manipulations common to most applications * Understands and uses the features common to most applications * Performs basic procedures to address software application problems
Competency: Core Software Applications	**Performs basic word processing operations**
Associated Skills and Knowledge	* Creates, opens and saves or deletes files * Selects, cuts, copies, pastes or deletes text * Performs operations to structure, format and spell-check documents
Competency: Core Software Applications	**Performs basic printing operations from common applications**
Associated Skills and Knowledge	* Identifies printers available for a given workstation * Identifies local versus networked printers * Adjusts the set-up, previews print jobs and performs print operations

CORE WEB TOOLS

Competency: Core Web Tools	Understands and uses common social networking and online collaboration tools
Associated Skills and Knowledge	* Locates and reads blogs and listens to podcasts; demonstrates familiarity with micro-blogging * Demonstrates familiarity with RSS and uses feedreaders or other means to manage feeds

Table Contd...

	* Demonstrates familiarity with instant messaging tools, social networking sites and social bookmarking * Demonstrates familiarity with photo-sharing, music-sharing and video-sharing * Demonstrates familiarity with online file-sharing and collaboration tools * Uses webconferencing programmes for synchronous, online meetings or learning * Identifies and uses help menus, tutorials and support communities to acquire the necessary skills * Locates and follows information sources to stay informed of new technologies and social tools

TECHNOLOGY COMPETENCIES: SYSTEMS & IT

Beyond the core technology competencies, there is an increasing variety and complexity of technology systems that drive library operations. Depending on the size and type of library, there may be strict divisions between the responsibilities of IT staff and other library staff, or the line may be more indistinct as it is for "accidental" systems librarians in small libraries. Find the right combination of competencies from this compilation to meet the needs of your library.

Many aspects of Systems and IT involve management skills.

DIGITAL RESOURCE TECHNOLOGY

With so many of a library's resources in digital format, especially in larger academic libraries, there is a host of new skills and knowledge involved in creating or selecting, organizing, managing and providing access to these digital resources. It's an interdepartmental effort within the library, crossing divisions between cataloging, preservation, systems

Table Contd...

and technology. Project management is pervasive in these efforts.

Competency: Digital Resource Technology	Selects, organizes and maintains the library's collection of digital resources
Associated Skills and Knowledge	* Defines, selects and manages a digital asset management infrastructure that supports access to the digital content * Establishes standards and best practices to assure effective retrieval of digital content * Understands and applies appropriate metadata schemas and the standards for expressing and storing these data * Demonstrates knowledge of multimedia file formats and of tools and processes available for digital file format conversion * Demonstrates working knowledge of best practices for digitizing various media * Defines and implements policies related to digital holdings, including collection, digital preservation, rights management, emergency plans, etc. * Works collaboratively with enterprise systems, Web services, e-resource management and interface services personnel
Competency: Digital Resource Technology	**Demonstrates working knowledge of programming languages applicable to digital resources**
Associated Skills and Knowledge	* Demonstrates working knowledge of XML, XSLT, XML Schema * Deploys XML-based APIs in integrating systems and services * Demonstrates working knowledge of

Table Contd...

	Web-based publishing tools and coding * Demonstrates working knowledge of Unix, relational database systems, METS and OAI * Performs system monitoring, testing and debugging
Competency: Digital Resource Technology	**Develops and manages interface services to provide integrated access to the library's resources**
Associated Skills and Knowledge	* Pursues the integration of discovery interface systems with the ILS and other sources of bibliographic metadata * Evaluates and implements federated search tools for streamlined access to library resources * Understands the principles of usability and the protocols for user testing; develops and maintains a robust practice of user testing on all interfaces * Pursues the integration of library resources with course management systems * Experiments with new tools for the delivery of library resources and services to users regardless of location and preferred platform * Defines and implements policies for resource delivery, authentication and identity management
Competency: Digital Resource Technology	**Pursues efforts to sustain and improve the digital resource systems and services**
Associated Skills and Knowledge	* Prepares the budget for support of digital resource technologies and in alignment with the library's overall budget * Generates objective data for the

Table Contd..

	evaluation of and ongoing redesign of user interfaces * Investigates, evaluates and keeps abreast of new developments in digital library systems and services * Investigates and evaluates new developments in discovery interface systems in alignment with user behaviour and expectations

ENTERPRISE COMPUTING

Many large libraries operate at the enterprise level of computing-a level of complexity introduced by the need to integrate multiple computer systems and networks and to accommodate access by a variety of remote users.

Competency: Enterprise Computing	**Performs enterprise computing management to integrate computing systems across a large organization**
Associated Skills and Knowledge	* Creates network connections among *local area networks* (LANs), mainframes and stand-alone computers, including legacy environments * Understands the architecture and scale of the enterprise system * Delivers hardware and software configurations for a variety of platforms and networks * Performs life-cycle management of firmware and applications, upgrading or replacing as warranted * Establishes and maintains an organization-wide e-mail system * Understands and manages the complexities of operating system upgrades on servers and workstations as appropriate * Manages multiple vendor relationships

	and licensing agreements * Ensures password protection and data security across the organization * Functions adeptly in basic programming and scripting languages * Understands and practices the principles of project management
Competency: Enterprise Computing	**Performs enterprise-level software management**
Associated Skills and Knowledge	* Understands and practices software version management * Defines schedules and implements software upgrade processes * Understands enterprise systems in use in parent organization and integrates library systems and services where appropriate and efficient * Understands principles of identity management and integrates library's need for authentication and authorization with parent institution's identity management system * Understands and practices good code distribution by designing and implementing architectures that efficiently distribute processing across available computing resources * Defines and manages processes to track incidents from receipt to resolution

HARDWARE

Every position in the library depends on the proper installation and reliable functioning of all of the computer equipment. The hardware is the skeletal structure on which all computing functions are hung.

Competency: Hardware	**Installs, configures and maintains computer equipment and peripheral devices**
Associated Skills and Knowledge	* Understands in detail the functions of the computer hardware, internal components, peripherals and external storage drives * Performs advanced troubleshooting methodologies for computer hardware and peripherals * Installs and configures a variety of computer components * Understands hardware performance and the impact of individual components on performance * Pursues the most effective and efficient ways to obtain technical support * Isolates, identifies and articulates problems with hardware
Competency: Hardware	**Installs, configures and maintains printers and scanners**
Associated Skills and Knowledge	* Connects printers, adds printer drivers and configures properties * Connects scanners, adds scanner drivers and configures properties * Supports users' access to networked printers and scanners * Isolates, identifies and articulates problems with printers and scanners

NETWORKING AND SECURITY

The network is the electronic nerve center of the library's operations and its intricacy increases with every new technology and new security threat. It's a high-wire act to keep on top of it all.

Competency: Networking and Security	**Installs, configures and maintains the library's local area networks (LAN)**
Associated Skills and Knowledge	* Understands network terminology, protocols, addresses and ports * Identifies and configures the key components for set-up of the local area network (LAN) * Understands the infrastructure that supports the library's LAN and identifies site-specific network needs * Identifies the options for network administration of hardware and software * Understands core differences between workstation and server configurations * Understands the operations of client/server and peer-to-peer networks, and the advantages of each * Understands and applies the principles of user ID and account management schema and tools
Competency: Networking and Security	**Understands and supports the library's telecommunications and wide area networks (WAN)**
Associated Skills and Knowledge	* Understands the relationship between a LAN (local area network) and a WAN (wide area network) * Assesses the library's overall Internet connectivity needs and works with appropriate agencies to ensure the long-term sustainability of high-speed connections that meet those needs * Understands IP authentication and related software for secure network access * Understands the basic concepts and terminology of telecommunications

Table Contd...

	* Understands the infrastructure that supports the library's telephony and wide area networks * Identifies a library's site-specific telecommunication needs
Competency: Networking and Security	**Installs, configures and maintains the library's wireless networks**
Associated Skills and Knowledge	* Identifies the library's site-specific factors and their impact on wireless signal transmission * Identifies the set-up options and the necessary equipment * Installs and configures the wireless components * Applies effective security protocols for all wireless networks * Identifies equipment needs for individual computers
Competency: Networking and Security	**Troubleshoots problems with the library's networks in order to maintain optimal operations for staff and users**
Associated Skills and Knowledge	* Applies strategies to isolate, identify and articulate problems with networks * Conducts effective technical support interviews * Locates and uses manuals and FAQs, and contacts appropriate sources for further technical support
Competency: Networking and Security	**Develops and implements practices for network security to ensure maximum protection of library systems and staff and user information**
Associated Skills and Knowledge	* Understands network security architecture and protocols * Understands hardware- and software-based security solutions

Table Contd...

	* Establishes a password management system and maintains secure passwords * Identifies, addresses and communicates potential and real security and privacy threats related to computer and Internet use * Identifies and develops a plan for regular and automated security maintenance tasks * Consults appropriate sources to stay informed of emerging security threats and the most current strategies and tools

OPERATING AND AUTOMATION SYSTEMS

Providing administration and support of the automation systems and the operating systems on the library computers and understanding the dependencies and workflows among systems are critical to maintaining a functional computing environment.

Competency: Operating and Automation Systems	**Installs, configures and maintains all operating systems functioning in the library environment**
Associated Skills and Knowledge	* Demonstrates general knowledge of operating systems available for use, including open-source and mobile systems * Selects, installs and configures appropriate operating systems * Understands the terminology, specifications and functions of the operating systems in use * Devises and executes a plan for operating system maintenance and update tasks * Troubleshoots problems with the operating systems

	* Devises and sustains effective back-up strategies * Understands and executes the process of imaging PCs * Manages the process for upgrading systems, including determining applications compatibility and planning data migration
Competency: Operating and Automation Systems	**Demonstrates advanced understanding of the library automation systems (ILS)**
Associated Skills and Knowledge	* Articulates the value and purpose of a library automation system * Understands the interrelationships and workflows of the various modules of the library's automation system * Uses standard or customised reports from the automation system for management of library operations * Establishes procedures to ensure current backups and regular updates to the automation system; schedules overnight procedures and processes * Ensures process for maintaining a log of system failures and problems * Performs regular evaluations of the systems and communicates with the vendor on failure, problems and services * Demonstrates familiarity with operating and database systems used by the ILS

PUBLIC ACCESS COMPUTING

Computers for public use are among the main attractions that bring people into the library. Public computing has come a long way since its introduction in the mid-1990s. In addition to the foundational knowledge in the other technology parts, the public's use of computers puts extra and unique demands on the set-up of the hardware, software, networks and security.

Competency: Public Access Computing	**Installs and configures the library's public access computers and networks to best meet the needs of library users**
Associated Skills and Knowledge	* Determines the needs for public access computers, wireless access and programmes * Understands the nature of security threats to a public access system * Selects and installs appropriate computer, networking and peripheral hardware for public use * Installs and configures appropriate operating systems and software applications for public use * Selects, installs and configures appropriate public access computer security measures * Configures public networks to secure and isolate them from nonpublic computers and networks * Selects, installs and configures access, bandwidth and content restriction measures as directed by library policy * Identifies and implements options for eservation, time and print management systems * Applies ADA recommendations for physical and electronic equipment * Understands pros and cons of open-source vs. proprietary software and identifies solutions that best meet user needs within organizational resources
Competency: Public Access Computing	**Maintains and troubleshoots the library's public computers, networks and security**
Associated	* Develops and executes plans for

Table Contd...

Skills and Knowledge	maintenance and update tasks of public computer hardware, operating systems, security and applications * Tracks and maintains software licenses to ensure currency * Keeps current of advances in tools and applications of benefit to users and determines the implications of deploying them on the public computers
Competency: Public Access Computing	**Develops, implements and communicates policies and practices for public access computing**
Associated Skills and Knowledge	* Establishes and publishes acceptable use policies for public access computers and wireless networks * Understands filtering issues in relation to E- Rate and LSTA funds; installs and configures filters as necessary * Understands the issues related to access to social networking sites and programmes

SERVER ADMINISTRATION

The complexity of computer networks breeds an increasing array of servers to deliver particular services to users. It may be necessary to select, configure and/or maintain any of a variety of server types appropriate to the library's needs.

Competency: Server Administration	**Configures and maintains the library's e-mail servers**
Associated Skills and Knowledge	* Understands the terminology and protocols of e-mail systems * Identifies and configures the key components for set-up of the e-mail server * Applies appropriate and effective security protocols for e-mail transmission
Competency:	**Configures and maintains the library's**

Table Contd...

Server Administration	Web servers
Associated Skills and Knowledge	* Understands the terminology and protocols of Web servers * Identifies and configures the key components for set-up of the Web server
Competency: Server Administration	**Configures and maintains the library's file servers**
Associated Skills and Knowledge	* Understands the terminology and protocols of file servers * Identifies and configures the key components for set-up of the file server
Competency: Server Administration	**Configures and maintains the library's print servers**
Associated Skills and Knowledge	* Understands the terminology and protocols of print servers * Identifies and configures the key components for set-up of the print server to host shared printers and process print requests over a network
Competency: Server Administration	**Configures and maintains the library's database servers**
Associated Skills and Knowledge	* Understands the terminology and protocols of database servers * Identifies and configures the key components for set-up of the database server
Competency: Server Administration	**Configures and maintains the library's other servers as needed**
Associated Skills and Knowledge	* Identifies and configures other server types as needed

Table Contd...

SOFTWARE APPLICATIONS

Many positions in the library require varying levels of proficiency with software applications, depending on which tasks need to be accomplished.

In addition, there is a layer of administration necessary to ensure that software is properly installed, licensed and ready to run when a user needs it.

Administration of Software Applications

Competency:	**Manages software applications for staff**
Administration of Software Applications	**and other nonpublic computers**
Associated Skills and Knowledge	* Evaluates and selects software applications appropriate for staff and other users * Installs and configures software applications * Isolates, identifies and articulates problems with software applications * Understands and manages licensing for all software applications * Understands the open-source options for software in libraries
Competency: Administration of Software Applications	**Provides administration for optimum performance of database programmes**
Associated Skills and Knowledge	* Monitors and implements procedures to improve performance * Implements measures to secure, back-up, restore and repair database information * Implements methods for sharing database information

Table Contd...

Database Application Proficiency

Competency: Database Application Proficiency	**Demonstrates beginner-level proficiency with database applications**
Associated Skills and Knowledge	* Designs a database to meet specified needs and identifies the data relation ships * Creates a basic database and accesses different views of the data * Creates and modifies tables, relational tables and forms * Runs basic queries and reports on data
Competency: Database Application Proficiency	**Demonstrates intermediate to advanced proficiency with database applications**
Associated Skills and Knowledge	* Applies advanced processes for retrieving and validating data * Applies advanced manipulations of tables and forms * Applies advanced methods for queries and reports on data

Document Management Programme Proficiency

Competency: Document Management Programme Proficiency	**Demonstrates appropriate level of proficiency with document management programmes**
Associated Skills and Knowledge	* Understands the file and workspace structure of the document management system * Adds new files, retrieves existing files, checks files in/out and edits files * Understands and uses collaboration and information-sharing features

Table Contd...

Electronic Publishing Programme Proficiency

Competency: Electronic Publishing Programme Proficiency	**Demonstrates beginner-level proficiency with electronic publishing applications**
Associated Skills and Knowledge	* Creates or opens files, chooses layouts and saves files * Inserts and manipulates text blocks and tables * Inserts and manipulates graphical shapes, images and clip art * Understands and applies the printing options
Competency: Electronic Publishing Programme Proficiency	**Demonstrates intermediate to advanced proficiency with electronic publishing applications**
Associated Skills and Knowledge	* Works with page masters and advanced layout configurations * Applies advanced techniques to text blocks, tables, paths and graphics * Creates customised publications, including books with table of contents and index * Optimizes publications for a variety of output options, including the Web and commercial printing

E-mail Programme Proficiency

Competency: Proficiency	**Demonstrates beginner-level proficiency E-mail Programme with e-mail programmes**
Associated Skills and Knowledge	* Receives, opens, forwards as needed or deletes e-mail messages * Composes or replies to, addresses and sends e-mail messages

Table Contd...

	* Sends, receives and saves attachments * Manages addresses/contacts * Creates folders and files messages for retrieval as needed * Identifies and uses Web-based e-mail programmes as well as desktop e-mail applications
Competency: Proficiency	**Demonstrates intermediate proficiency E-mail Programme with e-mail programmes**
Associated Skills and Knowledge	* Performs calendar operations to manage meetings and appointments * Configures rules, alerts and junk mail settings * Uses tasks, notes and journal features * Performs basic page set-up and print operations
Competency: Proficiency	**Demonstrates advanced proficiency with E-mail Programme e-mail programmes**
Associated Skills and Knowledge	* Manages e-mail archiving and data security * Uses remote access, instant messaging, fax and voice-mail features * Uses advanced features to manage contacts * Uses advanced calendar features to manage meetings and group schedules * Performs advanced printing operations

Photo-editing Programme Proficiency

Competency: Photo-editing Programme Proficiency	**Demonstrates beginner-level proficiency with photo-editing programmes**
Associated Skills and Knowledge	* Opens, saves and prints images * Resizes, crops, uses basic selection tools, and performs basic colour and contrast adjustments

Table Contd...

	* Reverses changes made to an image
Competency: Photo-editing Programme Proficiency	**Demonstrates intermediate to advanced proficiency with photo-editing programmes**
Associated Skills and Knowledge	* Uses the array of tools in the toolbox and image adjustment options * Uses a variety of detailed selection options * Uses layers, creates montages and applies special effects * Optimizes image for a variety of output options

Presentation Programme Proficiency

Competency: Presentation Programme Proficiency	**Demonstrates beginner-level proficiency with presentation programmes**
Associated Skills and Knowledge	* Creates, opens, runs and saves a basic presentation slide set * Applies slide designs, layouts and basic formatting * Inserts images, clip art and charts and modifies as needed * Understands and applies the printing options
Competency: Presentation Programme Proficiency	**Demonstrates intermediate to advanced proficiency with presentation programmes**
Associated Skills and Knowledge	* Creates and applies custom themes or templates and manages slide masters * Applies slide transitions, custom animations and action buttons * Applies advanced manipulation of images, clip art and charts * Inserts hyperlinks, sound clips and

Table Contd...

	video clips; records narration * Optimizes presentations for a variety of output options, including the Web or automated kiosk display

Spreadsheet Programme Proficiency

Competency: Spreadsheet Programme Proficiency	**Demonstrates beginner-level proficiency with spreadsheet programmes**
Associated Skills and Knowledge	* Understands the basic structure of workbooks, worksheets, rows and columns * Enters, saves, edits, finds and replaces, and filters data and text * Inserts rows, columns and worksheets * Copies and moves cells and worksheets * Applies basic formatting to cells
Competency: Spreadsheet Programme Proficiency	**Demonstrates intermediate proficiency with spreadsheet programmes**
Associated Skills and Knowledge	* Applies a variety of formatting options * Manages page settings, previews and print areas * Inserts hyperlinks, objects and images * Uses formulas and functions; finds maximum and minimum values * Creates basic charts to display worksheet data
Competency: Spreadsheet Programme Proficiency	**Demonstrates advanced proficiency with spreadsheet programmes**
Associated Skills and Knowledge	* Applies advanced formulas and functions * Performs advanced data analysis * Applies advanced number and condition formatting * Applies advanced data management

Table Contd...

	* Creates, edits and runs macros * Imports and exports data * Applies validation, protection and collaboration options

Web-based Office Application Proficiency

Competency: Web-based Office Application Proficiency	**Demonstrates proficiency with Web-based office applications for online collaboration**
Associated Skills and Knowledge	* Understands the advantages of using Web-based applications for collaboration * Identifies and selects appropriate online application tools * Identifies and uses help menus, tutorials and support communities to acquire the necessary skills

Web Site Design Programme Proficiency

Competency: Web Site Design Programme	**Demonstrates beginner-level proficiency with Web site design Proficiency programmes**
Associated Skills and Knowledge	* Creates site, adds pages, imports, edits and organizes content * Inserts and manipulates links, images, graphics and tables
Competency: Web Site Design Programme	**Demonstrates intermediate to advanced proficiency with Web site Proficiency design programmes**
Associated Skills and Knowledge	* Understands and applies Cascading Style Sheets (CSS) * Adds interactive features and flash objects * Performs advanced site testing, management and maintenance

Table Contd...

Word Processing Programme Proficiency

Competency: Word Processing Programme	Demonstrates beginner-level proficiency with word processing Proficiency programmes
Associated Skills and Knowledge	* Creates, opens and saves files * Selects, cuts, copies, pastes or deletes text * Performs operations to structure, format, spell-check and print documents
Competency: Word Processing Programme	**Demonstrates intermediate proficiency with word processing Proficiency programmes**
Associated Skills and Knowledge	* Inserts header, footer and page numbers * Inserts and formats columns and tables * Creates and applies styles * Inserts and manipulates images, charts and graphs * Formats and prints envelopes and labels
Competency: Word Processing Programme	**Demonstrates advanced proficiency with word processing programmes Proficiency**
Associated Skills and Knowledge	* Creates and uses master documents * Creates and formats footnotes, endnotes and a table of contents * Uses advanced features for formatting pages and tables * Creates and uses macros, forms, frames and controls * Understands and uses document security and collaboration features

TECHNOLOGY PLANNING

Technology planning is closely tied to other competency areas. The planning process is all about project management but with the demands of IT factored in; purchasing is entwined with budget and finance but informed by technical expertise.

Everyone agrees technology planning is critical in today's library.

Competency: Technology Planning	Formulates and implements an ongoing technology planning process
Associated Skills and Knowledge	* Identifies key players to form a productive technology planning team and orients the team with pertinent and current information and training * Collects relevant data and defines the criteria for upgrading or purchasing new equipment * Evaluates opportunities and requirements for expanded or new technology-based services * Establishes clear priorities for technology plans that align with the library's ongoing operations and strategic plan and the needs of the library users * Establishes sources and contacts to keep abreast of emerging technologies and how they impact library technology planning * Balances risk-taking with realism and alignment with library's priorities
Competency: Technology Planning	**Develops and maintains a library technology plan that meets current and future needs of the library community**
Associated Skills and Knowledge	* Investigates and analyses the needs of the community and environment to understand current and future needs and trends * Creates appropriate goals, objectives and activities that reflect analysis of community needs * Strives for compatible and stable

Table Contd...

	systems and configurations for maximum reliability * Develops and applies evaluation measures that gauge the success of the plan * Anticipates and predicts changes, trends and influences to effectively allocate resources and implement appropriate library technology initiatives * Incorporates ergonomics into technology facilities planning
Competency: Technology Planning	**Develops strategies and processes for purchasing technology for the library**
Associated Skills and Knowledge	* Prepares the budget for purchase recommendations based on the technology plan, factoring in total cost of ownership * Adheres to the library's established rules and procedures for purchasing, including procurement rules and bidding processes * Prepares a Request for Proposal (RFP) to support sound purchase decisions * Identifies and negotiates with technology vendors to obtain products and equipment that best meet the needs of the users * Leverages consortia and statewide procurement options * Maintains accurate records of transactions, specifications and standards * Understands the processes for and implications of applying for government funding programmes

TECHNOLOGY POLICIES

Fairness, efficiency, security and more depend on the clear definition and application of policies for technology use.

Competency: Technology Policies	**Creates, evaluates and implements policies and procedures for library technology**
Associated Skills and Knowledge	* Establishes network usage policies that balance convenience and usability with security concerns and wise stewardship of resources * Articulates and applies library policies on privacy, intellectual freedom and filtering as they relate to technology access and use * Seeks staff and stakeholder feedback during policies and procedures development * Explains the rationale underlying library technology policies and procedures and communicates effectively in nontechnical language * Continuously evaluates the needs for new or revised policies and procedures relative to changing technologies * Develops, reviews and maintains technology procedure manuals * Creates and regularly evaluates disaster preparedness and recovery plans for library technology

TECHNOLOGY TRAINING

There is a continual need for instruction as technology deployment intensifies in the library. Those who "get it" are in the best position to help those who don't. Seizing opportunities for informal knowledge exchange can often deliver the just-in-time learning that will ultimately provide better service to the library user.

Competency: Technology Training	**Provides training for staff and users on library technologies**
Associated Skills and Knowledge	* Articulates and demonstrates technical concepts and procedures to all levels of staff * Assesses technology trends that will affect the library and its users and advises all appropriate stakeholders in the organization * Aligns technology training with the library's overall objectives and efforts for staff and user training * Develops and delivers training events, following principles of learning theory and interactivity * Assists staff and public users in the use of software applications * Identifies resources available to users for instruction and training on software applications * Provides opportunities for staff to explore new technologies in the library environment

WEB DESIGN AND DEVELOPMENT

Library Web sites range from simple to complex, but they all share an awareness of how important it is in today's Web-enabled world to connect with the library community through the Internet.

Competency: Web Design and Development	**Designs a Web site for the library to provide virtual, 24/7 access to a portion of library services**
Associated Skills and Knowledge	* Understands the concept of a virtual branch and the importance of having a Web site for the library * Understands the basic criteria for designing and hosting Web sites

Table Contd...

	* Designs the user interface according to principles of usability and accessibility
Competency: Web Design and Development	**Implements and updates the library Web site**
Associated Skills and Knowledge	* Demonstrates proficiency with content management and/or Web site management systems * Demonstrates proficiency with Web site design software * Understands and applies the basic elements of HTML code * Understands the function of CSS and style sheets * Investigates emerging technologies for their potential to enhance delivery of information and services through the Web site
Competency: Web Design and	**Applies advanced Web technologies to the development of a library Web site Development**
Associated Skills and Knowledge	* Understands the architecture, protocols and terminology of the Internet * Uses appropriate scripting languages and applies standards for creating valid code to add functionality to the Web site * Evaluates and selects appropriate Web site management software * Writes code to ensure the usability and accessibility of the user interface * Understands and applies design parameters for Web site display on mobile devices * Understands and employs multimedia formats

Table Contd...

	* Builds dynamic pages with database integration * Sets up and monitors tracking of site statistics
Competency: Web Design and	**Implements and manages the library's presence on the Web to place the Development library's services in the path of the users**
Associated Skills and Knowledge	* Understands the importance of having a Web presence beyond the library Web site * Investigates and develops the library's presence on social networking sites * Evaluates and implements widgets and other tools for extending online access to library content
Competency: Web Development	**Demonstrates proficiency with video Design and and audio production programmes**
Associated Skills and Knowledge	* Records, transfers and edits video or audio files * Understands format options for video or audio files * Stores and displays video or audio files

11

Online Library Management System

INTRODUCTION

PURPOSE

The purpose of this application are as follows:

* The software is for automation of library.
* It provides following facilities to

Operator:

* Can enter details related to a particular book.
* Can provide membership to members.

Admin:

* Can read and write information about any member.
* Can update, create, delete the record of membership as per requirement and implementation plants.

SCOPE

The different areas where we can use this application are:

* Any education institute can make use of it for providing information about author, content of the available books.
* It can be used in offices and modifications can be easily done according to requirements.

TECHNOLOGY USED

* *Front End*: Servlets, HTML, Java script.
* *Back End*: MS Access, Apache Tomcat server.

ASSUMPTIONS

* This application is used to convert the manual pplication to the online application.
* Customised data will be used in this application.
* User does not have right to enter information bout books.

OVERVIEW

Project is related to library management which provides reading services to its members. Any person can become a member of the library by filling a prescribed form. They can get the book issued, so that they cab take home and return them.

FUNCTIONALITY

* Online membership.
* Keeps the track of issues and submission of books.

FEASIBILITY STUDY

In feasibility study phase we had undergone through various steps which are describe as under:

* Identify the origin of the information at different level.
* Identify the expectation of user from computerized system.
* Analyse the draw back of existing system (manual) system.

WORKING OF PRESENT MANUAL SYSTEM

The staffs of library are involved in the following tasks:

* Membership process: person have to fill membership form and they are provided with member id.

DRAWBACKS OF PRESENT SYSTEM

Some of the problems being faced in manual system are as follows:

* Fast report generation is not possible.
* Tracing a book is difficult.
* Information about issue/return of the books are not properly maintained.
* No central database can be created as information is not available in database.

PROPOSED SYSTEM

There will be three major components:

* Stock maintenance.
* Transaction entry.
* Reports.

Proposed system provides with following solutions:

* It provides "better and efficient" service to members.
* Reduce the workload of employee.
* Faster retrieval of information about the desired book.
* Provide facility for proper monitoring reduce paper work and provide data security.

DATA TABLES

Table 11.1. Members

Sl. No.	Coloum Name	Data Type	Length	Description
1.	Id_no	Text	50	Unique identification of the members
2.	Name	Text	70	Name of members
3.	Address	Text	100	Location of Members
4.	Date of Issue	Date/Time		Date of Registration
5.	Date of Expiry	Date/Time		Registration expiry date
6.	Status	Text	50	Permanent/Temporary

Table 11.2. Add Books

Sl. No.	Column Name	Date-Type	Description
1.	Book_name	Text	Title of the book
2.	Book_code	Text	Book identification number
3.	Author	Text	Author of books
4.	Date of arrival	Date/time	Date on which book was received
5.	Price	Text	Cost of books
6.	Rack_no	Text	Almirah no
7.	No_of_books	Text	Quantity of books
8.	Subject_code	Text	Unique identification no of particular subject

Table 11.3. Issue

Sl. No.	Column Type	Date Type	Description
1.	Id_no	Text	User identification number
2.	Book_name	Text	Title of books
3.	Issue_date	Date/time	Date on which book is issued
4 .	Due_date	Date/time	Due date on which book is to be returned

SNAPSHOTS

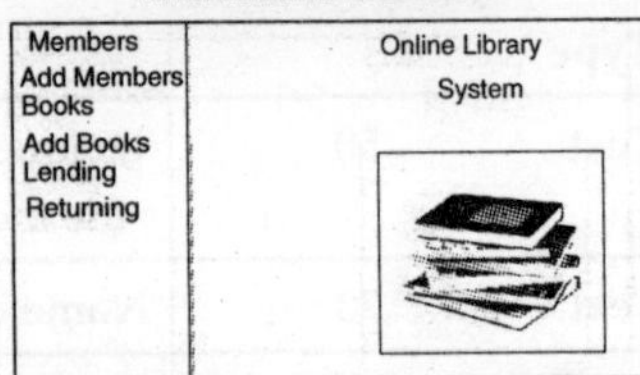

Fig. 11.1

Membership

IdNo Name
Address Date of Issue
Date of Expiry Status of Ms
Type of Ms Amount
ADD

Fig. 11.2

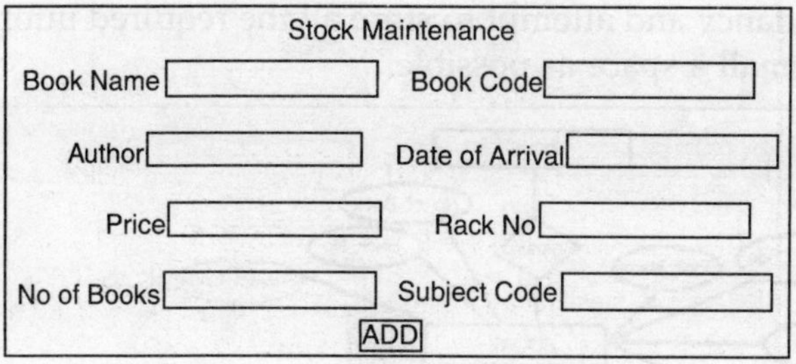

Stock Maintenance

Book Name | Book Code

Author | Date of Arrival

Price | Rack No

No of Books | Subject Code

ADD

Fig. 11.3

Issue of Books

Member Id No | Book Code

Date of Issue | Date of Expiry

ADD

Fig. 11.4

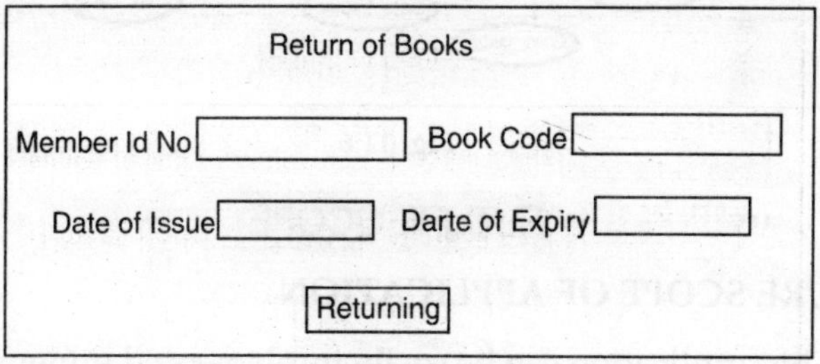

Return of Books

Member Id No | Book Code

Date of Issue | Darte of Expiry

Returning

Fig. 11.5

E-R DIGRAM

It is clear that the physical objects from the previous part – the member, books, library – correspond to entities in the Entity-Relationship model, and the operations to be done on those entities – holds, checkouts, and so on – correspond to relationships. However, a good design will minimize redundancy and attempt to store all the required information in as small a space as possible.

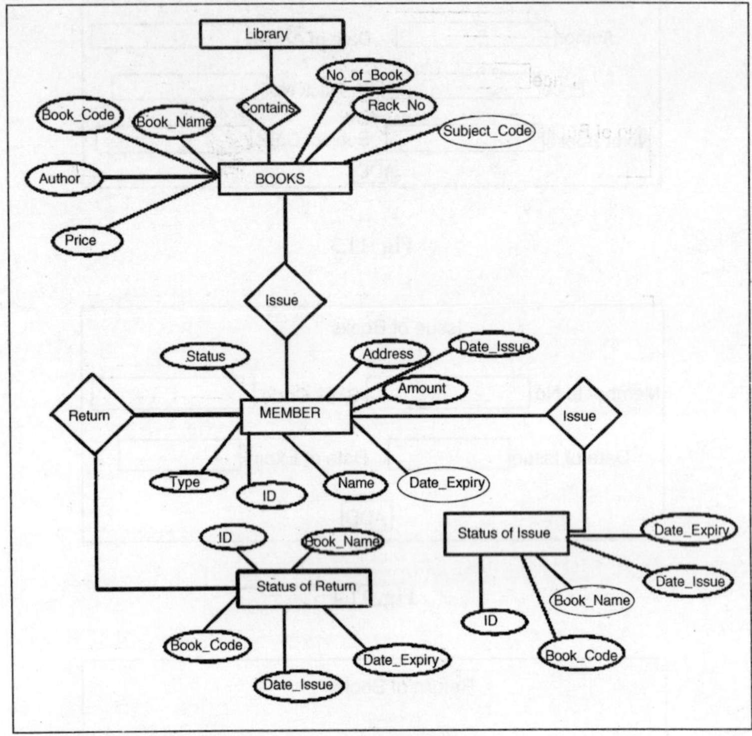

Fig. 11.6

FUTURE SCOPE

FUTURE SCOPE OF APPLICATION

This application can be easily implemented under various situations. We can add new features as and when we require. Reusability is possible as and when require in this application. There is flexibility in all the modules.

SOFTWARE SCOPE

* *Extensibility:* This software is extendable in ways that its original developers may not expect. The following

principles enhances extensibility like hide data structure, avoid traversing multiple links or methods, avoid case statements on object type and distinguish public and private operations.

* *Reusability*: Reusability is possible as and when require in this application. We can update it next version. Reusable software reduces design, coding and testing cost by amortizing effort over several designs. Reducing the amount of code also simplifies understanding, which increases the likelihood that the code is correct. We follow up both types of reusability: Sharing of newly written code within a project and reuse of previously written code on new projects.
* *Understandability*: A method is understandable if someone other than the creator of the method can understand the code. We use the method, which small and coherent helps to accomplish this.
* *Cost-effectiveness*: Its cost is under the budget and make within given time period. It is desirable to aim for a system with a minimum cost subject to the condition that it must satisfy the entire requirement.

Scope of this document is to put down the requirements, clearly identifying the information needed by the user, the source of the information and outputs expected from the system.

12

Academic Library Management in India: Challenges and Opportunities

INTRODUCTION

The 1990s have been one of the longest periods of sustained economic growth all over the world since the World War II. This economic growth has impacted all the spheres of human life including higher education. The academic libraries have also grown over a period of time in India and elsewhere. In general, information professionals and librarians have been coping well and addressing the many changes brought about by the electronic information revolution. There are increasing debates, discussions, seminars and other intellectual exercises on academic library management. Efforts are also made to identify the strengths and drawbacks of academic library system with the fond hope of improving the status of academic libraries in the developed and developing nations. The authors have made an attempt to present the salient features of academic libraries in India, focus the relevance of academic libraries in India and discuss the challenges and opportunities for academic libraries in India.

CONCEPT OF KNOWLEDGE MANAGEMENT

Broadly speaking, *Knowledge Management* (KM) is a process of creating, storing, sharing and re-using organisational knowledge to enable an organisation to achieve its goals and objectives of creating knowledgeable professionals and workforce. The advent of the "e-revolution", through the growth of global networks has accelerated the use of *knowledge management* (KM) especially in academic libraries. In the 21st Century KM is increasingly becoming a crucial tool in providing a dynamic and effective service to library users in India and rest of the world. Management gurus, such as Peter Drucker asserted, that for industries and institutions "the most valuable assets of a 21st century institution, whether business or non-business, will be its knowledge workers and their productivity". This affirmation was duly taken up by many academic libraries. Knowledge Management has already been successfully implemented in academic libraries and the policy makers, administrators, scientists and researchers have been actively involved in ensuring knowledge management through academic libraries.

ACADEMIC LIBRARIES IN INDIA

India is well known as the largest democracy in the world. Today there are a total of 237 universities, including 116 general universities, 12 science and technology universities, 7 open universities, 33 agricultural universities, five women's universities, one language universities and 11 medical universities along with 12,600 colleges that provide education in all disciplines. The number of teachers is 3.1 million, and 7.8 million students are enrolled in higher education. Schools of library and information sciences are also established all over the country with a view to create trained information workforce in the country. Indian academic libraries are managed on the basis of tested, tried and trusted principles of management.

INFORMATION AND LIBRARY NETWORK (INFLIBNET)

The University Grants Commission (UGS) has set up an autonomous Inter-University Centre in 1991 called INFLIBNET which is involved in modernizing university libraries in India. It connects the Indian libraries through a nation-wide high-speed data network. It promotes automation of libraries, develops standards, creates union catalogues of serials, theses, books, monographs and non-book materials; provides access to bibliographic information sources; creates database of projects, institutions, specialists; provides training, etc. Almost all academic libraries, especially university libraries, are members of INFLIBNET. It has also developed library automation software called SOUL which is distributed free of cost to its member libraries.

OTHER NETWORKS

Besides INFLIBNET, a number of other national networks and various library networks have also been developed including:

* NICNET (National Informatic Center's network),
* INDONET,
* ERNET (Education and Research Network),
* CALIBNET (Calcutta Library Network),
* DELNET (Developing Library Network), etc.

ADINET is associated with INFLIBNET, DELNET with NIC and MALIBNET with CFTRI. A good number of higher educational institutions are members of these networks. In particular, DELNET has 752 member libraries including 742 from India and 10 from outside which are engaged in compiling union catalogs, creating various databases of experts, providing training to library staff, ILL, online facilities, reference service, assistance in retrospective conversion, etc.

LIBRARY CONSORTIA

Many Indian university and college libraries are not in a position to subscribe to all the required journals and databases mainly due to lack of management support and financial constraints. The libraries are forming consortia in order to facilitate knowledge sharing at a much cheaper rate.

Some special libraries and organizations like:

* The *Indian Institute of Astrophysics* (IIA) Library,
* Inter-university Centre for Astronomy and Astrophysics (IUCAA) Library,
* National Centre for Radio Astrophysics (NCRA) Library,
* Physical Research Laboratory (PRL) Library,
* Raman Research Institute (RRI) Library,
* Tata Institute of Fundamental Research (TIFR) Library,
* Council of Scientific and Industrial Research,
* Department of Atomic Energy, etc., have established consortia to share electronic access to journal literature.

NISCAIR is developing a consortium for CSIR labs for accessing e-journals. Consortia in India are still a new concept that requires proper guidelines and methodologies. The UGC conducted a survey and found that about 142 university libraries had computer and Internet facilities which were interlinked to INFLIBNET. UGC has also launched a major initiative called UGCINFONET which provides high speed Internet connections in order to facilitate electronic access to professional literature including research journals, abstracts, review publications, and databases from all areas in science, technology, social sciences and humanities, and so on. Today, a number of professional journals are available over UGC-INFONET to all universities.

The subscription initiative under UGCInfonet is an important portal for sharing print as well as electronic resources amongst university libraries. INFLIBNET functions as a resource center with an aim to cater to the needs of its members for resources not accessible to them in electronic media or are available in print media.

INDEST CONSORTIUM

The *Indian National Digital Library in Science and Technology* (INDEST) Consortium was established by the *Ministry of*

Human Resource Development (MHRD). The ministry provides funds required for the subscription to electronic resources for 38 academic institutions, including the Indian Institute of Sciences, Indian Institute of Technology, Regional Engineering Colleges, Indian Institute of Managements, and about 60 centrally-funded/aided government institutions through the consortium. The INDEST consortium is the most ambitious initiative so far in the area of engineering and technology disciplines. The primary objective of libraries is to organize and provide access to information, and it remains the same although the format and methods have changed drastically.

RELEVANCE OF ACADEMIC LIBRARIES IN INDIA

Academic libraries are the treasure trove of knowledge which cater to the needs of scholars, scientists, technocrats, researchers, students and others who are directly associated with the mainstream of higher education. In this competitive age, the policy makers have to rise to the occasion and create a new generation of knowledge workers. The information personnel of the academic libraries are also called upon to equip themselves with the best tools, techniques, procedures and practices.

The ways in which people communicate, and acquire and share knowledge, will inevitably have an impact on the library, its services, and its staff. The academic libraries play an important role in the academic community by providing necessary forum and resources for faculty and students to do their research and advance their knowledge. In order to effectively meet the growing needs of the clients and achieve success in the management of academic libraries, the academic libraries need to actively address the many challenges for the design and delivery of innovative resources and services. Academic libraries are also required to play the role of scholarly partner in exploring new pathways to knowledge and acting upon this.

It is widely acknowledged that meaningful reference work and research support is absolutely essential to ensure successful dissemination of knowledge to the clients on the basis of meaningful team spirit and work. It is imperative that subject reference workers adapt to the reality of dealing with socially networked clients. Reference interaction has always been a conversation; moving towards reference in the social environment is therefore a natural development that has been shown to be not only practically viable, but also to benefit the community of users in the field of higher education. Academic libraries are required to develop know how and show how systems which are highly essential elements of meaningful academic library management.

CHALLENGES AND OPPORTUNITIES

The vision and mission of academic libraries are changing in India. These academic libraries now take on the key role of providing the competitive advantage to various universities, research and development organizations which play a pivotal role in the process of nation building. Academic libraries are positioning themselves to be the torchbearers and path makers of educational advancement by way of integrating knowledge systems and resources.

These academic libraries are required to do serious introspection on their roles, responsibilities and contributions. Comments and observations are noted very frequently on their strengths and limitations in various national and international forums. The vast literature gleaned from IFLA, ACRL and allied publications on academic libraries aptly reveal the changing roles and responsibilities of information professionals in the modern society. The academic libraries are also called upon to exploit all forms of digital and telecommunication technologies and explore new avenues and possibilities for the enhancement of knowledge resources which are available in different forms and places.

The builders and managers of academic libraries are also required to enrich computer security and authentication techniques which promote information diffusion. The information personnel are also required to enrich their professional competence and leadership qualities which would facilitate meaningful identification, location and evaluation of information resources in order to promote professional excellence among the user community. The "user-centred" paradigm has been adopted in the developed countries to create customizable interfaces and enrich the process of collection development in the academic libraries. The academic libraries really demand a well conceived, designed and maintained systems, practices and operations which would effectively meet the needs of different constituent groups and individual users. The administrators are mainly responsible for creating and sustaining software, hardware, human resources and data bases which would go a long way in promoting research and development in India. The proficiency of *library information science* (LIS) and information skills must be complemented by hardware and software skills for working in an *information technology* (IT) intensive environment.

CONCLUSION

The academic libraries have to be managed on the basis of constant introspection at the individual level and scientific evaluation at the institutional level in this age of knowledge management. Academic libraries in India are called upon to play a crucial and leading role over other types of libraries by transforming their information management skills, techniques, practices and resources. Redefining roles and responsibilities, constructive intervention of the organization leaders in institution building endeavors, positive involvement of information personnel in delivery system and constant evaluation of goods and services will make the Indian academic libraries highly appropriate and resourceful in future.

Bibliography

Acemoglu, D.: *Library Disaster Planning and Recovery Handbook*, New Delhi: Oxford University Press, 2002.

Ahluwalia, J.: *Insuring Library Collections and Buildings*, New York: UNDP, 2008.

Bardhan, P.: *Rural Libraries Management,* Amritsar: Guru Nanak Dev University, 2006.

Batra, G.: *Insurance and Risk Management for Libraries*, London: BBC Books, 2005.

Bhalla, G.S.: *Disaster Preparedness: Managing Library Liability,* Cambridge: Cambridge University Press, 2006.

Canagarajah, S.: *Management in the Library*, New Delhi: Council for Social Development, 2006.

Chadha G. K.: *Managing the Financial Risk in Library*, New Delhi: Oxford University Press, 2004.

Dahlman, C.: *Library Management in India: Strengths and Opportunitie*, London and New York: Longman, 2000.

Dasgupta, A.K.: *Insuring and Protecting Your Library's Collections*, London: Yale University Press, 2008.

Dearden, L.: *Training and Corporate Productivity in a Panel of Indian Libraries*, London: University College London, 2004.

Gupta, R.: *Library Administration and Management*, London: Sage Publications, 2002.

Gupta, S.P.: "*Libraries Face Many Exposures, Costly Losses*, Chicago: University of Chicago Press, 2006.

Krueger, O.: *Closing the Book on Library Losses,* Cambridge: MIT Press, 2000.

Nayar, Baldev Raj.: *Bonding with Your Employees and Board Members*, New York: Greenwood Press, 2000.

Pursell, G.: *Managing Legal Liability*, London: Sage Publications, 2002.

Rao, M.: *Library Management in India: Achievements and challenges*, Cambridge: Cambridge University Press, 2006.

Reynolds, Paul D.: *The Library and the Law: Injuries on the Job*, Kansas City: Kauffman Center, 2005.

Rodrik, D.: *Understanding Economic Policy*, London: Yale University Press, 2007.

Sanjaya, Lall: *Competitiveness, Technology, and Skills in Library Management*, Princeton: Princeton University Press, 2003.

Shankar, A.: *India's Library Management in the 21st Century*, London: Picador, 2002.

Tan, H.: *Models for Library Management*, London and New York: Longman, 2005.

Index